REGIONAL GREAT POWERS IN
INTERNATIONAL POLITICS

Regional Great Powers in International Politics

Edited by

Iver B. Neumann
Research Fellow, The Norwegian Institute of International Affairs
Oslo

St. Martin's Press

First published in Great Britain 1992 by
THE MACMILLAN PRESS LTD
Houndmills, Basingstoke, Hampshire RG21 2XS
and London
Companies and representatives
throughout the world

A catalogue record for this book is available
from the British Library.

ISBN 0-333-56419-7

Printed in Great Britain by
Antony Rowe Ltd, Chippenham, Wiltshire

First published in the United States of America 1992 by
Scholarly and Reference Division,
ST. MARTIN'S PRESS, INC.,
175 Fifth Avenue,
New York, N.Y. 10010

ISBN 0-312-08090-5

Library of Congress Cataloging-in-Publication Data
Regional great powers in international politics / edited by Iver B.
Neumann.
p.   cm.
Includes index.
ISBN 0-312-08090-5
1. Middle powers.   2. International relations.   3. World
politics—20th century.   I. Neumann, Iver B.
JX1395.R37   1992
327.1'1—dc20   92-3798
                                                  CIP

In memoriam
Professor John Vincent (1943–90)

Contents

Preface

This book is the fruit of a common effort over four years. We have incurred the usual debts of gratitude along the way. The Norwegian Institute of International Affairs and The Fridtjof Nansen Institute provided facilities. The Norwegian Research Council gave us some initial funding, and The Norwegian Ministry of Foreign Affairs provided a generous grant. Tore Gustavsen, Dagfrid Hermansen and Ann Skarstad were of great help. However, our main debt is to our faithful critics, professors Olav Fagelund Knudsen, Geir Lundestad, and R. J. Vincent.

The idea of addressing a book to the structural similarities of regional great powers active in international politics came to me during a course in classical theories of international relations conducted by that great inspirer of students and colleagues, John Vincent. When the project was well under way, he participated in two project workshops, and also agreed to write a piece. It was not to be. He died on 2 November 1990. We lost a source of inspiration and a contributor; the field of international relations lost one of its central thinkers. The book is dedicated to the memory of Professor John Vincent.

IVER B. NEUMANN

Notes on the Contributors

Nils A. Butenschøn is Associate Professor of International Relations in the Department of Political Science, University of Oslo, Norway. He is the author of a monograph on the historical and ideological preconditions of the State of Israel (*Drømmen om Israel*, 1984).

Veena Gill is Assistant Professor in the Department for Comparative Politics, University of Bergen, Norway. She was Lecturer at St Stephen's College, New Delhi, and is a graduate of the Jawaharlal Nehru and The Australian National Universities. She has written extensively on military-political relations in developing countries.

Andrew Hurrell, D. Phil. (Oxon) is University Lecturer in International Relations at Oxford University and fellow of Nuffield College. Formerly Assistant Professor of International Relations at the Johns Hopkins School of Advanced International Studies, Bologna, Italy, he is the author of *The U.S.-Brazilian Informatics Dispute* (1988) and is currently finishing a study of post-war Brazilian foreign policy, *The Quest for Autonomy*.

Arnfinn Jørgensen-Dahl, Ph.D., is Research Fellow at the Fridtjof Nansen Institute, Norway, where he is heading the Polar Programme. He has taught at several universities in Australia and at the National University of Singapore, and is the author of *Regional Organization and Order in South-East Asia* (Macmillan, 1982) and *The Antarctic Treaty System in World Politics* (Macmillan, 1991).

Samuel M. Makinda, Ph.D., is Lecturer in International Politics, Murdoch University, Perth, Australia. He was a Research Associate at the International Institute for Strategic Studies in London in 1989–90, and is the author of *Superpower Diplomacy in the Horn of Africa* (1987).

Iver B. Neumann is Research Fellow at the Norwegian Institute of International Affairs, Oslo, and a doctoral student at St Antony's College, Oxford, where he is finishing a thesis on Russian perceptions of West European cooperation. He is the author of a monograph on the postwar European order (*Splittelse og samling*, 1991).

Stein Tønnesson is Research Fellow at the International Peace Research Institute, Oslo, Norway. He is the author of *1946: Déclenchement de*

ix

la guerre d'Indochine (1987) and *The Vietnamese Revolution of 1945: Roosevelt, Ho Chi Minh and de Gaulle in a World at War* (1991).

Øyvind Østerud is Professor in International Conflict Studies in the Department of Political Science, University of Oslo, Norway. He is the author of a number of monographs in Norwegian as well as of *Agrarian Structure and Peasant Politics* (1978) and editor of *Studies of War and Peace* (1986).

Introduction

Iver B. Neumann

Contemporary sensibilities question the validity of all-encompassing systems theories, but also show growing impatience with idiographic empiricism. Theories of the middle range are very much in vogue. For the student of international relations, this is a theoretical climate conducive to the study of regions. Empirically, the end of the cold war may open up new regional space for regional great powers to exploit. These powers may to a greater extent provide for regional order. In that case, analyses which add the regional focus to the systemwide one may be especially timely.

A region consisting of a contiguous cluster of states is, on the one hand, an isomorphic subsystem of the international system. On the other hand, the lesser scale of the region combines with its defining geopolitical and cultural traits to make it a specific analytical concern. The region occupies the middle ground between bilateral relations on the one hand, and system-wide relations on the other.

The inequality of states is evident on the regional level of international relations, as it is on the global level. The empirical focus of the present book is *regional great powers*, which, as a category of states between great powers with systemwide interests and the all and sundry small states, are to be found somewhere in the middle of the hierarchy of states.

The term regional great power, although widely used, is not an analytical category devoid of problems. Since this is the subject of Chapter 1, a preliminary remark bearing on the choice of cases will have to do here. Someone who wants to carve up the world into regions is faced with a plethora of criteria. Although the standard work on the use of the term region in international relations does conclude that 'there is indeed, for each major aggregate, a core, a limited number of states found in each of the clusters', it stands to reason that different analytical needs make for different definitions of region.[1] Indeed, some students of international relations have suggested that we do away with the concept of region in favour of the concept of what they call 'security complexes'. Starting from the observation that 'the security implications of the anarchic structure do not spread uniformly throughout the system', Barry Buzan defined a security complex as 'a group of states whose primary security concerns link together sufficiently closely that their national securities cannot realistically be considered apart from one another.'[2] Although all the usual problems of delimitations remain, the major novelty of the concept is, arguably, to loosen the grip of territoriality. Whereas regions are invariably territorially contiguous, security complexes are not. Thus, the concept of security complexes would allow the analyst to treat for example the 1980s interstate dynamics on the ground in Southern Africa in terms of one security complex consisting of the same states as the traditional Southern African region, and one security complex consisting of the Soviet Union and the United States. The loss in territorial contiguity is compensated for by a gain in analytical contiguity. The major theoretical aim of this book, which is to find out how the systemic position of regional great powers make for similarities in policy problems and policy choices which cut across regional specifics, is not contingent on a detailed delimitation of specific regions. Therefore, we can afford not overly to disturb the sleep of conventional regions, but leave them lying where most cartographers and politicians have agreed to put them.

Even though we found it possible to avail ourselves of conventional regions, that did not in and of itself settle the question of which cases to investigate. This book concentrates on states which have been regional great powers during the period since the end of the First World War. There is a special emphasis on contemporary politics. We decided to leave out cases where a fully fledged great power is also a regional great power – the United States in North America is a case in point – simply because a great power is, by definition, not constrained by the existence of a category of states stronger than itself. This makes the character of its regional policy different from what it would have otherwise been. We also decided to leave out Western Europe. One reason for this is that the great power colonial histories of prospective candidates warrant their continued interest in other regions – France's policies in Northern Africa is a case in point. Another reason is to do with the sheer number of candidates, a question which is further muddled by the existence of the European Community in the postwar period.[3]

Regional great powerhood should be measured not in absolute power capabilities, but in capabilities relative to those of the other states in the region. In this case, powers such as Australia in Oceania, Sweden in Scandinavia or indeed Jamaica in the Caribbean, have a claim to regional great powerhood. Jamaica has a population of three million and scores low on most if not all conceivable indicators of political power. If Jamaica is a regional great power in the Caribbean, then Antigua is a regional great power in the Eastern Caribbean.[4] If Antigua, population 85 000, is a regional great power, then the sky is the limit. Our answer to this problem is again a commonsensical one: we have steered clear of small regions, and have kept an eye on absolute power capabilities. Israel, a tiny state with a population of about four million, is included because of the importance of the Middle East in international relations, and because of the theoretical interest it arouses as a dominant regional power in spite of limited quantitative resource base. The other cases include Brazil, India, Indonesia, Poland, South Africa and Vietnam.

To facilitate comparison and readability, the country chapters are written according to a common outline. Following a brief introduction of the country and its region, the authors address the questions of the country's self perception and declared policy, and its relations with great powers, regional challengers and other neighbouring countries. The discussion then turns to how these other countries have perceived the regional great power in question, and to the problems arising from differences between self perception and outside perception. Each chapter ends with an assessment of the main characteristics of the country's performance as a regional great power. There is also a conclusion at the end of the book, where the usefulness of the term 'regional great power' is discussed in the light of the findings.

NOTES

1. Russett, Bruce M., *International Regions and the International System. A Study in Political Ecology* (Chicago, IL: Rand McNally, 1967), p. 18.
2. Barry Buzan, *People, States, and Fear. The National Security Problem in International Relations* (Brighton: Wheatsheaf, 1983), pp. 105–6; for an application see Barry Buzan, Morten Kelstrup, Pierre Lemaitre, Elzbieta Tromer and Ole Wæver, *The European Security Order Recast. Scenarios for the Post-Cold War Era* (London: Pinter, 1990).
3. Numerous studies discuss the EC's state building potential, for example Johan Galtung, *The European Community: A Superpower in the Making* (London: Allen & Unwin, 1973).
4. Indeed, Antigua's power capabilities exceed those of its immediate neighbours in most regards, it plays a pivotal role in the Organisation of Eastern Caribbean States, and my impression from interviews with Antiguan staff of that organisation in 1988, was that they were very aware of this aspect of Antiguan foreign policy.

1 Regional Great Powers
Øyvind Østerud

THE PROBLEM AND THE PUZZLE

The category of states called 'regional great powers' is one which we feel, intuitively, must be affected by strategic postures and power relationships at the global level. It has often been argued that the *really* Great Powers may fortify regional alliance partners by relative retrenchment, or that superpower accomodation generally might increase the scope for regional assertiveness. On the other hand is the equally conventional view that powers at the local level reflect regional configurations relatively isolated from external control; the 'region' is a microcosm of the states system. For a variety of reasons, these are some of the murkier waters of international commentary. One may even ask whether 'regional great power' is a fruitful category at all, and if there is some sort of general role for states of this elusive standing.

Although the expression is widely employed in everyday language as well as in academic studies, the category of regional great powers has never been properly specified. It is as analytically evasive as it is intuitively important. The cluster of states in geographical regions, however delineated, is also a system with specific distributions of state power, territorial space, resources, and status. There may well be hegemonic relationships between regional polities; there may be more or less autonomous balances of power among them; and there may be historically contingent changes in the interstate 'correlation of forces' at the regional level.

Still, there is next to nothing on the regional great power in the academic literature on the grading or hierarchy of states. Martin Wight gives the category a passing note in his *Power Politics*.[1] He regards it as a subset of minor powers, together with 'middle powers', but with a geographically more restricted range: in a culturally united but politically divided subsystem of states, the features of the general states system may be reproduced in miniature. Within this limited framework some states may have more general interests and a capacity for acting alone – the regional great powers. Wight's examples are Egypt, Iraq and Saudi Arabia in the Arab world, Argentina and Brazil in South America and the Republic of South Africa on the African continent. He then proceeds to a more general

discussion of 'middle powers' in diplomatic history from the Vienna
Congress to the United Nations. Carsten Holbraad, equally, concentrates on
the multifarious indices of 'middle powers' – diplomatically, empirically,
and in the history of ideas – with hardly any place for a 'regional great
power' subset.[2]

The lacuna is also notable in the more general works on the gradation
or hierarchy of states. Hedley Bull concentrates on the role and character
of great powers generally, with respect to international order, while Robert
Klein, in his study of the historical evolution of the principle of sovereign
equality, likewise focuses on the centre stage of the states system.[3]

Neither is the category of regional great power recognised in a recent
study of the hierarchy of states, although hegemonic change and regional
rivalries are included in the analysis.[4] There are two fundamentally different inferences to be drawn from this neglect in the academic literature;
the category is either an analytical dead end, or it is still a worthwhile
challenge.

In any case, the topic is analytically evasive for three fairly distinct
reasons. Firstly, it is not clear how 'great powers' at a regional level
build a reasonably self-contained relationship irrespective of the wider
international system. They are of course affected by numerous links to
the wider order, where 'global' great powers play a vital role. If the
category of 'regional great power' shall retain any substance, however,
their standing cannot be purely derivative. The importance of the wider
international framework will have to be assessed.

Secondly, the criteria for great power status – globally or regionally –
are not evident. We might agree on a formal definition, but the empirical
specifications are still contestable. Some states might, for instance, have
a paramount standing in some respects, with more dubious substance in
other relevant spheres. Again, a status that seems adequate intuitively might
dwindle on further scrutiny.

Thirdly, a world 'region' is no given unit. It might, conventionally, be
synonymous with a continent. We might employ geographical delineations
like oceans, deserts and mountain ranges, realising that the relevance of
topographical characteristics are highly dependent on existing communications technology. We might employ political criteria, like alliance
configurations or spheres of influence, or we might use economic indicators, like commercial networks or conditions of production. We know,
accordingly, that different academic disciplines employ different territorial
delineations: the 'region' of the geographer is often at odds with the
'region' of the student of international relations. Furthermore, many
specific regions have been on the move in our politico-geographical

imagery. The 'Middle East' is not quite where it was 50 or 90 years ago. 'Eastern Europe' was a political as well as a geographical category from the late 1940s to the late 1980s, while it hardly remains more than a geographical conception after November 1989. Likewise, 'Mitteleuropa' has on and off been a plausible idea.

'Regional great powers', then, are hard to identify at the margins, when a 'region' has unclear or changing contours, and the 'power' in question has a dubious or equivocal standing, bending towards a wider global role or towards a minor local position. Any line of demarcation will be somewhat arbitrarily drawn, and any selection of 'regional great powers' is likely to rouse sensible controversy.

THE HIERARCHY OF POWERS

The states system is characterised by the striking contrast between the formal principle of sovereign equality on the one hand and the enormous empirical variation of constituent units on the other. States are conventionally differentiated according to size and population, according to economic prosperity and economic system, according to foreign policies and international role and according to power, however recognised. Hence the traditional ordering according to politico-strategical power: great powers, middle powers, small powers, micro-states. The idea of a hegemonic state, or of 'superpowers', are often added at the top of the hierarchy, while 'regional great powers' are down the list – somewhere.

The hierarchical states system may be conceived at three different levels of precision. The least sophisticated is just the idea of a multidimensional scale of inequalities, variation, differentiation, with the major categories as rather imprecise shorthand for chosen intervals on the scale. The more ambitious conceptual ordering is the identification of clusters of types in a hierarchical order, with some deeper systemic reality to the basic categories. Here, the idea of great powers – global or regional – acquires a theoretical meaning beyond the merely conventional shorthand. The most precise conceptual reference is hierarchy as a structural ordering principle of the international system. This is the notion employed in Kenneth Waltz's structural theory, with *hierarchy* as an alternative to the *anarchy* of the states system.[5] The idea of types of powers in our context is somewhere within the second range – more ambitious than a linguistic shorthand, but less precise than the structural principle of hierarchy employed by Waltz.

One group of criteria for the differentiation of states is the various empirical indices referred to above: size and population, economic prosperity, political régime, economic system, foreign policies, military power. Great powers, middle powers, small powers and so on may be defined according to their relative position on scales of these indicators, or certain combinations from them. The quantitative study of international relations offers several proposals of this kind. The first problem with a merely statistical ranking is that international roles, ambitions and political influence are left out or are only indirectly hypothesised, even if quantitative resources undoubtedly make up the backbone of the standing of 'powers'. The second problem is that the lower limit of a great power, or a middle power, or a regional great power, is quite arbitrary in these statistical terms. The third one is, further, that certain states may play a role far beyond their relative amount of the traditionally relevant resources, for reasons which beg for supplementary perspectives. The other group of criteria for differentiation is derived from typified models of the international system. The economic stratification into the First, Second and Third World (or more) is in fact more than an economic stratification, since it also involves an element of self-conscious mobilisation of organised 'estates' on the world scene, parallel to the constitution of the Third Estate during the French Revolution. This was in fact the linguistic point of departure for the French conception of *le tiers monde* in the early 1950s, and the Bandung Conference was the turning point for incipient third world mobilisation. The concept of the 'regional great power', then, might be connected to the major alignments and cleavages in the years after the Second World War: the newly independent states system in Africa and parts of Asia, the gap between the industrialised North and the underdeveloped South, the Cold War contest between East and West as it was played out in alliance patterns – or programmatic non-alliance – in regions peripheral to the rivalry. The tripartite classification of states is derived from all these three international cleavages – decolonisation, the development problem and the Cold War. Third World mobilisation has seen a fluctuation of 'regional great powers' in various phases of the period after the Second World War, as will be indicated below.

A widely different model is the spatial distribution within 'world systems analysis' as developed by Immanuel Wallerstein and associates.[6] Here, state structures and relative strength are derived from positions within a capitalist exchange system, that is, strong states of the dominant core, and weak states of the dependent periphery. An intermediate area – the mixed and composite *semi-periphery* – is a buffer zone, but also a politico-economic stage in its own right, with a range of medium powers that may play a paramount regional role. The semi-pheriphery, however, is the most indistinct category of the world-system model, and the corresponding regional states system is equally undecided. Still, the idea of regional great powers might have an analytical potential within this systemic conception.

The traditional ordering of powers might also acquire model-like characteristics when the categories have conceptual meaning beyond their position on a continuous scale, when there is a formal standing attached to the hierarchical order or when types of powers are specified in terms of particular international roles. These dimensions of a hierarchy of states should be considered in turn.

Great power standing has been intimately connected to relative military force. In a famous phrase, Leopold von Ranke argued that 'a definition of a great power [is] that it must be able to maintain itself against all others, even when they are united'.[7] Treitschke derived a slight modification of this criterion when he said that a great power is a power whose destruction would require a coalition of other powers.[8] Martin Wight states bluntly that 'great power status is lost, as it is won, by violence'.[9] Relative military force, then, has to prove itself in war, and the hierarchy of states is established and changed during the history of interstate conflict. While the 'global' great powers retain their capacity for self defence irrespective of other aspects of the international order, the standing of the *regional* great power is confined to local interrelationships, and therefore conditioned by the wider balance of forces; the regional hierarchy of states is never completely autonomous.

It is, however, far from evident that a great power will have to prove itself in war. Historically, this is a dubious criterion, since great power status has been acknowledged for potential rather than actual war-fighting. At present, no great power can fend off any attack, but acquires its standing by a credible capability for fatal retaliation. The rank of a modern 'superpower' – corresponding to the classical great power – is not acquired by actual violence, but by the credibility of a viable second-strike force. Correspondingly, regional great power status might also rest on reputation rather than proven performance.

There is a more formal aspect to the reputational criterion. In diplomatic history after the Congress of Vienna, types of powers have had a formal standing, recognised in treaties and international organisations. The classical great power concert was a system based on formal recognition, and the Charter of the UN specified an order with great power prerogatives. The formalisation of the grading of powers implies the possibility for non-correspondence between formal standing and real strength. Some of the formally recognised great powers may be great by courtesy, while some of the really great ones may suffer formal neglect. Diplomatic history is rife with divergences and incongruous time lags of this kind. It might be found as well in the organisation of regional states systems.

The final criterion on the standing of powers is not so much their resources as what they actually do; their interests and their international role. Conventionally, a great power is supposed to be a power with general, or world-wide, interests, while a regional great power, again, has notable interests within a wider regional area. Although such 'general interests' can hardly be described in the abstract and although the edges of this criterion are indeed vague, there may be a workable starting point here.

There is probably more to be said about the international role of great powers. They have, seemingly *per se*, a managerial role in the international system.[10] Firstly, they manage the relations between each other by means of military balances, diplomatic accomodations, linkage policies, codes of crisis management and so on. The international order of the Cold War has been described as an amazingly stable system dependent upon the managerial functions of the dominant powers.[11] Secondly, the great powers give organisational direction to the international system as a whole. The basic mechanisms here would be the counter-balancing of unequal alliances in the periphery, the policing of trans-border territories and spheres of influence, the control of unruly client states involved in regional conflicts or civil strife and the weight in the establishment of international régimes and rules of the game. The managerial role of great powers is here diagnosed in a purely descriptive way, without any evaluation attached to it.

However we define them, middle powers, or regional great powers, make up an ambiguous category, with a rather arbitrary lower limit. There are, furthermore, two distinct types of 'middle powers'. One type is constituted by states in an intermediate position in a hierarchy, however specified. Another is, linguistically, the states *in the middle*, in other words, the buffer states between powerful rivals or regional areas. The intermediate powers, neither great nor small, are hard to define clearly in politico-military or economic terms, except as a statistical medium category. Unlike the great powers, they seldom, and then only occasionally and rudimentarily, have a clear-cut formal status. For example, when the UN was established in 1945, some demand was voiced for recognising a group of second rank states by granting them priority as non-permanent members of the Security Council. Likewise, states informally recognised as regional great powers may experience preferential diplomatic treatment when wider interests are involved. A regional great power may be a middle power in the global context, but not necessarily so. It seems reasonable to argue that Israel qualifies as a regional great power in the Middle East, but most definitely not as a 'middle power' globally. The same goes for the Republic of South Africa in its area. On the other hand, a middle power generally is not necessarily a great power regionally, since it may exist in the close and dominated vicinity of really great powers, or of a number of other powers aspiring to a leading regional role. Generally, a middle power is defined within an international hierarchy of powers, while a regional great power is determined within a regional division of the globe.

In so far as the region is an international states system in miniature, the regional great power is just a great power writ small: it either has a dominant position within the regional hierarchy of states, or it is party to a regional balance of power system – presumably able to defend itself against a coalition of other parties. Even more important, perhaps, it has a managerial role at the regional level. It balances other forces, maintains codes of conduct, stabilises spheres of influence and polices unruly clients. These are some of the major functions to be identified and analysed.

THE EXPANSION OF THE STATES SYSTEM

In diplomatic terms, the grading of powers was introduced by the peace settlement after the Napoleonic wars. The European Concert was composed of the five great powers, Britain, France, Austria, Prussia and Russia. A class of middle powers was also recognised among German states. They comprised in particular the South German states of Bavaria, Wurttemburg and Baden, which sometimes tried to pursue an independent policy.[12] During most of the nineteenth century the modern states system remained fairly exclusively European.

By 1914 the European states system was remarkably changed. Austria had declined dramatically, while Prussia in particular had acquired a much higher standing. Italy claimed great power status after the unification in 1860, but never really made it. Two claimants outside Europe, however, now enlarged the geographical scope of the great power system: the United States, especially during the decades after the civil war, and Japan, which had modernised rapidly after the Meiji Restoration, formally aligned with Britain in 1902, and even proved victorious against Russia in the war of 1904–5.

The expansion of the states system is clearly reflected in the major international conferences.[13] Whereas the Congress of Vienna had been exclusively European, the conference in Paris in 1856 also included the Ottoman Empire, and thereby coopted Turkey. The Hague conferences in 1899 and again in 1907 enlarged the system considerably. In 1899 the USA, Mexico, China, Persia and Siam also took part, and European powers spoke on behalf of vastly expanded colonial empires. In 1907 the sixteen Latin American republics were included, on US initiative. The extended geographical scope of the system of states had crucial implications for the hierarchy of powers. The globalisation of the states system affected intra-European relationships as well as the balances between Europe and the external world. Extra-European rivalries and politico-economic projections led to rearrangements within Europe, particularly in the age of imperialism towards the turn of the century. New centres of political power emerged outside Europe, as demonstrated by the self-assertion of Japan in the Far Eastern crisis from 1895 to 1905. The grading of powers with the expansion of the states system was partly affected by the cooptation of non-European states, partly by peripheral self-assertion, and partly by imperialist rivalries.

The European system of the nineteenth century was also transformed by the principle of nationality. German and Italian unification altered the continental balance to the disadvantage of France. The break-up of empires meant new political realities in regional affairs, with nationalist Turkey as a new 'regional great power' in the Middle East, with a wholly new political geography in the old 'Mitteleuropa' and on the Balkan, and with a new territorial basis for countries like Poland and Czechoslovakia. The First World War was the major catalyst for these transformations.

Middle powers, or indeed regional great powers, did not figure formally within the League of Nations system, although the unstable power rivalries of the inter-war years granted them a structural space both in central Europe and in the Far East. The League became perhaps basically an international instrument of Britain and France, trying to contain the revisionist revanchism of Germany and its allies.[14] Unstable regional balances collapsed with the global ramifications of the Second World War, and heralded the more bi-polar world of the post-war years. The new bi-polarity, however, had significant modifications, and increasingly so. The bi-polar balance of power during the Cold War developed in notable contrast to the conception of a great power concert on which the United Nations was drafted. In the world of power politics, there were gross inequalities between the five permanent veto-invested members of the Security Council. France was coopted as a great power by courtesy – and of course as a future anchorage of Western interests in Europe; Britain, the hegemon of the age of imperialism, increasingly declined to a middle power status, and the membership of China became a pawn in the American-Soviet rivalry.

At the founding conference of the UN in 1945, there was also voiced some demand to recognise powers of the second rank by granting them priority in the selection of the non-permanent Security Council members.[15] These potentially formalised middle powers included Canada, Australia, Brazil, Mexico, Poland, Holland and Belgium. The last two candidates may – besides the courteous inclusion of Poland – seem particularly strange today, but they were of course colonial powers of considerable range in 1945. Generally, however, this list, and any such list, is highly contestable, and may create continuous jealousies and demands for revision. The idea of middle powers, then, was abandoned in the eventual arrangements of the UN.

Decolonisation, indeed, was the crucial process through which regional great powers emerged. The rise of the Third World, as a demand for politico-economic standing for a nascent global 'estate', was symbolised by the colonial defeat at Dien Bien Phu, and voiced in the Bandung Conference. The spirit of Bandung, however, was not carried by a faceless anti-colonial mass. The leading centres of Third World mobilisation, and later within the non-allied movement, were new 'regional powers' like India, Indonesia, Egypt and, somewhat later, Algeria. These countries had considerable size, a large population and some strategical assets in terms of resources or location. But first and foremost they had an ambitious and able political leadership. India's early position was greatly enhanced by the leadership of Nehru; Indonesia likewise gained much of its standing from president Sukarno; Egypt acquired a higher profile through the ambitions and role of Nasser; Algeria aspired to regional and Third World leadership during the presidency of Boumedienne. Even smaller countries like Cuba, Ghana and divided Vietnam played a role in Third World mobilisation, due to offensive leaders such as Castro, Nkrumah and Ho Chi Minh. The new regional and Third World leaders did, of course, not attain their position in a systemic vacuum, but they may have been necessary if not sufficient conditions for the standing of their states.

The history of Third World mobilisation, and the concomitant emergence of regional powers in the periphery of superpower rivalry, testifies to the importance of charismatic leadership in the hierarchy of states. Structural power base and ambition as well as natural resources and action may interact and compensate for each other, even if no general assessment of the range of such compensations is possible.

THE CHANGING INTERNATIONAL SYSTEM

Regional great powers in the modern world, however a 'regional power' is identified, operate in a wider context. The gradual relaxation of the post-Second World War bi-polar structure – expressed by the independent stance of China, the economic position of Japan and the NICs and the oil crises and the self-assertion of OPEC/OAPEC in the 1970s – implied higher standing for regional subsystems and their predominant states. Multi-polarity is *as such* a regionalisation of interstate power relationships.

The character of regional states systems is also, however, conditioned by the variation of Cold War strategies. On the Soviet side, the post-Stalin idea of peaceful coexistence implied intensified rivalries in the decolonising 'grey zone' between the power blocks. Non-communist, nationalist régimes in the Third World were no longer conceived as imperialist pawns, but as a potential area for friendship and cooperation to the ultimate disadvantage of the West, as a revival of the post-revolutionary front strategy of the early 1920s. Accordingly, several Third World states acquired Soviet economic and technical support, even if they eventually employed these externally supplied assets to gain a higher regional standing on their own. The vacillating loyalties of Egypt, Indonesia or Algeria during the 1960s are cases in point, and so are the shifting alliance patterns on the Horn of Africa in the late 1970s. North Vietnam remained the only former colony to achieve independence under a clearcut communist leadership, and Castro remained the prime example of a Third World leader converting to communism after fulfilling an originally non-communist revolution. The doctrine of peaceful coexistence was not only a strategy for Soviet influence. Incidentally, it also served to bolster non-communist régimes, with enhanced opportunities for regional governments to exploit the superpower rivalry.

American strategies of containment, on the other hand, were equally ambiguous. Periodically, containment implied a direct military response to perceived communist challenges, and involved intervention by force in shaken spheres of influence or even in the grey zones of rivalry. Periodically, however, it involved relative military retrenchment, with containment through support to regional alliance partners. There was a characteristic pendulum swing between 'symmetrical' and 'asymmetrical' containment strategies throughout the Cold War years.[16] The dilemma of indirect containment through strong regional allies, however, is the risk that the regional ally may use the supplies transferred to it for ends which are not in the interest of the supplier, be that in the form of regional assertion or otherwise. To 'play the China card' in anti-Soviet diplomacy, with partial US retrenchment, meant that the card could also be played according to local rules. The Nixon-Kissinger strategy of relative retrenchment, known as the Guam doctrine, meant that key allies like Iran or South Vietnam could transform their diplomatic position if the favoured régime collapsed. Even 'superpower', for short, is quite limited power in the peripheral zones of rivalry. Regional great powers have partly been produced as the incidental bi-product of incomplete attempts to control regional developments from outside.

Finally, it is quite likely that an end to the Cold War would mean even greater opportunities for regional great powers. The multi-polarity of the last decades would be fortified with the declining role of global great powers and with the declining intensity of the rivalry between them, even if some regional balances could shift dramatically. The 'hegemonic decline' of the US *per se* implies greater regional assertiveness. Likewise, a 'world without the USSR' – as a current expression goes – would have unpredictable consequences for the hierarchy of states in the Asian and eastern European rims of that state formation.

THE GEOPOLITICS OF REGIONAL POWER

There is complex interaction between political, socio-economic and geo-graphic elements both within regions and in their external relations. Any regional states system may be characterised and differentiated according to internal cohesion – culturally, politically and economically; according to infrastructure and communications; according to interstate relations like conflict, cooperation, and means of contact; and according to the regional hierarchy of powers.[17] Correspondingly, external and intrusive powers may affect regional affairs as to internal cohesion, communications systems, intensity of conflict or degree of cooperation, and power relations between regional states. The standing of powers, as we have seen, includes material capacities and location, military capabilities and motivational factors. The specification of regional great powers would require a comparative assessment of geopolitical characteristics like strategic location and size, centre-periphery structures, ethno-cultural diversity or cohesion, infrastruc-ture and economic base.

It is, however, hard to find general correlates between political standing and geopolitical features, even if the academic literature is rife with suggestions. One author argues that 'the initial geopolitical characteristic of the dominant state is that its original core area is located at the junction between the territory of its parent culture and that of a different culture'.[18] He cites historical examples like Castile and Austria between Christendom and Islam, but also has to recognise striking exceptions like the territorial expansion of the French state. Even if certain initial conditions and geopolitical correlates might explain historical cases of regional great power status, the explanations typically work only retrospectively, since *ad hoc* conditions, or the shadowy motivational factor, might account for the numerous power failures.

Most illuminating, perhaps, is the regional great power which aspired to a more comprehensive role, but which evidently failed because of geographic position and lack of resources for a wider power projection. Sweden, for one, was once a great power in the Baltic, but never gained a similar standing in the wider northern Europe. Poland, correspondingly, had dominated eastern Europe, but failed to attain a more comprehensive Slavic role. Italy, also, had acquired dominance in the eastern Mediterranean, while Mussolini failed to reassert Roman dominance in the wider Mediterranean area. There seem to be notable geopolitical differences between states which expanded to real great power status, and those which achieved only limited regional hegemony.[19]

The prerequisites and mechanisms of great power standing – global and regional – might be sought inductively and specifically. The general pattern, however, is likely to remain elusive. Still, a regional great power will at least be

- a state which is geographically a part of the delineated region
- a state which is able to stand up against any coalition of other states in the region
- a state which is highly influential in regional affairs
- a state which, contrary to a 'middle power', might also be a great power on the world scale in addition to its regional standing.

We may finally propose the major geopolitical regions and their candidates for regional great power standing.[20]

THE MAJOR CONTEMPORARY REGIONS – A TENTATIVE SUGGESTION

In *Europe* the most consistent candidates for great power status have been Germany, France, Russia and Great Britain, all based on a combination of military and economic strength. The modern states system itself originates in Europe, and the major states have also been great powers at the global arena. Germany has probably been the strongest continental candidate for regional great power status, and the paramount military conflicts in the area have been between Germany and various coalitions established to contain the German quest for power.

The Middle East and North Africa is characterised by several contenders for regional dominance, but no stable position for a singular great power has been achieved. Most Arab candidates have seen Arab unification as a vehicle to regional standing, while there is a basic conflict between Israel and all the other states. In its military standing Israel is a regional great power.

South Asia has a small number of states, with India as a dominant power in terms of population, military capabilities and economic strength. The wider influence of India is, however, somewhat frustrated by the conflict with Pakistan.

In *South East Asia* the state with the strongest power potential, Indonesia, is a regionally peripheral and insular country, without sufficient industrial, commercial and naval strength to dominate the adjacent area. The central area of the region is characterised by the polarity between Thailand and Vietnam, with Laos and Cambodia as buffer states. The advantage of Thailand in the rivalry with Vietnam has been the ASEAN cooperation and the alliance with China.

East Asia includes the Soviet Union, China and Japan, where all of them might be said to be great powers also in world politics. Regional affairs are dependent upon the tripartite relationship between these powers, and historically the rivalry has been expressed in wars over Korea and Manchuria. The potential for regional cooperation was aborted by the Japanese defeat in the Second World War, and by the the alliance patterns of the Cold War – as expressed most visibly in the sharp division of Korea. While the USSR also plays a role in Europe, *China* might alternatively be seen as a region in itself, with one imperial state including Tibet and Manchuria, and with a precarious independence of Mongolia and Taiwan – supported by alliances with the USSR and the USA respectively. A relatively weak economy, the burden of imperial cohesion, and the ideological isolation of the régime, have undermined China's standing as a real world power.

Australia and Oceania is a region dominated by Australia. Australia is, however, somewhat enclosed in the region, and this condition is underlined by the antagonism with Indonesia, which is in a way blocking the open access towards South East Asia.

Africa south of the Sahara has two major powers – Nigeria and the Republic of South Africa. The region is characterised by numerous weakly integrated states with poorly developed production capacities. It is, furthermore, characterised by the antagonism between the strongest state, the Republic of South Africa, and the majority of the population on the continent, including the majority within the republic itself. These factors have contributed to the isolation of black Africa in world politics.

South America is overall characterised by underdeveloped economies, weakly developed state apparatuses and the dominance of the United States. Brazil and Argentina are the major candidates for regional great power status.

North America is, of course, completely dominated by the United States, which is also the strongest single state in the world. The US is the only great power which has consistently played a major role in all the other regions over the last 50 years.

NOTES

1. Martin Wight, *Power Politics* (Harmondsworth: Penguin, 1979) p. 63.
2. Carsten Holbraad, *Middle Powers in International Politics* (London: Macmillan, 1984).
3. Hedley Bull, *The Anarchical Society: a Study of Order in World Politics* (London: Macmillan, 1977); Robert A. Klein, *Sovereign Equality among States: the History of an Idea* (Toronto: University of Toronto Press, 1974).
4. Ian Clark, *The Hierarchy of States. Reform and Resistance in the Internmational Order* (Cambridge: Cambridge University Press, 1989).
5. Kenneth Waltz, *Theory of International Politics* (Reading, MA: Addison-Wesley, 1979).
6. Immanuel Wallerstein, *The Modern World-System*, vol. I–II (New York, NY: Academic Press, [1974] 1980).
7. Leopold von Ranke, 'The Great Powers', in T. H. von Laue, *Ranke, The Formative Years* (Princeton, NJ: Princeton University Press, 1950).
8. Wight, *Power Politics*, p. 295.
9. Wight, *Power Politics*, p. 48.
10. Bull, *The Anarchical Society*, p. 200ff.
11. John L. Gaddis, *The Long Peace* (Oxford: Oxford University Press, 1987).
12. Wight, *Power Politics*, p. 63ff.
13. Hedley Bull and Adam Watson (eds), *The Expansion of International Society* (Oxford: Clarendon, 1984).
14. Clark, *The Hierarchy of States*; E. H. Carr, *The Twenty Years' Crisis* (London: Macmillan, 1939; 2nd edn 1946).
15. Wight, *Power Politics*, p. 64.

16. John L. Gaddis, *Strategies of Containment* (Oxford: Oxford University Press, 1982).
17. Louis J. Cantori and Steven L. Spiegel, 'The International Relations of Regions', *Polity*, II (1970): 397–425.
18. Geoffrey Parker, *Western Geopolitical Thought in the Twentieth Century* (London: Croom Helm, 1985), p. 64.
19. It was Stein Tønnesson who pressed for sticking one's neck out in this direction. I am grateful for his suggestions.

2 Brazil as a Regional Great Power: a Study in Ambivalence

Andrew Hurrell

INTRODUCTION

The view of Brazil as a major regional power or as a regional great power has a long history and has been very widespread. The picture of Brazil as the most powerful state in South America recurs constantly in newspaper articles and politicians' speeches, as well as in academic works. Such a view became most pronounced during the 1970s when the high growth rates of the so-called economic miracle seemed to establish the country as an upwardly mobile middle power, if not one moving ineluctably towards eventual great power status. To quote one typical example: 'Brazil possesses the will and the resources to reach for, and possibly, achieve, the status of a major international power by the end of the twentieth century'.[1] Writing more specifically in terms of relations with Latin America, Norman Bailey and Ronald Schneider argued in 1974 that: 'Supremacy, dominance or even paramountcy may well be within Brazil's reach by the 1980s'.[2] Such arguments persisted well into the 1980s despite the country's growing economic crisis. Writing in 1984, Wayne Selcher was unequivocal in arguing that 'Brazil's continental role has grown to clear primacy'.[3] Today those who view the post-Cold War order as being characterised by greater pluralism and the diffusion of power are once more pointing to Brazil as an increasingly important regional actor in the coming decade.[4]

The characterisation of Brazil as a regional power appears to make sense for two reasons: first, because of the extent to which South America does indeed form a coherent region. Although there may be a questionmark regarding the position of Mexico and Central America, the states of the South American mainland below Panama form a clearly demarcated region in geographic terms. The states within this region share a common set of historical traditions, especially as a result of the process of Iberian colonialism. There is a relatively high degree of cultural, ethnic, linguistic and religious homogeneity, with the Catholic Church playing a major role throughout the region. They confront similar problems of socio-economic development and their political systems derive from common roots and confront similar challenges. They face similar external constraints and there is a reasonable degree of commonality regarding their attitudes and policies towards both the West and the Third World.[5] Finally, there is a relatively high level of regional self-consciousness embodied in a complex network of both regional organisations and international legal régimes. The area thus appears to form a distinct region in the sense proposed by Cantori and Spiegel: 'two or more proximate or interacting states which have some common ethnic, linguistic, cultural, and historical bonds, and whose sense of identity is sometimes increased by the actions and attitudes of states external to the system'.[6]

Second, if South America forms a distinct region, then Brazil's powerful relative position within that region appears self-evident. Brazil's territory covers some 48 per cent of the total land area of South America. Its population (144 million in 1988) accounts for some 34 per cent of the total population of Central and South America and some 51 per cent of the total for South America. Its population is roughly equal to that of the next three most populous states taken together: Mexico, Argentina and Colombia. It has by far the most powerful economy in the region and its GNP in 1987 accounted for some 38 per cent of the total for Central and South America and 54 per cent of the South American total: US$ 77 billion more than those of Argentina, Chile, Colombia, Peru and Venezuela combined. By the mid-1980s Brazil produced over 50 per cent of the region's industrial exports and over 40 per cent of its manunfactured exports, well above Mexico (27 per cent) and Argentina (9 per cent). Militarily, Brazil has the largest armed forces in South America – 324 000 active forces as against 95 000 in Argentina, 101 000 in Chile and 120 000 in Peru.

Yet how realistic is this picture of Brazil as a regional great power? Is it merely the product of a past, pre-debt crisis age when dreams of *grandeza* (greatness) and *ufanismo* (national pride) clouded and distorted perceptions of the country's international role? Does such a view of Brazil still have some validity? If Brazil does have power, what is the scope and range of that power and how and over whom is it manifested? If Brazil is, in fact, not particularly powerful, why should this be, given the extent of its size and resources? What alternative picture should we have of Brazil's regional role? Is the 'end of the Cold War' likely to provide any kind of significant regional opening for Brazil? This chapter seeks to address these questions.

The rest of the introduction seeks to assess the character of Brazil's relations with the region against the three sets of theoretical assumptions that have underpinned most recent analyses of Brazilian foreign policy: capability theory, geopolitics, and dependency theory. Although in very different ways, all of these approaches have helped reinforce an exaggerated view of Brazil as a major regional power and it is for this reason that they are analysed here.

Capability theory

By far the most common basis on which Brazil is viewed as a regional great power concerns the country's overall power resources and the extent of these resources relative to the other states in the region. This is the most common basis for classifying states within a hierarchy of powers. It rests on a traditional, commonsense view of power that seeks to add together all the power resources that a country possesses in order to arrive at an overall assessment. What is needed is to isolate and evaluate the various components of national power on which the ability to coerce and to resist coercion are based.

Such an approach has had a significant impact on the analysis of Brazil's international role. Sometimes it is adopted explicitly, with the clearest example being Ray S. Cline's *World Power Assessment*.[7] A more sophisticated attempt to disaggregate the Third World using a broader range of indicators classifies Brazil as an 'Achiever', amongst whose characteristics are the possession of 'substantial power stocks' and a position as 'important in regional distributions of power and control'.[8] Far more frequently, however, such an approach is adopted implicitly. Indeed, almost every study of Brazil's foreign policy starts with a long list of the country's resources, with the implicit assumption that the mere possession of these resources must represent an important determinant of Brazil's international behaviour.

There can be no doubt that Brazil does rank as a regional great power in terms of resources. Its relative position within Latin America has already been mentioned. In addition, it is the fifth largest state in the world with an area larger than the United States, excluding Alaska. It is the tenth largest economy in the world (1987 GNP US$ 315 billion), roughly the same size as that of China (US$ 320) and considerably larger than that of India (US$ 241). By the 1980s it had become a significant exporter of a range of manufactured goods including aircraft, cars, capital goods. It is the world's second largest exporter of agricultural produce after the United States. It has the world's second largest reserves of iron ore and is the world's second largest exporter, the fourth largest producer of gold and has significant reserves of bauxite, uranium, copper, chromium, managnese, tin, zinc and lead. By the late 1980s, it had even managed to discover substantial reserves of oil, with domestic production accounting for around half of total consumption.

Behind these lists of power resources lies recognition of the tremendous process of economic development and modernisation that the country has undergone in the post-war period. From the mid-1940s to the mid-1980s Brazil grew at a yearly average of 7 per cent. It moved from a predominantly rural and agricultural country to an industrialised and urbanised society in little more than a generation. The urban population increased from 36 per cent in 1940 to 68 per cent in 1980 and to 75 per cent in 1988 (very close to the levels of Europe and America). The share of non-agricultural employment rose from 40 per cent in 1940 to 71 per cent in 1980. In 1964 coffee still accounted for over half of all export earnings with manufactured exports only accounting for 5 per cent of exports. By 1988 coffee's share had declined to 6 per cent with manufactured goods accounting for 58 per cent. This development, for all its incompleteness, distortions and inequalities, was comparable in its rapidity and intensity to that which occured in Germany and the United States in the course of the nineteenth century.

No one would deny that these resources have had a significant impact on Brazilian foreign policy. They provide a range of options and an ability to bargain effectively that the majority of developing countries simply do not possess. The problem, however, is that power is a complex and multi-faceted concept that is extremely difficult to measure in any clear-cut way. Indeed Brazil stands as perhaps the most striking case of the futility of grading states according to abstract lists of power resources. According to Ray Cline's 1980 *World Power Assessment* Brazil ranked third in the world in terms of 'perceived power', surpassed only by the United States and the Soviet Union. This is a meaningless and entirely fallacious way to approach Brazil's foreign and regional policy because it ignores two basic lessons of social power analysis. First, no attempt is made to relate this 'power' to any imaginable political context or situation, or, to use David Baldwin's unlovely term, to a specific 'policy contingency framework'.[9] As Baldwin suggests, we need to paraphrase Robert Dahl and ask: 'When you hear that Brazil is an influential regional great power, the proper question is: influential over what actors, in what period, with respect to what matters?' The second basic 'lesson' of social power analysis is that power must be related to an actor's intentions, objectives and values. Implicit in attempts to classify states according to their level of power lies a powerful residue of Realist dogma, namely that power will always be used to maximise international influence.

Brazil, even under a succession of military governments, stands as an object lesson that such assumptions are unwarranted. As we shall see, increasing international influence within South America has been one objective of Brazilian foreign policy, but only one of many and never the most important. First, the use of foreign policy to promote economic development has been a consistently more important goal, both as a central basis of government legitimacy and, in the minds of the Brazilian military, as the indispensable foundation for a *future* world role. Second, regional policy has consistently been viewed as secondary to relations with other more important areas. And third, foreign policy itself has rarely dominated the national agenda. This is particularly true of the period of marked introspection in the 1980s when the country was preoccupied by the dual task of economic modernisation and democratic consolidation.

It is also worth stressing that, at least since the time of Vargas in the 1940s, Brazil has not produced leaders who have placed great emphasis on forging a major international role or have seen an assertive foreign policy as central to their domestic political legitimacy. The contrast with other middle and regional powers is evident: think of Nehru, Nasser, or Sukarno. In addition, the successful assertion of regional power has often rested on a particularly powerful idea or a carefully crafted conception of power that is accepted both by all groups within the country concerned and by the outside world. Gaullist France (including its regional policy in Africa) and Nehru's India (with its special role in the Third World and Asia) are good examples. Such a pattern has not been the case in Brazil.

Geopolitics

The geopolitical approach is closely allied with capability theory both in its stress on power as the crucial determinant of a state's foreign policy and in the emphasis on Brazil's role as a future world power. Moreover, Brazilian geopolitical theories have had a great deal to say about the country's regional policy and its role as a regional great power. Strictly speaking, geopolitics denotes no more than a concern for geographical factors in international politics. In practice, the scope of most Brazilian geopolitical writing is much wider, covering what might be called 'Brazil's Grand Strategy' and including the relationships between geography and national security, economic development and the expansion of international influence. Moreover, most of geopolitical writing is explicitly prescriptive and, because of its widespread acceptance within the Brazilian military establishment, it has had a direct impact on the formulation of the country's foreign policy.

If we focus on the two most prominent post-war Brazilian geopoliticians, Golbery do Couto e Silva and Carlos de Meira Mattos, we can identify four basic characteristics.[10] First, at the heart of all Brazilian geopolitical writing lies a stark Realist picture of international relations. International life is seen as a ceaseless struggle for survival between states motivated by fear. As Golbery puts it:

> The incessant impulse that clearly dominates the entire Hobbesian dialectic . . . is the same great Fear, the cosmic fear . . . of the eternal insecurity of Man.[11]

This bleak social darwinist view of a never-ending struggle represents the clearest link between Brazilian geopoliticians and such earlier exponents as Kjellén, Haushofer and Mackinder.

The second characteristic is that survival is only possible within a strong nation state and that it is the fundamental duty of all states to maximise their power. To quote Golbery once more:

> The instrument of strategic action, in this era of total wars, can only result from the integration of all national forces, of all the physical and human resources available to each state, of all its spiritual and material capacity, from the totality of economic, political, psycho-social and military means that can be gathered for the struggle – in sum, from its National Power.[12]

A third characteristic is the belief that geopolitics represents an important means of uncovering both the determinants of national power and of understanding the bases of national politics:

> We therefore have a situation where Geopolitics, based on geographical science, and, in particular in that branch called Political Geography, serves as a geographical foundation stone and proposes directives [*diretrizes*] to National Politics, rooted in the basic concepts of space and position. [13]

What is it, then, that geopolitics is able to uncover? For both Golbery and Meira Mattos, geopolitical analysis reveals Brazil's vocation for greatness. On the one hand, Brazil possesses the necessary attributes and power resources to play a more significant role in world affairs. On the other, both see Brazil's progress towards such a role as being enhanced by its geopolitically 'privileged' position. This results from its extensive coastline, its many good ports, its natural dominance over the South Atlantic (especially the Atlantic Narrows between the Northeast of Brazil and West Africa), and, of particular importance, its natural predominance over Latin America.[14] According to Golbery, geopolitics helps to delimit 'platforms for expansion' and 'zones of influence in foreign areas both on land and sea'.[15]

Three areas have been consistently identified by Brazilian geopoliticians as possible targets for the external projection of power. In many of the earlier works, a great deal of attention is paid to the so-called heartland of Latin America, the 'magic triangle' in Bolivia formed by Cochabamba, Santa Cruz de la Sierra and Sucre. The second area is the South Atlantic down to Antarctica. And the third, particularly emphasised by Meira Mattos, is the Amazon Basin. Although Golbery claimed that Brazil was 'territorially satisfied' and that he was talking only of a cooperative expansion of influence, there is a strongly expansionist flavour to their writings which, not unnaturally, attracted a great deal of criticism from Brazil's Spanish-speaking neighbours, especially in the late 1960s and early 1970s. Brazilian geopolitical writings of this kind – and indeed most other geopolitical analysis – suffer from a serious flaw in that they use geography in a fundamentally misleading way. Golbery claims that geography lays down 'general directives' that enable politicians to 'decipher the main lines of the destiny of the nation'. In fact geopolitics can never form the bedrock of politics in this way because it is always necessarily based on some prior political or philosophical viewpoint. Geographical facts in themselves do not tell us anything about the behaviour of states unless we already have a picture of the interests, motives and objectives that govern a state's behaviour. Where geopolitics is all too frequently misleading is in suggesting that the features of the physical world show a preference for a particular viewpoint or in giving a scientific and objective gloss to a particular political opinion. It is on the strength of the underlying viewpoint, rather than on the validity of the geographical arguments that are used to buttress it, that the approach will stand or fall.

If we turn to the underlying assumptions we find a crude and extreme brand of Realism. Now what is interesting and important is not that such a viewpoint should have been held and should have influenced the policy of the Brazilian military towards its neighbours. Such a viewpoint *was* deeply held by the Brazilian military and through such important institutions as the *Escola Superior de Guerra* spread to other sections of the Brazilian élite. Moreover, as we shall seen, such a viewpoint *did* influence Brazilian policy towards the region. But the interesting point is the gap between the extreme nature of this geopolitical ideology and the relatively moderate course followed even by Brazil's military governments. (I stress the word 'relative': relative to, for example, South Africa, Israel, India or Vietnam). To take the most fundamental point: if international life in Latin America really was a ceaseless Hobbesian struggle, wouldn't you at least want to have a functioning military capability? Instead Brazil's military government spent very little on arms (a lower percentage of GNP than Austria) and developed no significant capability to project power beyond its borders. (As the quip goes, the Brazilian army *is* a political party, *thinks* it is a real military and *acts* like a national police force). Without too much exaggeration one might say that, whereas India from the 1960s on preached peace but built up a regionally overwhelming military force, Brazil preached conflict but remained militarily extremely weak and only partially sought to act out the geopolitical 'directives' of its own ideology.

As an approach to understanding the nature of regional power, geopolitics has little to offer. On the one hand, it relies too heavily on abstract indices of power and geographical 'privileges' without explaining the political context in which these might yield some concrete result. On the other, even under military governments, there was a significant gap between the so-called lessons of geopolitical analysis and the actual motivations and course of the country's foreign policy.

Dependency Theory

Dependency theory forms the third theoretical basis on which Brazil has been viewed as a major regional power. As has been frequently argued the term 'dependency theory' has been used to cover a variety of distinct, and often conflicting, theories. Amongst the range of theories, two are relevant for this chapter. The first relates to the concepts of 'associated dependent development' and 'dependent development' elaborated by Fernando Henrique Cardoso and Peter Evans.[16] In contrast to earlier ideas of the 'development of underdevelopment', Cardoso and Evans stressed the extent to which peripheral capitalist development was possible and was occurring – not least in the Brazil of the late 1960s and early 1970s. They saw Brazil as a prime example of a country which, because of changing patterns of global manufacturing, increased competition between transnational enterprises (TNEs), the size of its domestic market, and the strength of its state apparatus, was able in the 1970s to achieve high rates of economic growth. The core of such development was the alliance between the state and TNEs. Development could therefore occur in peripheral capitalist societies although the continuing central role of foreign capital ensured that it remained dependent, distorted and unequal:

> 'development' because it is characterised by the sort of accumulation of capital and increasingly complex differentiation of internal productive structure that was integral to the development of the 'core' countries, and 'dependent' because it is indelibly marked by the effects of continued dependence on capital housed in those countries.[17]

Such a view sought to explain the existence of rapid development within peripheral capitalist economies and the consequent increasing differentiation and inequality between them. In this sense it can be said to shed some light on the economic basis of Brazil's regional power.

Moreover, for all its flaws, the emphasis on the limits, constraints and distortions of the Brazilian development model and the continuing centrality of dependence on the international economic system has provided a far more adequate framework for understanding the economic crisis of the 1980s than the literature on Brazil as a future world power.

But whatever its strengths and weaknesses as a theory of *economic development* dependency theory has been particularly unilluminating as a guide to understanding the *foreign policies* of developing countries, especially large and complex countries such as Brazil. This is true in terms of Brazil's relations with the core capitalist countries where the structural power stressed by dependency theorists represents only part of the picture, albeit a very important part. It is even more true within the context of South-South relations. Indeed one of the major weaknesses in most dependency writing is that it provides little for understanding the character or content of relations *between* developing countries.

During the late 1960s and 1970s one variety of dependency theory attempted to overcome this weakness and to understand Brazilian regional policy within a broad dependency perspective. What emerged was the notion of 'sub-imperialism', which came in two variants. It was used first in a specific sense by Ruy Mauro Marini to describe the character of Brazil's overall political and economic system: 'the form which dependent capitalism assumes upon reaching the stage of monopolies and finance capital'.[18] The whole thrust of his work was to explain the internal reasons why Brazilian capitalism needed to expand beyond its borders. His particular explanation (based on the notion of 'superexploitation') was widely criticised but the term persisted as a label for a second and more general idea – 'to denote a subsidiary expression of US expansionism through the aegis of another country such as Iran or Brazil'.[19] Thus, according to a prominent proponent of this position, Paulo Schilling, 'one had to disguise North American domination and the best way for this was by choosing a junior partner, a straw man which would represent yankee interests in a united Latin American market'. Brazil thus 'fulfills its orders and functions as a gendarme'.[20]

As we shall see, the problem with this view was that it greatly overstated the closeness of the US-Brazilian 'alliance' and it played down Brazil's own reasons for pursuing an assertive regional policy in this period. Although the idea of Brazil as a 'sub-imperialist power' has some validity for the initial period after 1964, by the late 1960s the relationship with Washington had begun to erode. Brazil's moderately assertive policy towards the region of the early 1970s followed, then, from Brazil's own ambitions rather than from actions taken at the behest of the United States. It may have been 'imperialist' in a rather weak sense but it was only very partially a 'sub-imperialist' power. Moreover, even if it was a satisfactory basis for understanding Brazilian policy in the early-1970s, its relevance declined progressively as we move through the 1970s and into the 1980s.

Each of these theoretical approaches has helped reinforce an exaggerated and misleading view of Brazil as a major regional power. Abstract power capabilities, geopolitical 'necessities' and the dynamics of peripheral capitalist development all represent important elements in the overall picture of Brazil's international role. However, they distort our understanding of Brazil's regional position, first, by failing to place it within the broader context of the country's foreign policy and, second, by failing to consider the detailed evolution of Brazil's regional policy. It is to this story that we now turn.

REGIONAL PROFILE AND THE EVOLUTION OF REGIONAL POLICY

One major problem with the notion of South America as a distinct and homogeneous region is that it underplays the very important sense in which Brazil has been historically distinct and distant from the rest of South America. This distinctiveness resulted partly from the character of Brazilian society: linguistically distinct as a Portuguese-speaking country; culturally distinct as a result of the differing patterns of Portuguese colonialism (and, very importantly, decolonisation); racially distinct because of the small size of the Indian population and the large section of the population of African origin. For cultural models and for political ideas Brazilian élites looked not to their neighbours or indigenous traditions but first to Europe and subsequently to the United States. Miami is still the first foreign city to be visited by most Brazilians. Distance was reinforced by geography and the sheer difficulty of establishing regular communication with the other capitals of post-independence South America. Again it is still far easier and cheaper to get from, say, Rio to Miami than from Rio to Lima. The separation of Brazil from the rest of the region also resulted from the pattern of economic development established during the colonial period and the extent to which economic ties both in the colonial and post-colonial periods were tied firmly to the core capitalist countries. Finally, Brazil's very size and apparent natural dominance led to a deep-rooted and persistent fear within Spanish-speaking America of Brazilian expansionism and its potentially hegemonic position within the region.

Brazil's relations with Argentina represent the obvious exception to this picture of distance and minimal interaction. Here the relationship was intense and the historic rivalry between the two countries formed the distinguishing feature of the international relations of the southern part of the region. Two points should be stressed here: first, that although rivalry predominated, relations in the twentieth century have been a complex mixture of conflict and cooperation.[21] And second, that from the time of Barão do Rio Branco in the early twentieth century down to the 1970s, Brazil looked to the United States as a prime means of balancing the power of Argentina, a tactic which only served to reinforce the distance and difference between Brazil and its neighbours.[22]

Let us now look in a little more detail at the evolution of Brazil's regional policy since the late 1960s. At the risk of some oversimplification, two distinct phases can be isolated, the first from 1969 to 1979 and the second from 1979 to the 1990s.

Suspicion and Hostility, 1969–79

The foreign policy of the military government that took power after the coup of 1964 was firmly anchored on relations with the United States. Under the first two military presidents – Castello Branco (1964–67) and Costa e Silva (1967–69) – there remained some interest in pursuing regional economic integration and in the formation of a regional anti-communist alliance. However, by the late 1960s, the historic distance between Brazil and its Spanish-speaking neighbours was once more all too evident. Relations between Brazil and the other major states of the region varied from cool to openly hostile. The size of Brazil combined with the extremely rapid economic development of the years of the 'economic miracle' rekindled traditional fears of Brazil's expansionist and hegemonic ambitions.

Such fears and suspicions were strengthened by the rhetoric of *Brasil potencia* that dominated the foreign policy of the Médici government (1969–74). The image stressed by the Médici government was of a rapidly developing middle power moving towards First World status and having little in common with the other countries of the region. As the foreign minister, Mario Gibson Barbosa put it:

> I would say, before anything else and quite simply, that Brazil is a rising power. I do not believe that it is possible to argue with this assertion. This statement . . . is not a product of *ufanismo* [national pride] with which people used to describe in our textbooks, the riches of our country, but on the contrary results from a serious realisation of what we already are.[23]

Spanish American fears were also fuelled by the very visible influence within the military government of the kinds of geopolitical thinking described earlier, with its talk of 'moving frontiers' and historic missions to regional predominance. Moreover, the reassertion of the special relationship between Brazil and the United States that followed the 1964 military coup sharpened the traditional Spanish-American view of Brazil as a trojan horse for US imperialism and it was in this period that the view of Brazil as a 'sub-imperialist' power was most prevalent. Political distance was increased by the ideological divide that separated Brazil's government from Allende's Chile, Velasco's Peru, Lanusse in Argentina and Torres in Bolivia, and there was no longer any possibility of constructing the anti-communist regional front with which the Brazilian military government had toyed in the 1964 to 1969 period.

Finally, the Brazilian government had come to see little scope for the attempts at greater regional economic integration that had been proposed in the 1960s. Indeed, although Brazil continued with rhetoric of the need for Latin American unity, its attitude towards regional organisations was at best ambiguous. On the one hand, multilateral regional organisations could usefully complement Brazil's economic diplomacy and help prevent the emergence of a united anti-Brazilian grouping. On the other, as an economically more advanced country, it was increasingly wary of any moves towards integration that would involve making concessions to weaker members. Above all, Brazil was reluctant to allow Latin American economic or political solidarity to interfere with its own bilateral relations with the United States. Despite two major regional tours by the foreign minister, Mario Gibson Barbosa in 1971 and 1973, relations remained strained. The focal points of opposition were Venezuela and Argentina. Relations with Venezuela had deteriorated in the 1960s as a result of Venezuela's decision to sever relations with Brazil following the 1964 military coup, and were further strained by Brazil's abrogation of its oil-purchase agreements and its progressive switch to Middle East oil. Caracas was also deeply concerned with expansion of Brazilian influence in the Amazon basin following the launch of the *Programa de Integracão Nacional* in 1970. This involved the extensive colonisation of the Amazon and the construction of a network of strategic highways (especially the Transamazon) and owed much of its inspiration to the ideas of Brazil's geopoliticians, especially General Golbery.

In the case of Argentina, the close ideological ties that had existed between Presidents Costa e Silva and Ongania were ended by the arrival in power in Buenos Aires in 1971 of General Lanusse. The new government in Buenos Aires preached ideological pluralism, improved relations with Allende's Chile and favoured the lifting of the Cuban suspension from the OAS. More importantly, it sought to intensify Argentinian ties with the Andean Pact in order to form a united anti-Brazilian front (this, at least, was how it appeared to Brasilia). The increased tension drew on the general suspicions outlined above but developed around three principal areas of discord.

In the first place, there was an increase in rivalry for influence in the buffer states of Bolivia, Paraguay and, to a lesser extent, Uruguay. The Médici and Geisel governments placed a strong emphasis on the expansion of Brazil's political and economic presence in these states. Relations with Bolivia had been difficult until the August 1971 coup which brought the pro-Brazilian Hugo Banzer to power and in which Brazilian involvement appears to have been reasonably clearly established. Brazil's exports to Bolivia rose from US$ 3.9 million in 1969 to US$ 126 million in 1979. Brazilian investment in Bolivia grew rapidly and, as in Paraguay, there was extensive colonisation by Brazilians in the border regions. In November 1973 Brazil and Bolivia signed an agreement under which Bolivia would supply Brazil with 240 million cubic feet of gas per day over a twenty year period in return for Brazilian investment in the steel industry. This was followed by further agreements in May 1974 and October 1978 when it was agreed to increase the supply of natural gas from 240 to 500 million cubic feet. Political ties between Brazil and Stroessner's Paraguay were close, with a succession of presidential visits. Brazil's exports to Paraguay rose from US$ 6.5 million in 1969 to US$ 324 million in 1979 and imports from just US$ 387 000 to US$ 71 million. The construction of new bridges, new road and rail links and the use by Paraguay of the Atlantic port of Paranaguá helped to draw the landlocked country into Brazil's economic orbit, as did the fact that, by 1973, there were around 40 000 Brazilian 'colonists' in the Paraguayan region of Alto Paraná.

The second focus of friction developed over the use of hydroelectric resources of the Paraná river. This development lay at the heart of Brazilian policy in Paraguay. The 1966 Ata das Cataratas had both ended the disputed claim to the area around the Sete Quedas falls and had laid the basis for future agreement on the use of the Paraná river. Further meetings in March 1969 and July 1971 between the Paraguayan and Brazilian presidents prepared the ground for the signature in April 1973 of the Itaipu Agreement which envisaged the construction of a 12.6 million KW hydro-electric plant – the world's largest hydro-electric project. Argentinian opposition to these developments had been growing in the late 1960s but re-emerged as a bitter source of discord in mid-1972 and continued to dominate relations until 1979. Third, the nuclear rivalry between Brazil and Argentina, visible since the Brazilian decision in the late 1960s to move ahead with the acquisition of nuclear technology, grew more intense and was sharpened immensely by the 1975 Brazil-West German nuclear agreement, the largest ever transfer of nuclear technology to a developing country.

The 'Latinamericanization' of Foreign Policy since 1979

This pattern of relations between Brazil and its Spanish-speaking neighbours which varied from coolness to outright hostility began to change in the late 1970s. An early sign of change was Brazil's proposal in November 1976 for the creation of an Amazon Pact to assist the joint development of the Amazon Basin. After considerable initial difficulties, Brazil was successful in overcoming the suspicions of the seven other countries involved and the treaty was signed in 1978. Whilst the treaty fitted the traditional Brazilian aim of trying to minimise its isolation and allay the fears of its neighbours and whilst it hardly led to any particularly notable concrete results, it does provide an indication of a more activist approach to the expansion of political ties with the region.

Far more significant were the initiatives taken by the government of President Figueiredo (1979–85). Economic relations continued to expand. Brazilian exports to the region rose by 69 per cent between 1979 and 1981 to US$ 4264 million and in 1981 Latin America's share of total Brazilian exports (18.4 per cent) surpassed that of the United States for the first time. There was also an important shift in political attitudes. Building on the improvement of relations with Peru and the launching of the Amazon Pact, Brazil embarked on an intensive campaign to improve political relations. On one level, the new policy was visible in the language used to describe foreign policy. To quote foreign minister Guerreiro in 1980:

> A fundamental fact is our identity as a Latin American country . . . We are Latin Americans, what has been lacking was to exploit the conse-quences of our identity.[24]

On a more practical level, clear evidence of the new policy could be seen in the unprecedented range and frequency of political contacts between Brazil and other governments in the region. Between 1979 and 1981 Figueiredo paid official visits to Venezuela, Paraguay, Argentina, Ecuador, Bolivia, Peru, Colombia and Chile: a striking contrast to the normal dominance of visits to the United States and Europe. There was also a marked improvement in relations between Brazil and the Andean Pact.

The early years of the Figueiredo government also saw the first signs of the rapprochement with Argentina. In October 1979, Brazil signed an agreement with Paraguay and Argentina which effectively ended the protracted dispute over the Itaipu dam. This was followed in May 1980 by Figueiredo's visit to Buenos Aires during which a package of ten agreements was signed.

These included an agreement on nuclear cooperation, covering joint research and the transfer of some nuclear materials. In August 1980 Videla paid a return visit to Brasilia, during which a further seven protocols and conventions were signed extending the nuclear agreements. As a visible sign of the new climate, 1980 also saw the resumption of joint naval manoeuvres.

On the Brazilian side, the most important factor behind this shift in policy was the growing perception that its earlier regional policy had been thoroughly counter-productive. Talk of Brazil's emergence as a great power and Golbery's geopolitics had merely served to exacerbate Spanish-American fears and to create the very situation that Brazil feared, namely the formation of a united anti-Brazilian grouping. Moreover, such a policy had become an obstacle to other more important Brazilian goals, especially the expansion of economic ties and the promotion of Brazilian exports. Finally, if the central theme of Brazilian policy was to diversify its external relations and to increase the range of its foreign policy options, then it became increasingly illogical to all but exclude Latin America from that process.

For Argentina, the most immediate push came from the traditional logic of balance of power politics. 1979 saw a marked deterioration in Argentinian-Chilean relations over the Beagle Channel dispute, with the two countries on the brink of war in late 1979. The immediacy of this threat underlined the logic of rapprochement with the old adversary, Brazil. Moreover, it had become clear by this time that the special relationship between Washington and Brasilia had unravelled – the most visible signs being the bitter disputes of the Carter years over human rights and nuclear proliferation. The old Argentinian fear of Brazil as a 'sub-imperialist' power had therefore become increasingly outdated and irrelevant.

Rapprochement was also assisted by the nature of the issues. On the one hand, it was clear to Argentinian policymakers that there was little that they could do about the Itaipu project which was by then nearing completion. Indeed dragging out talks until this point had been the chief Brazilian tactic. On the other hand, although the nuclear rivalry was far from dead, the very visible failures of the Brazilian nuclear programme and the technical weakness of the West German-supplied technology eased Argentinian fears in this area.

After this initial improvement, relations with Argentina slowed in the early 1980s. The Falklands/Malvinas War of 1982 was a worrying sign that the extreme 'territorial nationalism' in Argentina had not disappeared, that geopolitical thinking still dominated the minds of many, and that armed conflict might actually be possible within the region – a contingency that had seemed remote for most of the post-war period. Moreover, Argentinian rearmament after the war fuelled fears both within Brazil and beyond that the region might be moving towards an arms race. In the early 1980s a number of commentators were predicting that the region was becoming more conflictual and more like the rest of the developing world. First, the struggle for natural resources had, it was argued, drastically increased the stakes of many historical disputes: hydroelectric resources on the River Paraná between Brazil and Argentina, access to off-shore oil, fishing and seabed minerals in the case of Chile and Argentina (and, in many Latin American minds, Britain and Argentina); access to oil once more in the border disputes between Peru and Ecuador, Venezuela and Guyana, and Venezuela and Colombia. Second, it was argued that the re-emergence of superpower rivalry in the Third World had increased the stakes and intensity of regional insecurity, above all in Central America. Third, many saw the overall decline of United States hegemony and the virtual death by 1982 of the Inter-American Military System as reducing the ability of

Washington to maintain 'discipline' within its own sphere of influence. And finally, many noted the continued prevalence of extreme geopolitical thinking amongst the militaries of the Southern Cone and the fact that arms spending and the capabilities of national arms industries appeared to be increasing.

However, at least within the region of Brazil and the Southern Cone, this gloomy picture has not materialised and the differences between the region and other parts of the developing world have become more apparent. Not only have Chilean-Argentinian relations improved but the return to civilian rule in March 1985 saw a significant acceleration in Brazil's moves towards closer relations with the region. This was visible in the official statements proclaiming Brazil's Latin American identity; in the far more prominent Brazilian role in the new multilateral groupings such as the Cartegena Consensus, the Contadora Support Group and, most importantly, the Group of Eight and the Rio Group; and in Brazil's policy of restoring relations with Cuba in 1986 and seeking to bring Cuba back into the Latin American fold.

But it has been rapprochement with Argentina that has produced the most concrete results. In November 1985 Presidents Sarney and Alfonsin signed a trade agreement which sought to progressively dismantle trade barriers over a ten year period. They also agreed to form joint working parties on the exchange of primary and capital goods, science and technology, transportation, communications and energy. A flurry of schemes for increased economic cooperation led in July 1986 to the signature of the *Ata para a Integração* (Integration Act). This was followed in November 1988 by the signature of the *Tratado de Integração, Cooperação e Desenvolvimento* (Treaty of Integration, Cooperation and Development). The most recent phase occurred in July 1990 with the decision to establish a full common market by the end of 1994.[25] In April 1991 Paraguay and Uruguay were formally included in this process of economic integration.

The durability of the Brazilian-Argentinian rapprochement can be explained by a combination of domestic, regional and global developments. The broader impact of the international system will be examined in the next section. Here three points should be stressed: the increased stability in the nuclear relationship, the impact of domestic political change, and shifts in the economic policies of the two countries.

First, there is the important element of stability that has been achieved in the nuclear relationship. The failures of the Brazilian nuclear programme both increased the need for cooperation and reduced Argentinian fears of rapid and destabilising Brazilian progress in this area. Brazil had much to gain from cooperating with Argentina's more advanced nuclear technology, whilst Argentina realised that it no longer had to fear a rapid Brazilian push to acquire a nuclear weapons capability. Morever, both countries continued through the 1980s to see the acquisition of technology in this area as important to their long-term development (and perhaps, at some later point, military) objectives and to view themselves as having a common position against attempts by outside powers to limit the proliferation of nuclear technology.

Increased mutual confidence on the nuclear question followed from a far greater degree of transparency. This has been perhaps the most important result of the low-level technological cooperation that gradually expanded through the 1980s. But it was also the result of greater public openness. Thus Brazil gave Argentina prior notice of its public announcement in late 1987 of the existence of the secret so-called 'parallel' nuclear programme and of the functioning of a domestically-built gas centrifuge enrichement facility. Most dramatically, confidence was enhanced by Sarney's visits to Argentina's nuclear facilities in 1987 and 1988, and Alfonsin's visit in 1988 to the hitherto officially unacknowledged Brazilian facility at Aramar.[26] President Collor's formal renunciation of Brazil's parallel nuclear programme in September 1990 further enhanced this increased confidence.

The second point concerns the role played by domestic political developments. The literature on Third World insecurity has rightly stressed the extent to which conflict and insecurity result from the internal weaknesses of many post-colonial states: the fragility of state structures and the difficulties of sustaining political legitimacy; the problems of maintaining economic development; the existence of ethnic and religious division; the growth of secession movements and so on. If we adopt Barry Buzan's usage of the terms 'weak' and 'strong' states to cover the degree of domestic social cohesion, then it is clear that both Brazil and Argentina are somewhere in the middle of the league.[27] Their 'weakness' in this sense has been well illustrated by the painful process of democratic transition and the protracted problems of democratic consolidation. Yet, as against the situation in Peru or Central America, there is little spill-over between the domestic difficulties of the two countries and their international rivalry. In contrast to, for example, the situation between India and Pakistan, Brazilian-Argentinian competition has been largely a case of traditional inter-state rivalry with little or no attempts to interfere in the domestic affairs of the other state.

The one area where domestic factors have mattered is in the nature of the respective governments. Clearly harmony was not likely to be furthered by the existence of insecure military governments, heavily influenced by extreme and often paranoid geopolitical fears (for example, that Brazil was building the Itaipu dam in order to threaten Buenos Aires with flooding) and, in the case of Argentina, inclined to use an aggressive foreign policy in order to buttress their declining political legitimacy. The move towards civilian rule has therefore been an important factor in the rapprochement. Their common interests as newly democratic governments facing similar problems and threats has been a frequent theme of the rhetoric of the post-1985 period. The agreements and presidential meetings have explicitly sought to provide mutual support for the process of democratic consolidation. Indeed some commentators have even suggested that the new era of greater international harmony in the region can be seen as an extension of the Kantian liberal peace.[28]

The link between democratisation and improved relations is important but should not be exaggerated. In Brazil there has been great continuity of foreign policy despite changes in the form and complexion of governments. Indeed the Brazilian policy of improving relations with Argentina began under a military government. In addition, the military remain politically powerful in both Brazil and Argentina. In Brazil their political role was explicitly recognised by the 1988 Constitution and the military successfully fought off proposals for a civilian minister of defence and for a parliamentary system that would make the five military ministers in the cabinet answerable to Congress. Given the extent of military power, the rapprochement with Argentina cannot therefore be seen solely as a policy of the civilian government. Whilst the greater enthusiasm of the civilian élites and of President Sarney was crucial, it would have been unlikely to develop this far without general agreement of the military and without a parallel shift in military thinking. In Argentina, the important point is not the total disappearance of the political power of the military (which clearly has not occurred) but rather the disrepute of aggressive and unsuccessful military adventures brought about by the Falklands/Malvinas fiasco.

Whilst the impact of political change has been generally positive, the role of the third factor, economic developments, has been far more ambiguous. The severity and uniformity of the economic crisis and the impact of the so-called 'lost decade' of Latin American development, served to underline common interests and common perspectives between the two countries. The negative external environment re-emphasised the need to broaden and strengthen the regional market and to institutionalise the economic interdependence that had been growing through the 1970s. There was therefore a need to present a united front against a hostile world particularly as regards trade and debt issues.

Yet against these pressures to cooperate, the economic crisis itself made the consolidation of the rapprochement more difficult. The onset of the debt crisis in 1982 had a disastrous effect on inter-regional trade, with Latin America's share of Brazilian exports falling from 19.3 per cent in 1980 to 9.7 per cent in 1985, rising slightly to 11.4 per cent in 1989. Trade with Argentina expanded slowly but the overall salience remained low. Recession in both countries has made it difficult to persuade businesses to take advantage of the new opportunities offered by the integration agreements, whilst macro-economic policy and strategies for dealing with the foreign debt in the two countries have been erratic and rarely in line.

Those taking an optimistic view of the July 1990 agreement on the creation of a free trade area can point to the gradual emergence of a more balanced trading relationship, especially since what had appeared to be an entrenched Brazilian trade surplus ended in 1989 following a particularly notable increase in Argentinian capital goods exports to Brazil. Moreover, the prospect of moves towards freer trade may be based on more deep-rooted and parallel shifts in the macro-economic policies of the two countries. In both there has been a marked shift towards a greater reliance on market mechanisms; a desire to restructure and reduce the economic role of the state; and, externally, a determination to reduce trade and investment barriers and to place far greater emphasis on the importance of integration into the world market.

Yet, despite the increased convergence of economic policies, progress is unlikely to be fast: stabilisation plans in both countries have caused deep recession and an eventual expansion of bilateral trade will remain dependent on broader economic recovery in the two countries and the ability of the new economic policies to attract foreign investment. Just as distrust remains strong within the military, so there are powerful business lobbies whose opposition to further integration will have to be overcome. The existence of a deep-rooted security community will therefore remain dependent on the successful expansion of economic ties, as well as on an increase in the still very low level of societal contacts.

EXTERNAL CONSTRAINTS

The pattern of international relations within a region such as Latin America results from the interplay of domestic, regional and global factors. It is for this reason that it is often so difficult to demarcate a region and define a regional power in purely regional terms. Whilst it is clearly misleading to view the pattern of Brazil's relations with its regional neighbours as in some way derivative of the dynamics of the global international system, the broader international context cannot be ignored. This section draws together the two main sets of factors that have been at work on this level: First, the constraints that result from proximity to the power of the United States; and, second, the changing relative position of Brazil's hemispheric relations within the country's broader foreign policy.

For most of the post-war period it was common to argue that the international political system acted as a significant constraint on Brazil's capacity to act as a major regional power. According to this argument, Brazil's rise to regional predominance in the post-war period which should have followed from the decline of Argentina was nullified by the expansion of the United States' sphere of influence to cover the entire region. What had been a largely autonomous regional balance of power was therefore overshadowed by Brazil's position within a US dominated power system and by the constraints of the Cold War.

Such a view cannot stand as a sufficient explanation of Brazil's regional policy. But there are elements here that are important. The combination of the Second World War and the Cold War did lead to the creation of a US dominated power system based on its position as the dominant trade partner and provider of aid, investment and technology; the creation of the so-called Inter-American Military System; the dominance of North American cultural influences; and a degree of ideological consensus between Washington and Brazil's governing élites. Brazil's position within the United States' sphere of influence therefore meant that there was no empty backyard or *chasse gardée* of the kind that France was able to develop in Africa: an area of low strategic priority to both superpowers (at least up to the mid-1970s) in which historical and cultural ties, a willingness to intervene militarily and the position of bridge to Europe enabled Paris to carve its own sphere of influence.

But it was not solely the presence of US power within the region that militated against a larger Brazilian role. Central to the history of US-Latin American relations has been an alternative conception of regionalism, vigorously propounded by the United States and successfully implemented in the institutional structure of the Inter-American System. Brazil, then, was not only a rather separate member of the Latin American family. In addition the notion of Latin America as a distinct region had to contend with an alternative regionalist conception, which stressed inter-American solidarity and the common interests of the western hemisphere as a whole and which would inevitably be dominated by the 'colossus of the North'.

Brazil's geopolitical position also worked against attempts to manipulate superpower rivalry for its own regional advantage. What David Vital has called 'contingent power' deriving from the manipulation of Great

Power rivalry has represented an important source of potential leverage for would-be regional powers.[29] Given the overall character of post-war Brazilian foreign policy (aimed at economic development and economic rather than military power), such a policy was undercut both by the dangers of this strategy (in the form of US antagonism and the withdrawal of US aid, loans and investment) and by the marginal economic gains that might have resulted from closer relations with the Soviet Union. Attempts to diversify relations to include the Soviet Union certainly played a significant role in Brazilian foreign policy in the 1970s. But anything beyond expansion of low-level economic ties was precluded both by the absence of significant economic complementarity and by the dangers of antagonising the United States.

Lastly, and in many ways most significant, was the impact of a United States sphere of influence on the pattern and distribution of military power within the region. Brazil's location within a US dominated security system drastically reduced the need to build up a large military capability against extra-regional threats. There was never a convincing need for a serious defensive capability against extra-regional powers which would inevitably have upset the regional balance of power and given Brazil the capacity to develop a more assertive regional role. The obvious but very important contrast here is with India. For India the need for defence against major outside powers (above all China) led to a clear perceived need to create a large and powerful military. This, in turn, inevitably altered the balance of power of India's relations with Pakistan and its other weaker neigbours. On this argument the relatively low level of conflict in post-war Latin America is thus not so much a result of an activist policing role by the regional hegemon, but rather that the isolation of the region enabled it to escape the destructive interaction between regional and extra-regional power balances that has so bedevilled the Middle East or the Indian sub-continent.

But what of the argument that the existence of a US sphere of influence offered Brazil opportunities rather than constraints? The idea of building a regional role around a special relationship with a major extra-regional power has been a common feature of the post-war world, although the relative importance of this extra-regional support has varied from case to case: Israel's regional power is dependent on the continued support of the United States. Cuba's regional role in Africa derived in large part, from its alliance with the Soviet Union. India's relationship with the Soviet Union has buttressed its regional power in the sub-continent.

Such a notion has been present in Brazilian foreign policy. It formed part of Vargas's strategy in the Second World War and his plans for the post-war world. It also played a central role in the foreign policy of the Brazilian military following the military coup of 1964. The foreign policy of the post-1964 government was based upon a re-assertion of the special relationship with the United States with strong ideological foundations. Thus Brazil supported US Cold War positions by, for instance, breaking relations with Cuba, gave vocal support over Vietnam (there were even discussions about sending Brazilian forces) and, most notably, dispatched Brazilian troops to the Dominican Republic in 1965. In the minds of President Castello Branco and his advisers was the idea of what General Golbery had called a *barganha leal*, the loyal bargain by which Brazil would be rewarded for its special relationship and fidelity to the anti-communist cause: rewarded by increased economic aid and investment, increased military assistance, and recognition of Brazil's role as the dominant power (its *real estatura*) in the region. For Golbery, not only did Brazil possess a number of important assets of great value to the United States in its global struggle with the Soviet Union, but geographical distance meant that Brazil's role within South America did not need to clash with that of the United States:

> We can also invoke a 'manifest destiny', even more so because it does not collide in the Caribbean with that of our more powerful brothers to the north.[30]

Yet, already by the late 1960s, the idea of this kind of privileged relationship had begun to unravel. For the United States, once the perceived threat of 'another Cuba' in Latin America began to recede, Brazil (and the region as a whole) lost its priority on the US foreign policy agenda, an agenda increasingly dominated by the Vietnam War and by the growth of superpower détente. Moreover, the deterioration of the political situation in Brazil and the moves towards still greater repression and brutality pushed Washington to distance itself from Brazil's military government (aided by powerful criticism in Congress of human rights abuses in Brazil). Finally, however much Washington valued Brazil as a regional ally, it was unwilling to see the balance of power within the region disturbed by an overmighty Brazil. As in the past it sought to balance its relations with Spanish and Portuguese speaking Latin America.[31]

Thus, whilst Washington continued to pay rhetorical deference to Brazil's position (as in the rhetoric of the Nixon Doctrine and in Nixon's famous remark in 1971 that 'as Brazil goes, so will go also the rest of the Latin American continent'), the relationship became gradually more distant and the number of points of friction increased, especially over economic and trade issues. Indeed Brazil is a good example of how the Nixon Doctrine, which explicity focused upon the development of a new security role for major regional powers, did not provide an especially accurate guide to policy. As Robert Litvak puts it:

> On the periphery, the transitional and ambiguous nature of the Nixon Doctrine was evidenced in the awkward, uncoordinated manner in which the Administration conducted relations with those countries which were nominally targetted to be recipients of any regional devolution of American power – Brazil, Zaire, Iran and Indonesia.[32]

With the gradual unravelling of the attempts of the early military governments to revive the special relationship with the United States, Brazil entered a period of sustained foreign policy activism that lasted from the early 1970s to the onset of the debt crisis in 1982. This activism was driven principally by economic motives and was focused heavily on the expansion of economic relations. The expansion of power political influence remained very much in the background. Still more important for the argument of this chapter was the fact that this activism was aimed overwhelmingly at the expansion of Brazil's relations beyond the hemisphere. The achievement of regional predominance was *not* a central aim of policy (except perhaps, as we have seen, in terms of Brazil's smaller neighbours to its south). The dominant theme of foreign policy was the construction of a broader international role through an extensive policy of diversification. This would both help underpin Brazil's economic development by providing new export markets, new sources of oil, and new sources of technology, loans and investment, and help reduce the historic constraints imposed by its geopolitical position within a US sphere of influence. This activist policy led to the expansion of relations in four areas: first, with Western Europe and Japan (where Brazil could play upon the common perception that it was indeed an emerging major power); second with the Soviet Union and the socialist countries; third, with the developing world, particularly Africa and the Middle East; and fourth, with the Third World movement in its demands for a New International Economic Order.

This activist policy of diversification came under increasing strain with the growing economic crisis of the 1980s. Indeed much of the explanation for the 'Latinamericanization' of Brazilian foreign policy in the 1980s reflects the absence of the kinds of alternative options that Brazil had sought to develop in the 1970s. Thus well before the last North/South summit at Cancun in 1981 it had become clear that the Third World movement had failed in its calls for a radical reform of the international system. Brazilian markets in many parts of the developing world, especially

Africa and the Middle East declined significantly – even if they did not disappear altogether. Although great hopes continued to be placed on relations with Europe and although there was much European rhetoric about support for democracy in Latin America, there was little in the way of concrete assistance. Japan remained the focus of great expectations. But, whilst the Japanese economic role continued to grow, Tokyo remained wary of increasing its economic stake in Brazil given the severity of the economic crisis and the extent of political uncertainty and confusion that followed the end of military rule in 1985.

Much of Brazil's return to the region can therefore be explained by the relative absence of alternatives. Moreover the difficulty of finding significant external economic assistance is set to remain. The collapse of communism in Europe, German unification and the movement towards completion of the EC's internal market by 1992 have led to a period of introspection in Europe that is likely to continue well into the 1990s. More importantly, the need to promote economic reform in Eastern Europe has served to increase the number of middle-income countries competing for a limited amount of economic aid, foreign investment and technical help.

Yet if one set of external factors worked to push Brazil towards the region and thereby revive the possibility of a more assertive, perhaps even dominant, regional role, the changing position of the United States worked to complicate the picture. On the one hand, US policy in the Reagan years aimed explicity at the reassertion of US hegemony over the region and was openly antagonistic towards any emerging regional groupings whether political (for example over Central America) or economic (for example the series of sporadic attempts by the major debtors to coordinate debt strategy). On the other hand, the debt crisis meant that Washington was once more the critical focus for Brazilian foreign policy. Not only did the US relative share of Brazilian trade grow significantly but, more importantly, it was Washington that would determine the management of the debt crisis, either directly or through its influence over US-based financial institutions. Brazil's 'return to the region' therefore coincided both with a reassertion of US hegemony over the region and with a strikingly negative shift in its own bilateral relationship with the United States.

The dominant role of the United States is also set to remain. In many areas of the world, it is argued, the end of the Cold War will work to the benefit of would-be regional powers. On the one hand, the interest of the superpowers in exploiting regional insecurity will diminish. On the other, their mutual withdrawal will lead to an increase in 'regional space'. However, in Latin America there can be no easy assumption of a significant decline of US hegemony. The extent of US power remains overwhelming and, in the absence of alternatives, the economic condition of the region will continue to be critically influenced by US economic policies and by US preferences over the management of the debt crisis. Moreover, 'Monroeist' tendencies in the United States are far from dead and it is noteworthy that Cold War rationales for US intervention have quickly been replaced by historically more deep-rooted arguments: the need to keep order, to extend democracy and to protect US economic interests.

Finally, the fear of emerging regionalism in other parts of the world has led Washington to think once more about a revived and extended western-hemisphere bloc and strengthened inter-American regional cooperation. Such a trend can be seen in the proposals for a Free Trade Agreement with Mexico (and, more recently with Chile) and in Bush's Enterprise Iniative for the Americas speech in July 1990 and his 1990 tour of the region. It is too early to tell how much of this rhetoric will be incorporated in concrete US policy. Much will depend on the results of the Uruguay Round, on the evolution of the EC after 1992, and on the future state of US-Japanese relations. But it does suggest two things: first, that one of the most interesting issues for the 1990s will be the relationship between the new regionalism developed between Brazil, Argentina and possibly Chile on the one hand, and the broader hemispheric regionalism promoted by Washington on the other; and second, that success for hemispheric regionalism will naturally tend to undercut any Brazilian attempt at a broader and more significant regional role.

CONCLUSION: WHAT KIND OF REGIONAL POWER?

This chapter has sought to outline and explain the evolution of Brazil's regional policy through two distinctive periods. In the first period, relations were characterised by mutual suspicion and hostility and there was certainly a considerable amount of rhetoric about Brazil's position as an emerging great power and about its 'natural' predominance within Latin America. In the period since 1979 the direction and nature of Brazil's regional policy has changed very considerably. The suspicion and hostility of the earlier period has given way to a more active and cooperative approach, as well as to a relatively durable and solidly based rapprochement with Argentina that represents a basic change in the pattern of Latin American international relations.

The character of relations has certainly changed. But what kind of regional *power* has Brazil become? Let us think first in terms of relational power: the capacity to use military resources or to exploit economic ties to force a direct change in the policies of another state. From this perspective Brazil's power is strongest *vis-à-vis* the border states of Bolivia, Paraguay and Uruguay. As we have seen, it was here that the geopolitical ideas of the military did produce some concrete results during the 1970s. The Brazilian military was prepared to intervene in the internal affairs of these states, most notably in Bolivia in 1971 and in the form of cross-border anti-subversive activities in Uruguay by the Brazilian secret services. By the end of the decade, its economic influence within this region had certainly increased very significantly. The increase of trade relations, the construction of external communication links, border colonisation and, above all, the Itaipu dam project had brought this sub-region firmly within Brazil's economic orbit. Moreover much of Brazil's economic dominance in this area remains. Thus in 1989 Brazil accounted for 27 per cent of Paraguayan exports (as against 1.7 per cent in 1970 and 30 per cent in 1980) and 15 per cent of its imports (as against 3.2 per cent in 1970 and 25 per cent in 1980). In 1989 Brazil accounted for 22 per cent of Uruguayan exports and 27 per cent of Uruguayan imports and supplied 32 per cent of Bolivian imports (up from 22 per cent in 1980). In other ways, however, its economic power in this area has declined with a heavily indebted Brazil no longer able to advance the kinds of export credits and technical assistance that it had provided in the 1970s.

But beyond the border states, the limits to Brazil's economic power remain very visible. For Brazil the salience of the region fell back in the 1980s after the rapid gains of the 1970s: in 1989, for example, Latin America's share of Brazilian exports stood at 11 per cent – as against 10 per cent in 1964 and 19.3 per cent in 1980. More important is Brazil's limited salience as an economic partner for the majority of major Latin American states. Thus in 1989 Brazil accounted for only 1.2 per cent and 1.9 per cent of Mexican exports and imports (as against 2.8 per cent and 2.4 per cent in 1980); 2.0 per cent and 3.8 per cent of Venezuela's exports and imports (3.4 per cent and 2.3 per cent in 1980); 4.4 per cent and 6.0 per cent of Peru's exports and imports (3.4 per cent and 3.0 per cent in 1980); 0.2 per cent and 4.6 per cent of Colombia's exports and imports (1.9 per cent and 2.8 per cent in 1980); and 4.8 per cent and 11 per cent of Chile's exports and import (9.1 per cent and 7.8 per cent in 1980). Argentina occupies an intermediate position here with a gradual expansion of trade since the mid-1980s. Thus Brazil's exports to Argentina rose from US$ 548 million in 1985 to US$ 710 million in 1989 and imports increased from US$ 469 million to US$ 1239 million. In 1989 Argentina accounted for 2.1 per cent of Brazilian exports and 6.5 per cent of its imports and

Brazil accounted for 7 per cent of Argentinian exports and some 18 per cent of imports.

Militarily, even during the 1970s when geopolitics and national security doctrines exercised their greatest hold over the country's military rulers, Brazil made little or no attempt to build up its military capabilities, in stark contrast to the majority of other would-be regional powers. Although it developed an important arms industry, production was almost entirely for export and there was little attempt to modernise Brazil's outdated military equipment. The army continued to be mostly trained and deployed for internal security duties and the capacity to project power towards Brazil's borders remained extremely limited. This pattern continued through the 1980s. It is true that the period between 1982 and 1986 saw a concerted effort within the Brazilian military to rethink its role and strategy (partly as a response to the more troubled regional climate, but partly as an effort to find an alternative and more professional role as the country moved very gradually towards civilian government). Yet although there were modest increases in defence spending (from US$ 1.7 billion in 1981, to US$ 1.8 billion in 1983, to US$ 2 billion in 1985 and 1986), most of these re-equipment plans have remained unfulfilled. This has been largely the result of the financial constraints of the debt crisis, but also reflected the failure of the army to agree on a radical shake-up of its structure that would have involved moving towards a much smaller, more mobile, and more professional force. Moreover, even the most radical plans accepted that too great an escalation of Brazil's military capability would be counter-productive. Had, for example, Brazil acquired significant numbers of the *Osório* main battle tank, being developed for export to the Middle East, the regional military balance of power would have been irrevocably altered. Thus, despite the gradual modernisation programme and despite the emergence of an increased power projection capability (as for instance in the Amazon), Brazil does not have the power to project serious military power beyond its own borders. In addition, increased competition in the world arms market (worsened in the short term by Iraqi default and the UN blockade) makes it likely that the viability of Brazil's arms industry will come under increasing strain in the 1990s.

One might argue that such an emphasis on relational power is too narrow. What of the 'managerial' role of regional powers? There may be something in the argument that the shift towards a more activist and cooperative policy has strengthened Brazil's capacity to shape the pattern of events in the region and to set the regional agenda in its own interests. As and when Brazil's economic growth resumes, such a framework based on economic cooperation will entrench the country's predominance within the region but without antagonising its regional neighbours. There are, however, clear limits to the validity of such a view. F. S. Northedge has argued that a 'state may be said to have power in the international system when another state recognises that it cannot be ignored when issues have to be determined'.[33] On this basis Brazil could be said to have significant power *vis-à-vis* Bolivia and Paraguay.

Similarly, the 'Brazilian factor' remains a continuing (although far from dominant) element in the overall formulation of Argentinian foreign policy. But beyond that the overall foreign policies of the majority of states in the region are determined with little or no reference to Brazil and its regional policy. As other chapters in this volume demonstrate, such a picture stands in striking contrast to the situation in the Middle East or the Indian sub-continent.

What accounts for this gap between Brazil's apparent 'natural' regional dominance and its actual limited regional role? The conventional explanation for this striking contrast is to stress the constraints that result from the continuing power and presence of the United States. Brazil's regionalist ambitions have been undercut by US claims to view Latin America as its own sphere of influence. Brazil has therefore been unable to develop an assertive regional role because of the policies of its far more powerful neigbour to the north. As we have seen, these constraints are indeed important but they represent only one part of the picture.

At the extra-regional level, there is the role played by Brazil's relations with other parts of the world apart from the United States. In the 1970s the central thrust of foreign policy (labelled first 'responsible pragmatism' and then 'universalism') was the diversification of the country's external relations and the expansion of relations with Europe, Japan, China, the Soviet Union and the Third World. Despite the rhetoric about 'geopolitical necessities', Latin America was simply not a major priority of Brazilian foreign policy in this period. Although the relative priority of the region has certainly increased in the 1980s, relations with these other areas have remained significant. Latin America has certainly become far more important for Brazil, but it is still far from being the sole, or even major, focus of Brazilian foreign policy.

At the regional level, proposals for a more assertive role have been undercut by increased Brazilian awareness that any such policy would only reawaken traditional Spanish-American hostility towards Brazil and would thus prove thoroughly counter-productive. To this logic was gradually added the perceived benefits of cooperation: first, the need of the countries of the region to present a united front in negotiations with an increasingly hostile outside world. Second, the concrete economic and security benefits of cooperation, visible above all in the process of rapprochement with Argentina that has gathered pace through the 1980s.

Finally, there is the overwhelmingly economic orientation of Brazilian foreign policy. Brazilian foreign policy has not aimed at expanding international influence but rather at furthering the country's economic development and increasing its international economic power. There is a strong argument that the 'power' that stems from regional influence is of little relevance in pursuit of this objective. What matters are the kinds of 'soft power' described by the modernist writers on international relations: power that derives from successful operation within a highly interdependent world economy, from the capacity to bargain effectively across a range of economic issues, and from the successful manipulation of economic and environmental interdependence to one's own advantage.[34] Of course, regionalism may be of some use here. Regional cooperation may enable a state to bargain more effectively with outside powers on debt or trade issues. But, although this aim formed a major part of the rhetoric of Latin American regionalism in the 1980s, its results proved meagre. For all the talk about a new era of Latin American solidarity, it is important to remember that the countries of the region were unable to develop a common policy on the single most important external issue of the 1980s, namely the management of the foreign debt. Regional cooperation may also of course provide economic benefits in the form of increased trade. But even here there must be some doubts as to whether the small-scale regionalism of the kind that is being promoted between Brazil and Argentina makes a great deal of economic sense. Except for 'macro-regionalism' (for example, the European Community, a Western Hemisphere bloc, or Japan and South Asia), are regional spheres of influence any longer economically viable? It is doubts of this kind that are pushing many in Latin America to think more seriously about the acceptability of some kind of Western Hemispheric economic unit.

The chapter has argued, then, that the common perception of Brazil as a major regional power is misplaced. It both rests on misleading theoretical assumptions and fails to take account of the specific evolution of Brazil's foreign policy. As against the popular view, Brazil cannot be seen in a meaningful sense as a regional great power. Despite the country's vast power potential and despite what appears to be its 'natural' dominance over the region, its actual influence has been limited by a series of deliberate policy choices, by the dynamics of the regional balance of power and, to a lesser degree, by broader international constraints. On the one hand, Brazil is a country whose governments have not placed a particularly high priority on expanding international influence, especially in the power political arena. On the other, in so far as Brazil has sought to expand its international influence and the range of its international economic ties, it has done so on a broader stage than the purely regional one. In contrast to several of the other states examined in this volume, the achievement of regional predominance has not generally been seen as essential to the country's broader international role.

NOTES

1. Riordan Roett, 'Brazil Ascendant: International Relations and Geopolitics in the Late 20th Century', *Journal of International Affairs*, IX (1975): 139–54 at 139.
2. Norman Bailey and Ronald Schneider, 'Brazil's Foreign Policy: A Case Study in Upward Mobility', *Inter-American Economic Affairs*, XXVII (1974): 3–25.
3. Wayne Selcher, 'Recent Strategic Developments in South America's Southern Cone', in Heraldo Munoz and Joseph Tulchin (eds), *Latin American Nations in World Politics* (Boulder: Westview, 1984), pp. 101–18 at p. 101.
4. Earl Ravenal, 'The Case for Adjustment', *Foreign Policy*, LXXXI (1990–91): 3–19.
5. Andrew Hurrell, 'Latin America, the West and the Third World', in Robert O'Neill and R. J. Vincent (eds), *The West and the Third World* (London: Macmillan, 1990), pp. 153–69.
6. Louis J. Cantori and Steven L. Spiegel, *The International Politics of Regions: A Comparative Approach* (Englewood Cliffs, NJ: Prentice Hall, 1970), pp. 6–7.
7. Ray S. Cline, *World Power Assessment: A Calculus of Strategic Drift* (Boulder: Westview, 1980); Wayne Selcher, 'Brazil in the World: A Ranking Analysis of Capability and Status Measures', in Wayne Selcher (ed.), *Brazil in the International System: The Rise of a Middle Power* (Boulder: Westview, 1981), pp. 25–63.
8. Davis B. Bobrow and Steve Chan, 'Simple Labels and Complex Realities: National Security for the Third World', in Edward Azar and Chung-in Moon (eds), *National Security in the Third World: The Management of Internal and External Threats* (London: Edward Elgar, 1988), pp. 44–76 at p. 65.
9. David Baldwin, 'Power Analysis and World Politics: New Trends versus Old Tendencies', *World Politics*, XXXI (1979): 161–94.
10. The single most important work is Golbery do Couto e Silva, *A Geopolítica do Brasil* (2nd edn; Rio de Janeiro: José Olympio, 1967); also Carlos de Meira Mattos, *A Geopolítica e as Projeções de Poder* (Rio de Janeiro: José Olympio, 1977).
11. Golbery, *A Geopolítica do Brasil*, pp. 8–9. A similar, if marginally

less obsessive, Realism is apparent in Meira Mattos, see especially his discussion of Morgenthau in Mattos, *A Geopolítica e as Projeções de Poder*, pp. 59–63.

12. Golbery, *A Geopolítica do Brasil*, p. 13.
13. Ibid., p. 166; also Carlos de Meira Mattos, *Geopolítica e Destino* (Rio de Janeiro: José Olympio, 1975), p. 4.
14. Golbery, *A Geopolítica do Brasil*, pp. 48–9.
15. *Ibid*, p. 35.
16. Peter Evans, *Dependent Development. The Alliance of Multinational, State and Local Capital in Brazil* (2nd edn; Princeton, NJ: Princeton University Press, 1981); Fernando Henrique Cardoso and Enzo Faletto, *Dependency and Development in Latin America* (Beverly Hills, CA: University of California Press, 1979), especially the introduction.
17. Evans, *Dependent Development*, p. 112.
18. Ruy Mauro Marini, 'Brazilian Subimperialism', *Monthly Review*, February 1972, p. 15.
19. NACLA, 'Brazil: The Continental Strategy', *Latin America and Empire Report*, IV (1975): 4.
20. Paulo Schilling, *Brasil Va a La Guerra* (Buenos Aires: Schapire, 1974), p. 31; also his *Expansionismo Brasileiro. A Geopolítica do General Golbery e a Diplomacia do Itamarati* (Rio de Janeiro: Global, 1981).
21. Helio Jaguaribe, 'Brasil-Argentina: Breve Análise das Relações de Conflito e Cooperação', in Helio Jaguaribe, *O Novo Cenário Internacional* (Rio de Janeiro: Editora Guanabara, 1986), pp. 164–92.
22. The classic study of this subject is E. Bradford Burns, *The Unwritten Alliance. Rio-Branco and Brazilian-American Relations* (New York, NY: Columbia University Press, 1966).
23. Gibson Barbosa, speech to the *Escola Superior de Guerra*, 17 July 1970, *Documentos de Política Exterior*, IV, p. 160.
24. Speech to the *Escola Superior de Guerra*, 4 September 1980 (mimeo).
25. Sonia de Camargo, 'Caminhos que se juntam e se separam: Brasil e Argentina, uma visão comparativa', *Política e Estrategia*, X (1986): 372–403; Sonia de Camargo, 'Brasil e Argentina: A integração em questão', *Contexto Internacional*, IX (1989): 45–62.
26. Monica Hirst and Héctor Eduardo Bocco, 'Cooperação nuclear e integração Brasil-Argentina', *Contexto Internacional*, IX (1989): 63–78.
27. Barry Buzan, *People, States and Fear. The National Security Problem in International Relations* (London: Wheatsheaf, 1983).
28. Philippe Schmitter, 'Idealism, Regime Change and Regional Cooperation: Lessons from the Southern Cone of Latin America' (mimeo 1989).
29. David Vital, *The Survival of Small States* (Oxford: Oxford University Press, 1971).
30. Golbery, *A Geopolítica do Brasil*, pp. 50–1.
31. This repeated the pattern of events in the 1940s when Vargas had constructed a very close economic, political and military relationship with

the United States in the hope of cementing a preferential relationship. Yet, to Brazil's intense annoyance and frustation, instead of receiving preferential treatment and the major share of post-war US assistance, Washington sought to balance its ties with Brazil by improving relations with Peron's Argentina.

32. Robert Litvak, *Détente and the Nixon Doctrine* (Cambridge: Cambridge University Press, 1984), p. 137.
33. F. S. Northedge (ed.), *The Use of Force in International Relations* (London: Faber, 1974), p. 12.
34. Robert Keohane and Joseph Nye, *Power and Interdependence* (2nd edn; Glenview, IL: Scott, Foresman and Company, 1989).

3 India as a Regional Great Power: in Pursuit of Shakti

Veena Gill

INTRODUCTION

Contemporary international relations theory is marked by its relative neglect of regional subsystems. Barry Buzan in a recent study laments that in 'the absence of any developed sense of region, security analysis tends to polarise between the global system level on the one hand, and the national security level of individual states on the other . . . Both perspectives miss the regional level, which comprises the dynamic of security relations among the local states'.[1] In the case of South Asia, this is a problem well illustrated by the few studies whose point of departure is the complex of intraregional security relations.[2] South Asia is marked by a relative absence of regional cooperation and an asymmetry of power relations where, at least since the vivisection of Pakistan in 1971, India predominates.

It is generally argued that India has a position of dominance in the South Asian subcontinent broadly commensurate with its size, population, military capabilities and relative internal stability.[3] This status was amplified by its role in the creation of Bangladesh in 1971, it was verified by Indian interjection to resolve Sri Lanka's ethnic conflict in 1987 and vindicated in the military action in the Maldives to contain an attempted coup against President Gayoom in 1988. Moreover, India has aspired to a global role, for example in its leadership of the non-aligned movement.

The South Asian subcontinent covers an area of appoximately 4 468 000 sq. kilometres and includes Bangladesh, Bhutan, India, the Maldives, Nepal, Pakistan and Sri Lanka. To the northwest is Afghanistan, included in West Asia. China, which shares a common border of about 3 000 kilometres with India in the Northeast, is defined within East Asia and Burma as a part of Southeast Asia. Although they constitute a part of the security scenario and have geographical, historical and cultural linkages to the subcontinent, these powers are considered parts of other regional subsystems.[4]

South Asia, bounded in the north by the Himalayan chain of mountains, lies across the Indian Ocean, by the side of the Persian gulf and the Malaccan straits. The countries of the region have a common history, culture and in most cases a common colonial heritage. The British Indian empire included areas that are now part of Pakistan, Bangladesh and Burma. The British exercised paramountcy over the Himalayan kingdoms of Sikkim, Bhutan and Nepal, and maintained spheres of influence in Tibet and partly in Afghanistan. Ceylon (Sri Lanka) was administered as an independent British colony.

In sharp contrast to certain other regions such as Western Europe or Southeast Asia, South Asian countries have neither a common definition of external threat to their regional security nor do they have common developmental strategies. India is the only country that has a common border with all the other states. Physically, the other states lie apart from each other, and most of their interaction is through India. Cultural ties – ethnic, linguistic and religious – cut across the region's political boundaries. India, being the largest and most heteregenous state, represents the mainstream of social similarities and diversity. In view of the presence of common ethnic and religious groups, the question of national identity *vis-à-vis* Indian influence is a sensitive one for other countries of the region. The shared history of colonialism and its legacy of territorial division and demarcation of boundaries is divisive, witness the separation of east Pakistan – now Bangladesh – from west Pakistan by a territorial mass of over a thousand kilometres and the conflict over the northern territory of Kashmir between India and Pakistan. Disputed boundaries, territories and waterways (India and Bangladesh) are the major cause for conflict. Table 3.1 illustrates the enormous differences between India and the other states.

As compared to other South Asian states India has the largest armed forces establishment. What is more, it has demonstrated the willingness and ability to use it for furthering its regional interests. It produces an impressive array of weapons and equipment for internal consumption and export to developing countries. It is at present the only South Asian country with a demonstrated nuclear capability, although Pakistan is fully committed to and fast approaching the same goal. It has the best record of political stability in the subcontinent, characterised by nonviolent régime succession. It has a secure industrial base (ranked ninth in the world), and skilled and technical manpower (ranked third in the world) and is self-sufficient in food production. Although India is a regional giant in relative terms, it must be noted that the growth of its military and economic power is severely constrained by its enormous growing population (2 per cent annually), acute balance of payments deficit largely due to dependence on oil imports (in 1988 minus US$ 6870 million) and high rates of inflation (8.8 per cent in 1987). The moral fibre is undermined by high unemployment (10 per cent in 1987), increasing disparities of income, caste and social unrest, and vulnerability of popular and public institutions to political manipulation and control.[5]

REGIONAL PROFILE: FROM SECURITY TO HEGEMONY

India's principal security concerns are Pakistan, China and the presence of great powers in waters contiguous to its coasts. Subordinate concerns are its smaller neighbours, islands and littoral states in the Indian ocean.[6] National security policymaking in India as in many other developing countries is made by leaders rather than institutions. In the history of independent India, two leaders stand out from the others, for their contribution of distinct security concepts and policies. They are Jawaharlal Nehru, its first prime minister 1950–64, and his daughter Indira Gandhi, prime minister 1966–84. While Nehru succeeded in projecting India as an international actor over and above its modest power base by virtue of its leadership of the Non-Aligned Movement, Indira Gandhi was able to secure for the country military power and the status of regional leadership.[7]

During Nehru's tenure the focus of Indian security policy was global

TABLE 3.1   *Size of Population, GDP, Area and Armed Forces in South Asian Countries, 1989–90*

	Population (mill)	GDP (mill US$)	Area ('000 sq. km)	Armed Forces
Bangladesh	109	19 320	144	103 000
Bhutan	1.4	300	47	203 000*
India	816	237 930	3 288	1 262 000
Maldives	0.2	70	0.3	26 000*
Nepal	19	2 860	141	35 000
Pakistan	106	34 050	804	550 000
Sri Lanka	17	6 400	66	65 000

* Men fit for military service

SOURCES: *World Development Report* (New York, NY: The World Bank, 1990); US Central Intelligence Agency, *Handbook of the Nations* (9th edn; New York, NY: Central Intelligence Agency, 1989); *The Military Balance 1990–1991* (London: Brassey, 1990).

rather than regional. The key to India's globalism was diplomacy and mediation, not military power. Indian foreign policy was to be guided by the principles of nonalignment, aimed at consolidating Indian independence and securing an honoured status in the international hierarchy of states. With the emergence of the two power blocs, this was sought through a policy of peaceful coexistence with the communist bloc and the avoidance of military entanglements with the West. The objective of this policy was to increase India's autonomy of action and minimise external great power influence that could compromise its security interests. Nehru proposed already in 1946 that India should 'keep away from the power politics of groups, aligned against one another, which have led in the past to world wars and which may again lead to disasters on an even vaster scale'.[8]

Nehru believed that India – in the light of its geographical location, cultural contributions to world civilisation and power potential – was destined to play an important role in world affairs. He sought to establish an international image for the state commensurate with its size, resources and presumed role. In an address to Asian nationalists in 1947 he said:

> We stand at the end of an era and on the threshold of a new period of history . . . Asia, after a long period of quiescence, has suddenly become important again in world affairs. . . . It is fitting that India should play her part in this new phase of Asian development . . . we have no designs against anybody; ours is the great design of promoting peace and progress all over the world. Far too long have we in Asia been petitioners in Western courts and chancelleries. That day must now belong to the past . . . we do not intend to be the playthings of others.[9]

Indeed in the first two decades of independence, India acquired an importance in international politics out of proportion to its power capabilities. As leader of the nonaligned movement India's services were solicited in mediating and negotiating international conflicts, as in Korea, Indo-China, the Middle East and the Congo. Nonalignment provided it with an unusual form of power in international politics – moral influence; India as the spokesman and leader of oppressed mankind.[10]

To the extent that Nehru had a regional vision it was for an all Asian unity and not a South Asian regional power structure managed by India. The military aspects of regional security were not a priority. He drew instead upon the Buddhist precept of *Panchshila* (five principles of peaceful coexistence) involving neutrality, noninterference and nonalignment in respect of equal and bigger neighbours. Nehru's belief in a united Asia was premised on amity between India and China and *Panchshila*, drafted by Nehru and Zhou Enlai in 1954, was a non-military solution to their respective security interests in the Himalayas. Nehru accepted China's control over Tibet in exchange for India's influence in Nepal, Bhutan and Sikkim. India's attitude to the Himalayan frontier in the 1950s and 1960s was a response to the contextual adversity arising from China's military intentions and role in Tibet and the Sinkiang. It was in the light of these considerations that the British treaties with Sikkim of 1861 and 1918, Bhutan of 1910 and Nepal were renegotiated in 1949 and 1950, confirming their status as protectorates of India. Nehru was not unconcerned about the requirements of India's regional security, but India's relations with its neighbours in the period 1947–62 were not informed by a regional Indocentric strategic conception and policy.[11] For example, Sikkim as an Indian Princely State could have been easily and legitimately integrated into the Indian Union in 1947, but Nehru refrained from pressurising The Maharaja Tashi Namgyal. India consolidated its security interests in the Himalayan kingdoms mainly through a policy of economic diplomacy and political support. Citizens of Nepal and Bhutan (and Sikkim, too, prior to its integration into India in 1975) have free access to institutions and employment opportunities in India. India's contributions are an important part of the budget of Nepal and Bhutan. Developmental assistance in terms of loans and grants was initiated in 1951 and 1958 respectively.

India's policy towards its smaller South Asian neighbours in this period was marked by bilateralism and patronage. The Sri Lankan idea of regional community, especially economic cooperation, was received coolly by the Indians, who saw a clear advantage in bilateral dealings with smaller states. Little *Realpolitik* consideration was given by the Nehru régime to the fact that India's neighbours did not share its beliefs in non-alignment and the post-independence status quo in the subcontinent favouring India. Pakistan had entered into a mutual security agreement with the United States in 1954. In 1962 when China attacked India, Nehru was forced to admit that security threats had to be countered by military force and not diplomacy. In the light of regional circumstances a major reappraisal of Indian foreign policy resulted. Nehru sought and received military equipment from the United States, Britain and Canada. India's stance as an independent nonaligned state stood discredited.

In the postwar configuration of bipolarity, India's stance of nonalignment was initially received with coolness in the United States and antipathy in the Soviet Union. The Soviets considered Indian leaders as reactionaries and pro-imperialists. It was in the period after Stalin's death that the Soviets realised India's potential as a useful ally in South Asia. Their subsequent cooperation was based on securing their respective interests. Nehru was interested in securing the Soviet Security Council veto on disputed Jammu and Kashmir, as well as economic aid. The Soviets were interested in countering Western naval power in the waters contiguous to South Asia. In 1957, and later in 1962 and 1964, India used the Soviet veto to block UN resolutions proposing a UN force for a demilitarised Kashmir and a solution to its dispute with Pakistan over that territory. In the light of the dispute between the Soviet Union and China on their common borders, Nehru hoped that a Soviet connection would also provide a guarantee of India's security *vis-à-vis* China, and links between the two countries were reinforced after the 1962 war with that country. India purchased 100 Soviet MIG 21 fighter planes (and concluded a manufacturing agreement). This was followed in subsequent years with the acquisition of a wide range of military equipment from the Soviet Union.

India sought economic and military support from the Soviet Union primarily to counter the effects of Pakistan's military alliance in 1954 with the United States. Nehru had initially sought a peaceful solution to India's conflict with Pakistan over Kashmir, which included a war in 1947–48, and had brought the matter before the UN. His diplomatic initiative was aimed at excluding external interference in regional politics, and isolating the region from the cold war rivalry of the great powers. His failure to secure a favourable response in the UN from the Western powers was owing primarily to their divergent strategic views on the prevailing regional balance of power. There was little doubt that the United States and Britain did not share Nehru's perceptions of India's greatness. By entering into a strategic alliance with Pakistan in 1954, the Americans had revealed their partiality for British strategic thinking, which saw Pakistan as 'the fulcrum of Asia', located as it is at the crossroads of Central, West and South Asia. Pakistan provided the United States with intelligence and military bases in this first round until 1968. Pakistani élites, who had since the partition a well based mistrust of India's regional intentions and who had never been reconciled to India's claims of predominance, hoped that their military and economic relationship with the United States would enable Pakistan to at least challenge if not secure a power parity with India.[12]

There is no doubt that this initial external influence in regional politics hopelessly complicated and exacerbated Indo-Pakistan hostility and relations. India had sought the patronage of the Soviet Union to guarantee its security, power and dominance. Pakistan directed its efforts through Western alliances to challenge and establish military and defence parity or near equality with India. Indian élites were forced to accept that India's manifest claims for greatness would be both questioned and challenged by its neighbours and rivals. In 1965 Pakistan and India fought two inconclusive wars over disputed territories.

India's regional record in the first two decades after independence (1947–1964) under Nehru's leadership was a mixed one. While India was able to consolidate its hold over the small Himalayan kingdoms, it was forced to admit that its claim to dominance in South Asia was both questioned by its rival South Asian state, Pakistan, and discredited by the defeat inflicted upon it by its Asian neighbour China in 1962. In the absence of a clear perception of India's regional role and the consequent absence of a regional strategic policy and power resources, India's claim for greatness remained rhetorical and unsubstantiated. India's relative success at the global level as a diplomatic mediator disproportionate to its tangible power resources were possible mainly due to the emergence and crystallisation of the Cold War, which empowered Nehru with the force of the Non-Aligned Movement.

The rise and growth of Indian military power in South Asia is a post-1966 phenomenon. It was under the leadership of Indira Gandhi that an Indian regional strategic perspective and policy emerged. In the period 1966–84 India was able to establish a forceful (although not unquestioned) regional presence through a policy of offensive military power, combined with the astute personal diplomacy of its Prime Minister. Indira Gandhi's primacy of power politics as an instrument of policy was her major contribution to Indian security strategy.[13] In the years 1966–84 India visibly expanded its military establishment, with the objective of establishing its predominance in South Asia. India's defeat of Pakistan in 1971 and the 'liberation' of Bangladesh is a landmark in India's quest for regional great power status.

The reappraisal of Indian foreign policy initiated by Nehru after India's débâcle with China was carried to its logical conclusion by his daughter. As in the time of her father, Indian security policymaking remained the prerogative of the Prime Minister and a few individuals. This is documented by her Principal Secretary who writes: 'I do not recall a single occasion during the last 31 years when problems of our country's security were discussed seriously or in depth.'[14]

Indira Gandhi and Nehru were poles apart in their leadership styles and strategic thinking. Her political rhetoric and strategy was pragmatic and informed by *Realpolitik*, while her father's was guided by moralism and idealism. Indira Gandhi's security perspectives are illustrated by her statement that her father 'was a saint who strayed into politics' while she was 'a tough politician'.[15] Building upon Nehru's legacy but reformulating and redefining it, she gave a new meaning to the concept of non-alignment. It was used by her as a flexible strategy for securing diplomatic, military and economic support from the great powers as and when it suited India's national interests.

The Rivalry between India and Pakistan

A distinctive characteristic of South Asian regional politics is the rivalry between India and Pakistan. The two countries have fought three wars over their disputed territorial claims; in Jammu and Kashmir in 1947–49 and again in September 1965, and in the Rann of Kutch in April-May 1965. The fourth war in 1971 led to the military defeat and dismemberment of Pakistan. India's military 'liberation' of Bangladesh dramatically illustrated India's ambitions for regional dominance while reducing Pakistan's capabilities to challenge it. The India-Pakistan conflict predates the creation of the Pakistan state.[16] The rejection by Indian political leadership of the (Pakistan) Muslim League's 'two nation' theory and the partition of the subcontinent in 1947 after the withdrawal of the British made Pakistani leaders feel that India was not reconciled to the existence of Pakistan. This theme has been reiterated in speeches made by its leaders Ayub Khan, Zulfikar Ali Bhutto and Zia-ul-haq.[17] Adding to this was India and Pakistan's common experiences of communal violence during mass migrations at the time of partition, disagreements over the sharing of assets and liabilities including military stores of the undivided India and disputes over the accession of native states, most important being those of Junagadh, Hyderabad and Jammu, and Kashmir. India in its turn has hardly disguised its aspirations for regional leadership, which has been a source of provocation to Pakistan.

Pakistan does not accept India's regional hegemony. The primary aim of the foreign policy of Pakistan is to achieve equality of status with India. Pakistan is determined to alter the imbalance of regional power, and has sought to accomplish that aim by securing the military and economic assistance of external powers. Important security relationships have evolved in the course of Pakistan's history with the United States, latest when the Carter doctrine of 1980 assigned Pakistan a key role in the defence of US interests in West Asia, with China, and with the Islamic countries in the Persian Gulf and the Middle East, especially after 1971. In the past two decades Pakistan's leadership has embarked upon a programme for the acquisition of a nuclear capability. A nuclear device with a complementary delivery mechanism is a top priority on Pakistan's defence agenda. This policy is based on Pakistan's assessments that it can neither catch up on India's superiority in conventional arms nor match India's defence spending capability. Pakistan's nuclear ambitions have put a severe strain upon India's continuance of a non-nuclear weapons policy in the 1990s. While India's principal security objective has been to limit the presence of external powers in South Asia (it considers its own proximity to the Soviet Union as a response to the US and Chinese security relationships with Pakistan), Pakistan has sought to alter the regional status quo by courting foreign powers willing and able to assist it. India's response to the foreign military assistance elicited by Pakistan has been to conclude a competitive arms agreement with the Soviet Union (1984, 1986). India is among the top four non-communist recipients of Soviet arms exports.

An interesting dimension of India-Pakistan hostility has been the two countries' implicit support of subversive and terrorist groups in each others domestic politics. India's assertions of support from Pakistan to Sikh extremists in Punjab are countered by Pakistan's accusations of Indian support of anti-government demonstrations in Sind.

In 1985–86, joint efforts to merge the Pakistan proposal for a no-war pact with India's proposal for a treaty of peace and friendship failed. India feared that Pakistan's security relationship with the United States would result in Pakistan providing it with a base for operations and thus endangering its regional security environment. It therefore insisted upon a Pakistani commitment against this possibility and the acceptance of bilateralism in the spirit of their Simla agreement of 1972 in resolving their problems. Pakistan rejected these demands. It cited the crisis on its western borders as the reason for its reluctance to agree to the no-bases condition and it was not prepared to give up its option of raising the Kashmir issue in international fora. The only positive result of these talks was an agreement in 1986 not to attack each others' nuclear facilities. In January 1986 the ruling Muslim League passed a resolution opposing normalisation of relations with India without first solving the Kashmir issue.

Pakistan and India's efforts to improve their relations in recent years have resulted in the establishment of a bilateral joint commission and the formation of The South Asian Association for Regional Cooperation (SAARC). This has been possible however only by ensuring that their sensitive political and military issues are placed outside the agenda of SAARC meetings. Suspicious of India's efforts to forge cooperation and India's regional role Pakistan has described India as 'a crocodile in the waters of the Indian Ocean' and 'a shark in the waters of the SAARC'.[18] Pakistan's own role in SAARC was made clear in an article by the Pakistani defence expert General Akram in 1985. He wrote:

Pakistan's strong position vis-à-vis India raises its stature in the eyes of the smaller powers which look to a strong, a vibrant Pakistan as a source of comfort and assurance. . . . Pakistan is in an ideal position to ensure that no one state acquires a dominating position in the region to further its own narrow national interest.[19]

Pakistan's objectives are to complicate Indian aims for regional great power status. It has used SAARC in recent years to project India as a threat to smaller neighbours and itself as the only state capable of countering this threat and protecting them. The rationale for the smaller South Asian states to establish a regional association was indeed to counter this threat collectively.

India and its Smaller Neighbours

A senior Indian Foreign Ministry official stated in the late 1980s that 'India is the centre of the region, so the region is India, and it is our job to protect it from outside'.[20] India's regional policy is informed by the view that India's security is symbiotically related to the security of the entire subcontinent.

Three important questions arise in the context of India's relations with its smaller neighbours.[21] First, what role does India want these states to play in the context of its adversarial relations with Pakistan and China? Second, to what extent have these states facilitated regional penetration by external great powers? Third, has India's regional dominance compromised or enhanced the sovereignity of its weaker neighbours?

India's security concerns for its northern borders are to an extent based upon British India's strategic perspectives on the Himalayan kingdoms. British policy saw the creation of Tibetan and Afghan buffers against the Chinese and Russian empires, bilateral treaties with Nepal and Bhutan, a base in Sri Lanka, and the courting of friendly relations with the rulers of these states. As already mentioned, India renegotiated these treaties with the Himalayan kingdoms. After China's military action in Tibet in 1959, India in 1962 and the Indo-Pakistani conflict in 1965, India was forced to admit China's assertion in regional affairs, and sought to counter it by integrating the Himalayan states more closely to its defence system. In the context of its conflict with Pakistan over Kashmir, India was interested in securing a stable frontier in the north and northeast. India's role in the creation of Bangladesh opened the way for a treaty of peace and friendship signed in 1972. While the treaty underlined their coordination in responses to international issues and spelled out their common security perspectives, no formal security relationship was specified, and since the overthrow of Mujib's régime in 1975 Bangladesh's security perceptions have not converged with India's.

India's defence planners perceive Sri Lanka as a vital link in their overall defence strategy. Sri Lanka's proximity to India and its geo-strategic location in the Indian ocean makes it an important security concern. Sri Lanka has always been wary of its giant neighbour, and apprehensive of its cultural and political domination. In order to ward off a possible Indian aggression Sri Lanka concluded a defence arrangement with Britain prior to its independence in 1948. A British naval base was stationed at Trincomalee and an air base at Katunayaka.

India's relations with Sri Lanka in the 1950s and 1960s were marked by cordiality and a common approach to international power conflicts in their refuge in non-alignment. In 1970–71 they jointly proposed to make the Indian ocean a zone of peace. India and Sri Lanka were both agreed in opposing the presence of external great powers in waters contiguous to their coasts, and safeguarding the Indian ocean from their rivalry. Their friendly relations were reversed after both their respective Prime Ministers, Srimavo Bandarnaike and Indira Gandhi lost their political office in 1977. Sri Lankan president Jayawardene sought a diversification of trade and foreign policy. To the chagrin of India, Sri Lanka tried to opt out of the region and connect itself with Southeast Asia by applying for membership of ASEAN. Bilateral relations have been strained over the ethnic conflict in Sri Lanka and India's military role in trying to solve it. During the early 1980s India provided training facilities and military supplies to Tamil terrorists who were fighting Sri Lanka's security forces. In 1987 an Indo-Sri Lanka agreement was concluded establishing an Indian peace keeping force in in the northeast region of the country, of about 45 000 troops. In 1989 Sri Lankan leaders, perceiving a threat from what they saw as India's imperialist aims, asked for the withdrawal of Indian forces. India responded promptly and was out by March of the same year. However, Rajiv Gandhi strongly criticised President Jayawardene's handling of the ethnic conflict at the non-aligned meeting in Harare. He is reported to have said: 'We do not know what Sri Lanka is wanting to do . . . If they do not like our help we are prepared to step out'.[22] The Indian peace keeping force stayed 32 months, lost at least 1200 men and spent around US$1 billion for what the former Indian High Commissioner in Colombo Mr Dixit termed 'a necessary projection of Indian power'.[23] India's three years mediation in the ethnic crisis was a failure. The Indian view of its role is illustrated by a statement made by the Indian deputy high commissioner in Colombo: 'We have achieved our main objectives – bringing the [Tamil]

Tigers into the democratic process, getting the Tamils regional autonomy and safeguarding the unity of Sri Lanka'.[24] A more widely held view is that this is the biggest Indian military failure since the 1962 war with China. India was unable to stop Sri Lanka's induction of men and hardware from extraregional sources, that is the use of British and Israeli mercenaries. The mutual reciprocity of its foreign policy postures with the US, China and Pakistan are perceived by India as an attempt to counter Indian influence.

Generally India's relations with its smaller neighbours in the 1950s had been stable and conducive to India's security interests. Nehru had been able to secure the commitment of Nepal, Sikkim and Bhutan's rulers to India's strategic concerns, in exchange for India's political and economic support to their régimes. Nehru's policy and rhetoric of globalism rather than regionalism and the pursuit of an international status for India projected a less threatening image and role of India to its smaller neighbours.

Since the 1960s the rationale, content and form of India's security relationships have been questioned and opposed by these small states. These neighbours have highlighted their divergent security perceptions by pursuing independent foreign policies and initiating strategic concepts that are largely incompatible with, if not completely antagonistic to, India's perceived regional security interests. They have asked for terminations or modifications of treaties with India. Nepal's zone of peace proposal, Bhutan's aspirations to pursue an independent foreign policy, including towards China, Bangladesh and Sri Lanka's endorsement of Pakistan's proposal for a nuclear weapons free zone in South Asia, and Bangladesh's initiative for SAARC illustrate their differences from India on regional security issues.

A variety of factors account for the divergence of strategic perspectives between India and the smaller regional states. Three major explanations are: (1) that India's relations with its smaller neighbours have been hegemonistic, resulting in their differences over what constitutes their respective security threats; (2) that India's regional great power status is perceived as reducing the autonomy and independence of their domestic and foreign policies; and (3) that 'anti-Indianism' in the region is a consequence of fundamentalist and 'delayed' nationalist tendencies in these regional states.[25]

Can India aspire for regional leadership without arousing fear among its smaller neighbours? Inequality of power relations do not in themselves create conflict and discord. Dovetailing security perceptions are conceivable despite power disparities among states, and cooperation in the pursuit of common goals is possible among unequal states. The problem is not the difference in military strength as such, but rather India's preference for military force rather than diplomacy in consolidating its influence. The installation of King Tribhuvan and a constitutional monarchy in Nepal in 1950–51, India's integration of Sikkim in 1975, the liberation of Bangladesh from Pakistan in 1971, India's intervention in Sri Lanka in 1987 and Maldives in 1989 are illustrations of India's offensive regional policy. While India's self-assertiveness and absolute military strength have grown immensely in the last few decades, India has been unable to convince the smaller South Asian states of its ability to guarantee stability in the region: Pakistan's challenge to its regional preponderance, India's own inconclusive efforts at militarily resolving the Kashmir question, its vulnerability *vis-à-vis* its greater Asian neighbour China, all tend to undermine its credibility as a regional great power.

Sri Lanka's and Nepal's courting of China in recent years is an effort to balance India's regional profile as well as to secure alternative sources of military and economic support. Bangladesh has taken steps to normalise its relations with Pakistan as a counterweight to India, and increased contact with China and the USA to secure its development needs. India's neighbours question its defence guarantees and fear its protection.

EXTERNAL CONSTRAINTS: GREAT POWER INTRUSION

India's major security preoccupation in the period of Indira Ghandi's leadership was to consolidate its sphere of influence in South Asia while minimising the possibility of interference by external powers. In this context a prime objective was to elicit compliance from the great powers on India's regional leadership. Soliciting the support of the Soviet Union was not difficult for India in the light of their mutual perceptions of strategic, economic and political interests in the period under review. Still, there were occasions on which there was a divergence of views; these included Pakistan in the late 1960s and China in the 1970s; the Non-Proliferation treaty; and the Soviet proposal for collective security in Asia. The strategic environment in South Asia, which changed with the Soviet invasion of Afghanistan, resulted in their friendship ties being strenghtened again. Pakistan was elevated to the status of a 'frontline state' for the Americans and was supplied with sophisticated arms. This fact together with Pakistan's efforts to acquire a nuclear capability dramatically altered the strategic environment for India. The Chinese intrusion into the Sumdorong Chu valley in Arunachal Pradesh in August 1986 aggravated border relations and caused apprehensions in India. These developments were perceived similarly by India and the Soviet Union, which resulted in their close cooperation on regional issues. Soviet support for India's regional leadership was reiterated by Soviet Deputy Foreign Minister Mikhail Kapitsa in 1985. He said: 'We want to be friends for all countries of South Asia. We hope these countries are able to sort out their problems with India, because if they do not and there is a problem between India and its neighbours we will side with India'.[26] In 1986 the two countries signed important agreements on economic, cultural and foreign policy matters at the conclusion of President Gorbachev's visit to India. An important objective of this visit was to seek India's support for the Soviet proposal for Asia-Pacific security, outlined by Gorbachev in Vladivostok in July 1986. This strategy can be seen as a counter to what could be called an 'Eastern NATO', that is the evolving Washington-Tokyo-Seoul relationship. According to Moscow the Eastern NATO aims at the strategic encirclement of the Soviet Union.[27] India is seen as an important ally in countering this aim; however, it has not endorsed the Soviet Asia-Pacific security proposal. On this issue it is clear that Soviet and Indian perceptions are at variance. India's response to the proposal is that bilateral and regional mechanisms should be used to enhance stability in the region rather than external great power interference. In addition the UN system should be strenghtened for international peace.

On other matters of strategic global significance, such as nuclear disarmament), and of regional importance, such as the heavy arming of Pakistan and China's relations with India and the Soviet Union, there are compatible perceptions of interests illustrated by Gorbachev's statement:

> Indo-Soviet relations rest on the reliable foundation of our Treaty of Peace, Friendship and Cooperation. Its supreme meaning lies in a reciprocal commitment to act, should a complicated situation arise for one side or both. Such situations did arise. Both the Soviet Union and India have remained faithful to their commitment.[28]

In retrospect the Soviet Union has played a key role in supporting Indian objectives for regional dominance. A major alteration in the Indo-Soviet equation is not likely in the forseeable future, Soviet efforts to improve relations with China notwithstanding.

Securing American acceptance of its dominant regional role or at least minimising the latter's interference in the region has been more difficult. A fundamental problem for regional great power aspirants such as India is their limited resource capabilities, which make them dependent upon external sources for advanced military and economic technologies. Indian élites have given priority to both an expansive indigenous defence production programme and diverse sources of arms supply, with the obvious aim of widening their security options. These policy goals have made assistance from the West, especially the United States, contingent. The United States however has not neccessarily shared India's regional security perceptions or aspirations for regional leadership as conducive to furthering its own strategic interests in the region.

According to one analyst there is an inherent conflict between different US goals in South Asia.[29] On the one hand American officials recognise that India will have a formidable military capability by the end of the twentieth century, and will be able to use this power to help or obstruct US strategic aims in the Indian Ocean. According to a US State Department official:

India could be a power that contributes to world stability as the United States will see it, and want to shape it in 1995 and the year 2025, and a power with which we could work together much as we try to work together with other major powers now to enhance our long-term national security aims. And that I think is an exciting possibility that perhaps [opens] a new chapter in United States-Indian relations.[30]

This opinion apparently informed US policy in the mid-1980s, resulting in the US accomodating India's requests for advanced military and economic technology. In May 1985 the countries signed a Memorandum of Understanding on transfer of high and strategic technology. Most noteworthy here is the American willingness to consider the sale of advanced General Electric 404 engines for use in prototypes of the light combat aircraft being developed by India, and the supercomputer which can be used for simulating nuclear explosions. India has asked for it for a monsoon reserach project. These important agreements notwithstanding, there is as yet no substantive military supply relationship between the countries. In terms of actual arms sales in the period 1979–83, as much as 70 per cent of India's military hardware was purchased from the Soviet Union. The US sales were only 2 per cent of the value of the purchases from Moscow.

There is no doubt that the US hopes to benefit from reducing India's military dependence on the Soviet Union. India's interests are also served by widening its foreign policy options. On the other hand the United States' concrete strategic policy in South West Asia assigns a key role to Pakistan. The strategic importance of that country has obliged the US to be responsive to Pakistani sensitivities *vis-à-vis* India. Pakistan, which has a close military relationship with China, has also provided the US with a diplomatic opening to that country. The US-sponsored military buildup and modernisation of Pakistan's armed forces operate indirectly in the South Asian context as a constraint upon regional expansionist Indian aims. In 1982 a five year package of US military aid to Pakistan worth US$ 3.2 billion was initiated. The second US military aid package is for about US$ 4.2 billion spread over six years. US military assistance to Pakistan has been perceived by Indian élites as altering the basic regional power balance. Indira Gandhi and later her son Rajiv Gandhi as Prime Minister (1984–89) have sought US assurances that it will limit military assistance to Pakistan both qualitatively and quantitatively. US naval deployment in the Indian Ocean is another related concern for India's policymakers, who do not discount their possible use in the event of an Indo-Pakistani war. Still, India has little cause for apprehension considering the fact that the US has kept out of the 1965 and 1971 India-Pakistan conflicts and Pakistan has no assurance of US intervention in a bilateral conflict with India. Americans argue that US relations with Pakistan pose no threat to India, and that they are not interested in interfering in South Asian bilateral problems since they are fully aware that intervention will only invite greater Indian reliance on the Soviet Union as a counterweight.[31]

India's ability to direct regional affairs is strongly inihibited by its adversarial relationship with China. China does not accept India's regional claims and has sought to undermine them through a policy of military and diplomatic support to neighbouring South Asian states – Pakistan, Nepal, Bhutan, Burma and Bangladesh. It has signed border demarcation agreements with Burma and Nepal in 1960–61, with Afghanistan in 1962 and with Pakistan in 1963, to assure these small states of its non-belligerent security policy. India perceives a long-term threat from China, taking the cue from China's nuclear programme, its security relationship with Pakistan and its efforts to secure influence with smaller regional states. The perception is reinforced by Chinese support, including arms, for dissidents in India's northeastern states – Assam, Mizoram, Tripura, Nagaland and Arunachal Pradesh. The Chinese on their side have denounced India's integration of Sikkim into the Indian Union in 1975 as an 'illegal annexation'. It does not accept India's advisory role in the foreign affairs of Bhutan. China has supported Bangladesh on the issue of sharing the Ganges waters with India and has favourably acknowledged Nepal's proposal of 1975 to declare itself a peace zone. In the formulation of its regional policy India is profoundly influenced by the Pakistan-China nexus. In 1968 Bhutto acknowledged China as Pakistan's most reliable ally, whose interests *vis-à-vis* India coincide with those of Pakistan. China has officially supported Pakistan in its Kashmir conflict with India, and from the 1960s became the main supplier of arms and aircraft to Pakistan. Between 1964 and 1979, China offered in all about US$ 620 million in assistance to Pakistan, which amounted to 13 per cent of China's total aid programme. In the context of Sino-Soviet conflict and India-Soviet amity China has reacted adversely to India's formal military and economic ties with Moscow, fearing its encirclement. Since the outbreak of Sino-Indian conflict in 1962, relations between the two powers have been hostile. Attempts at normalisation were made after 1976 when the two countries resumed full diplomatic relations.

In recent years China has offered a package deal to resolve its territorial disputes with India. In 1980, Deng Xiaoping outlined a proposal guaranteeing India's claims in the northeast in exchange for its control over Aksai Chin in the west. India has rejected the offer in the rounds of talks during the last several years. India seeks acceptance of its control over Kashmir and Sikkim which China refuses. The resolution of the border disputes between the two countries is compounded by the fact that it affects other neighbouring countries. It involves determining the trijunction with Burma and Bhutan, and it affects the Sino-Bhutan border settlement as well as the status of Sikkim and Kashmir. In the meantime an unresolved border continues to be a heavy burden on India's defence forces. India has stationed mountain divisions trained for high altitude operations and Indian Air Force squadrons in border areas and expanded its regional logistics network and the flexibility of its nuclear capabilities as a counterpoise to China's forces.

CONCLUSION: ASPIRATIONS AND REALITIES

India's quest for regional greatness is complicated by three factors; one, the influence of extraregional great powers in South Asia; two, its own resource limitations that constrain it from using economic diplomacy rather than military force in its relations with regional states; and third, its own and neighbouring states' domestic political problems.

Maintaining hostile or friendly relations with its neighbours for the exigencies of domestic politics was particularly evident under Indira Gandhi.[32] India's policy towards Sri Lanka was also guided by domestic considerations given the proximity of India's Tamil state to Sri Lanka. There were instances of Nepal and Bangladesh acting as sanctuaries or support bases for extremist, subversive and secessionist forces working against India. In the northeast, Gurkhas of Nepalese origin demanded a separate state to be called 'Gurkhaland'. The long lasting agitation in the Indian state of Assam, involving the status of Bengali refugees, was intricately related to the creation of Bangladesh. Easy geographical access has encouraged political opposition in India's neighbouring countries to seek shelter and sanctuary in Indian territory. As a result, ruling élites have found it politically expedient to invoke anti-Indian symbolism and policies to deal with their domestic political adverseries. This is evident in the politics of Pakistan, Nepal, Bangladesh and Sri Lanka.

Internal and interstate political problems have been further exacerbated by the penetration of external actors such as the US, the USSR and China. These powers have pursued their strategic interests by extending their cooperation to these countries in their domestic and interstate conflicts. China's offer of a non-aggression pact to Nepal in 1960, its decision one year later to construct the Kathmandu-Kodari road linking Nepal with Tibet, and its insistence on dealing with Bhutan directly for the settlement of the border demarcation and other bilateral issues, were attempts to reduce India's influence.

While India's industry and agriculture has recorded impressive growth rates, India labours under the economic strains of a burgeoning population, growing inequalities of income, high inflation, indebtedness and unemployment. Although India has given priority to a military buildup, it judges its options to use economic aid diplomacy rather than muscle power to be limited. Thus, its regional policy remains unidimensional. In the period 1985–1989 India's defence budget has doubled from less than US$ 4.5 billion to over US$ 9 billion per year, with the most striking growth taking place in the navy. The reasons for this are to be sought in the US military presence at Diego Garcia, the vulnerability of the Andaman, Nicobar and Lakshadweep island chains, and the need to defend coastal waters, including commercial assets such as offshore oil installations.

Some military analysts see India's arms modernisation programme as designed to provide a military support to its 'status elevation demands upon the international community', suggesting that its regional policy and naval buildup are elements of a conception of India as an emerging global power; that is a fully fledged great power, and not just a regional one.[33]

India has sought and managed to create a sphere of influence in South Asia. Its pursuit for power has, however, been littered with obstacles. India has been forced to accept that its regional dominance is neither inevitable nor guaranteed. It has also experienced that military might is a necessary but not a sufficient condition for regional greatness. There is a growing sentiment in New Delhi that military concerns need to be linked to India's economic concerns. In the words of a senior Indian bureaucrat:

'When you pass a certain stage of industrialisation, war ceases to be an effective policy'.[34] India's economic aims seem to match its military goals in the 1990s as illustrated by the technological and industrialisation programme initiated by Rajiv Gandhi in 1986. The changes in India's strategic environment after the mid-1980s, with the withdrawal of the Soviet Union from Afghanistan and an American acceptance of India as a regional power, are conducive to a more stable regional environment. The revision by the United States and the Soviet Union of their regional priorities makes it easier for India to assume the role of regional stabiliser.

In the recent past there has also been a shift from 'high politics' to 'low politics' in South Asia, where some suggest that economic development issues have assumed greater importance than national security issues.[35] At the regional level, the emphasis on economic concerns is exemplified by the formation of the South Asian Association for Regional Cooperation in 1985. The economic concerns of South Asian countries, and of China, and their search for foreign investment and technology from the Western powers may bring about a change in existing regional alignments.

Nevertheless, despite recent economic activities of South Asian states, the structure of their regional rivalry and conflict persists. India's relations with its neighbours are strained, and marked by divergent regional security perceptions. Pakistan's nuclear programme poses a special challenge.

Through the past few decades India has shown a tremendous resilience against domestic, regional and international strains and has established a forceful presence in its region. Judged by the standards of its ability to project its influence and military power in South Asia, India is a regional power. In terms, however, of its dependence upon one great power, the Soviet Union, and its inability to insulate the region from the external great power influence of China and the US, it does not qualify at present as a fully fledged great power.

NOTES

1. Barry Buzan in Barry Buzan and Gowher Rizvi, *South Asian Insecurity and the Great Powers* (New York, NY: St. Martin's, 1986), p. 4.
2. S. D. Muni: 'South Asia', in Mohammed Ayoob (ed.), *Conflict and Intervention in the Third World* (London: Croom Helm, 1980), pp. 38–72; Surjit Mansingh, *India's Search for Power* (New Delhi: Sage, 1984); G. W. Chowdhry: *India, Pakistan, Bangladesh and the Major Powers* (New York, NY: Free Press, 1975); Stephen P. Cohen (ed.), *The Security of South Asia* (Chicago, IL: University of Illinois Press, 1987); Michael Brecher, 'International Relations and Asian Studies: The

Subordinate State System of Southern Asia', *World Politics* XV (1963): 213–35.

3. For example John Mellor (ed.), *India: A Rising Middle Power* (Boulder, CO: Westview, 1979); Onkar Marwah and Jonathan Pollack, *Military Power and Policy in Asian States: China, India and Japan* (Boulder, CO: Westview, 1980). In contrast, Buzan and Rizvi, *South Asian Insecurity and the Great Powers*, argue that the distribution of power in South Asia between India and Pakistan is bipolar.

4. Mansingh, *India's Search for Power*.

5. US Central Intelligence Agency, *Handbook of the Nations* (9th edn; New York, NY: Central Intelligence Agency, 1989).

6. Onkar Marwah, 'India's Military Power and Policy', in Marwah and Pollack, *Military Power and Policy in Asian States: China, India and Japan*, pp. 103–4.

7. Mansingh, *India's Search for Power*, p. 25.

8. Jawaharlal Nehru to the Constituent Assembly, 8 March 1949, quoted in Mansingh, *India's Search for Power*, p. 14.

9. Quoted in Mansingh, *India's Search for Power*, p. 14.

10. As Carsten Holbraad points out, *Middle Powers in International Politics* (London: Macmillan, 1984), p. 71, John Holmes, director general of the Canadian Institute of International Affairs, characterised India under Nehru as a great example of a middle power because of its active diplomacy in the conflict between the two blocs.

11. A similar view is expressed by Ashok Kapur, 'The Indian Subcontinent: The Contemporary Structure of Power and the Development of Power Relations', *Asian Survey* XXVIII (1988): 693–710, who states that there is no evidence to validate the notion of an undeclared claim to Indian hegemony in the Nehru Period (p. 703). On the other hand Leo Rose in James N. Rosenau *et al.* (eds), *World Politics* (New York, NY: Free Press, 1976), p. 214, argues that the basic principles underlying India's regional policy since 1947 has been to establish its regional hegemony.

12. For an excellent study on the evolution of Pakistan's foreign policy see S. M. Burke, *Pakistan's Foreign Policy: An Historical Analysis* (London: Oxford University Press, 1973); also Mohammad Ayub Khan, *Friends Not Masters* (New York, NY: Oxford University Press, 1967).

13. Mansingh, *India's Search for Power*, especially Chapters 1 and 2.

14. P. Haksar cited in Noor A. Husain, 'India's Regional Policy: Strategic and Security Dimensions', in Cohen, *The Security of South Asia*, pp. 27–79 at p. 32; see also Raju G. C. Thomas, 'Defense Planning in India', in Stephanie G. Neuman, (ed.), *Defense Planning in Less-Industrialised States* (Toronto: Lexington, 1984), pp. 239–64.

15. Indira Gandhi, cited in Husain, 'India's Regional Policy: Strategic and Security Dimensions', *The Security of South Asia*, p. 32.

16. D. C. Jha, 'The Basic Foundations and Determinants of Pakistan's Foreign Policy' and B. N. Goswami 'The Elites and the Formulation

of Pakistan's Foreign Policy: The Early Years' in S. Chopra (ed.), *Perspectives on Pakistan's Foreign Policy* (Amritsar: Guru Nanak Dev University Press, 1983), pp. 1–38 and 39–49 respectively.

17. Ayoob, *Conflict and Intervention in the Third World*; *Times of India* interview with President Zia-ul-haq, 1 March 1981.

18. Samuel Baid, 'Stalemate in South Asia', in Satish Kumar (ed.), *Yearbook on India's Foreign Policy* (New Delhi: Sage, 1988), p. 112; for an excellent study of Indo-Pakistan rivalry see Gowher Rizvi in Buzan and Rizvi, *South Asian Insecurity and the Great Powers*, pp. 93–126.

19. Cited in Baid, *Yearbook on India's Foreign Policy*, p. 121.

20. Reported in *Asiaweek*, 1 September 1989, p. 24.

21. U.S. Bajpai, *India's Security* (New Delhi: Lancers, 1983), pp. 115–121; also S. D. Muni, 'India's Political Preferences in South Asia', *India Quarterly* XXXI (1975):23–35; Ralph R. Premdas and S. W. R. Samarasinghe, 'Sri Lanka's Ethnic Conflict: The Indo-Lanka Peace Accord', *Asian Survey* XXVIII (1988): 676–85; Lok Raj Baral, 'Nepal's Security Policy and South Asian Regionalism', *Asian Survey* XXVI (1986): 1207–19.

22. Reported by Baid, *Yearbook on India's Foreign Policy*, on p. 126.

23. Reported in *Financial Times*, 24 March 1990, p. 3.

24. Ibid.

25. See Bajpai, *India's Security*, pp. 115–21; also Rizvi in Buzan and Rizvi, *South Asian Insecurity and the Great Powers*, pp. 126–56.

26. Cited in Satish Kumar (ed.), *Yearbook on India's Foreign Policy* (New Delhi: Sage, 1988), p. 187.

27. Cf. Kumar, *Yearbook on India's Foreign Policy*, p. 191.

28. Cited in Kumar, *Yearbook on India's Foreign Policy*, p. 191.

29. Dilip Mukerjee, 'India's Relations with the United States: A New Search For Accomodation', in Kumar, *Yearbook on India's Foreign Policy*, p. 205. His analysis is based on two US state department documents, the National Security Decision Directives 99 of July 1983 and 147 of October 1984.

30. Cited in Mukerjee, 'India's Relations with the United States: A New Search For Accomodation', in *Yearbook on India's Foreign Policy*, p. 205.

31. R. K. Jain (ed.), *US-South Asian Relations 1947–82* (New Delhi: Radiant, 1983).

32. Shashi Tharoor, *Reasons of State: Political Development and India's Foreign Policy under Indira Gandhi, 1966–1977* (New Delhi: Vikas, 1982).

33. See for instance American analysts Jerrold F. Elkin and W. Andrew Ritezel 'The Indo-Pakistani Military Balance', *Asian Survey* XXVI (1986):518–38 at 521.

34. Reported in *Asiaweek*, 1 September 1989, p. 27.

35. This is the view expressed by, for example, Raju C. Thomas, *Indian Security Policy* (Cambridge, MA: Harvard University Press, 1986).

4 Indonesia as a Regional Great Power

Arnfinn Jørgensen-Dahl

INTRODUCTION

To identify where in the rather malleable international landscape of 'regions' Indonesia belongs is perhaps easier in its case than in the case of other candidates to 'regional great power' status. One scholar once wrote that 'regions are what politicians and peoples want them to be'.[1] For scholars, governments, and the international business community it is now conventional to regard the ten countries which comprise Southeast Asia a region distinct from others. In addition to Indonesia, the countries are Brunei, Burma, Cambodia, Laos, Malaysia, Philippines, Singapore, Thailand, and Vietnam. These ten are in many respects very different. Yet, despite dissimilar political creeds and ideological disputes, ethnic cleavages and contrasting modes of economic and political organisation, a sense of regionalism has emerged among important segments of their populations. It is, to be sure, unevenly distributed and has taken shallower root in some countries and populations than in others. For the purposes of this chapter, however, it is sufficient to note that the existence of a sense of regional attachment among influential and decision-making élites in the ten countries is a well documented phenomenon, and is reflected in many of the policies which they pursue.[2]

Of the countries of Southeast Asia, none stands out as markedly from a demographic and geographical point of view as Indonesia (see Table 4.1). Indonesia's population is the fifth largest in the world and is almost three times that of its nearest regional rivals – the Philippines and Vietnam. Its territory is also almost three times that of Burma, the second largest country in Southeast Asia. It is the world's largest archipelagic state. Some 13 600 islands, of which about 6000 are inhabited, cover a land and sea area which stretches some 5100 kms from east to west and some 2000 kms from north to south. Its great strategic importance derives in considerable measure also from the fact that through its waters pass some of the world's most important sealanes which, via the Indian, link the Atlantic and Pacific Oceans.

TABLE 4.1   *Population, area and income of states in Southeast Asia*

Country	Pop. (mill. 1950)	Area sq. km.	GDP bill US$	GDP per cap (US$)
Indonesia*	190.1	1 919 440	80.0	430
Brunei	0.4	5 770	3.3	9600
Burma	41.3	678 500	11.0	280
Cambodia	7.0	181 040	0.9	130
Laos	4.0	236 800	0.6	150
Malaysia	17.5	329 750	37.9	2270
Philippines*	66.1	300 000	40.5	625
Singapore	2.7	622	27.5	10 300
Thailand*	55.1	514 000	64.5	1160
Vietnam*	66.2	329 560	14.2	215

* In the case of Indonesia, Philippines, Thailand and Vietnam the figures refer to
  GNP and GNP per capita.
SOURCE: *The World Factbook 1990* (Washington, DC: Central Intelligence
Agency). The GDP and GDP per capita figures are estimates for 1989 as are
the other figures.

Measured in terms of Gross National Product (GNP), the Indonesian
economy exceeds the next two on the list – those of Thailand and the
Philippines – by 25 and 100 per cent respectively. If, however, one turns
to level of economic development and uses GNP per capita as a rough
measure, it occupies a much more modest position. Although its GNP per
capita is twice that of Vietnam's, it is barely a third of Thailand's, less than
a fifth of Malaysia's, and less than five per cent of Singapore's.

Indonesia's economy is still largely agricultural. It has, however, for
some considerable time been rather dependent on the export of oil and
gas which, until the early 1980s, allowed it to pursue a fairly autarkic
development policy. A large domestic market did not, however, protect
it from the collapse of oil prices in the 1980s, which brought about
a reconsideration of its economic policies. In addition to traditional
commodities such as rubber, coffee, palm oil, logs, tin and other minerals,
emphasis was put on broadening the manufacturing sector. From having
followed an import-substitution policy it is now moving slowly towards
a more outward and export oriented policy. Although trailing the other
ASEAN members in this respect and carrying Asia's largest public and
private external debt, Indonesia's economic prospects in the years ahead
look fairly bright especially if oil and gas prices should remain at a
reasonably high level throughout the 1990s.[3] With the partial exception
of the Philippines, it and its fellow ASEAN members during the last

couple of decades have been and continue to be among the world's high performers in terms of economic growth.

The creation of wealth, however, is one thing, its distribution is another, especially in a country as far-flung and vast as Indonesia. As in so many other parts of the developing world, excessive inequality and poverty have been and are conspicuous features of the social landscape of Indonesia. When these maladies have not led to greater social unrest, the reason is in some measure to be found in economic policies which have sought their alleviation. Whilst disagreement exists about the extent to which the declared aims in the social field of the various economic five-year plans have been achieved, the government seems at least attentive and sensitive to criticism that they have not. Corrective measures have been introduced, and although the record may be spotty, a moderate easing of income inequality has probably taken place in parts of rural Indonesia coupled with a general improvement as far as the level of absolute poverty is concerned. In the urban areas the record seems somewhat less reassuring.[4]

Social deprivation of various kinds is not its only domestic problem. Cultural and ethnic variety of the complicated and sometimes even extreme sort found in Indonesia has often proven not to be the best foundation on which to fashion and conduct a reasonably coherent foreign policy. Like the other countries of Southeast Asia, Indonesia is a multi-cultural society, only more so than most others. There lives within its boundaries no less than 350 ethnic groups.[5] Yet, although the two cannot be entirely separated in so far as one feeds on the other, it is regionalism of the domestic variety rather than ethnic diversity as such which has posed the greatest challenge to the stability of the Indonesian polity. Especially during the first decade after independence antagonism between Java, as the centre of the republic and the seat of dominant political power, and the Outer Islands became the source of several regionally based rebellions. Regionalist and even separatist sentiments are still found in parts of the far-flung archipelago as, for example, in northern Sumatra, which has been a traditional centre of opposition to rule from Jakarta.[6] Domestic discontent of this sort has also been exploited in the past by outsiders who have seen in it a tempting vehicle for the pursuit of their own ends.[7] Nor has Indonesia remained untouched by the religious ferment which has gripped the Islamic world in recent times. It is the world's largest Islamic country but with its own particular brand of schisms within the one dominant religion. Successive Indonesian governments have had an ambiguous attitude towards Islam, with a tendency to view it as a divisive rather than a unifying force.[8] A somewhat different but important issue concerns the role of the Chinese minority in Indonesia. As in other parts of Southeast Asia, the Chinese community occupies a pivotal position in the economy and is therefore also a target of much resentment.[9] Both the religious and minority issues are factors of some import on Indonesia's relations with the outside world.

Since 1966 the political power structure of Indonesia has been dominated by the military. Even before that time the country's armed forces occupied a politically very prominent position. They were, however, held at bay by a combination of the strength of the Indonesian Communist Party (PKI) and the charisma of President Sukarno, whose adroit manipulation of the hostility between the armed forces and the communists from about 1958 until 1965/66 kept him on top of the political power totem pole. The coup attempt of 1 October 1965, which gradually brought about the demise of Sukarno in March 1966, and the destruction of the PKI as a political force, proved to be a turning point, and elevated the military to the top of the political hierarchy, a position which they maintained under the leadership of President, erstwhile Lieutenant General, Suharto.

As in other countries under military rule, the armed forces in Indonesia rely on the possession of overwhelming coercive power to maintain their dominance of the political system. Though persuasive, coercive power alone, however, provides a poor basis for claims to legitimacy.

> The Indonesian army differs from most armies that have seized political power in that it had never previously regarded itself as an apolitical organization . . . Indonesian army officers have always concerned themselves with political issues . . . Their right to participation was given formal recognition through appointments to the cabinet, the parliament, and the administration . . . and . . . the army's non-military role was accompanied by an ideology justifying its new activities . . . The army's continued domination of the state . . . is justified on the grounds that civilians still need the strong leadership that only the army could provide.[10]

For better or worse, military rule has imposed on the Indonesian polity a greater degree of stability than was the case before they took over the reins of power. At some 280 000 men, the size of the Indonesian armed forces are second in the region only to those of Vietnam and equalled only by those of Thailand.[11] The relative political stability on the domestic scene under Suharto has also given to Indonesia's foreign relations more coherence and continuity than before, a point which will be revisited later.

Ranking it only on the basis of the elements referred to in this brief overview, suggests that Indonesia has as good a claim to a regional leadership role as any of its regional cohabitants. The question now is whether its policies and the views of others reflect its evident ambitions in this regard.

REGIONAL PROFILE

Since it gained independence in 1949, Indonesia's foreign policy has twice undergone changes which have been perceived as major by the outside world, and have affected in almost equal amounts both relations with the great powers and its regional neighbours. To the Indonesians themselves, however, they have appeared in a more mellow light. A change of policy which transfers favours from one great power to its principal opponent is likely to be seen by others as rather dramatic. But inside the country itself it may appear less so and be thought of as part of a continuous policy of, say, national survival. Although more or less abrupt change has taken place, it is therefore no accident that constancy and continuity appear equally salient to the eyes of writers and observers when they consider the long haul of Indonesia's foreign relations.

Many of the central features of today's foreign relations go back to the early days of the republic. Its devotion to non-alignment as a foreign policy 'principle' was acquired already during the period of self-proclaimed independence before Indonesia gained formal independence in December 1949. This was at a time when the post Second World War bipolar structure had bedded down firmly in its cradle in Europe, and shortly thereafter found its most telling expression as far as Asia was concerned in the Korean War. The somewhat wayward course over the years of the commitment to non-alignment when translated into policies has not altered its position as a guiding principle for successive Indonesian governments. Non-alignment as a policy takes, of course, as its most important point of reference the great powers and their relations, and it thus involves at least three parties – the non-aligned itself and two great powers to which it tries to remain equidistant. Each of the great powers has its own views of what is important and not important in the policies of the others and therefore of what constitutes 'correct' non-alignment. The great powers have in fact found it far from easy to fathom the purpose and motive behind what to them appeared as the erratic twists and turns of policy of states whose commitment purportedly was to non-alignment. The deep ideological conflict with attendant, strongly opposed views and values which animated the bipolarity in the 1950s and 1960s could, on the other hand, but make it extra difficult, even well-nigh impossible, for any non-aligned country, however hard it tried, to pursue policies which in all and sundry respects were seen as non-aligned by both the United States and the Soviet Union.

The fact that non-alignment was subject to widely different interpretations exacted its toll on Indonesia's relations with the great powers. They were made no easier to handle whenever the great powers seized seemingly tempting opportunities to meddle illicitly in its domestic affairs in order to further their own interests. Account must also be taken of the effects of some of Indonesia's own actions and behaviour which endeared it to neither the great powers nor its regional neighbours.

Relations with Great Powers

Of all Indonesia's great power relationships the one with the United States has been on the whole most satisfactory. This is not to say, however, that the relations between the two have not had to weather some troublesome moments and times. Sukarno's Guided Democracy rule from about 1958 to 1965–66 proved in this respect the most taxing period of all. It started none too well. Considerable as the capital of good-will was that the United States had acquired by lending diplomatic support to the Indonesian independence struggle in its last stages, the US drew heavily on it when it more or less openly supported the anti-government forces during the so-called PRRI/Permesta regional rebellions in 1958.[12] Although it fairly soon thought better of it and abandoned this position, damage had been done to its standing in the eyes of many Indonesians. In the last round of the conflict between Indonesia and the Netherlands over Irian Jaya in 1961–62 the United States, however, exerted helpful influence which in the end led to the transfer of Irian Jaya to Indonesia. Its attempts to follow an even-handed course during the other important issue of the time – Indonesia's policy of Confrontation with Malaysia during 1963–66 – and to bring about a negotiated settlement ended in failure, and the US subsequently adopted a position in favour of Malaysia and its allies. This change on its part was brought about as much as anything by the increasingly erratic behaviour of President Sukarno who, among much else, on the very last day of 1964 withdrew Indonesia from membership in the United Nations.[13]

The political end to Guided Democracy and Sukarno came in March 1966, and a new era in Indonesian-United States relations began under the so-called New Order military régime headed by Suharto. A new course was set for Indonesia's foreign policy in which elements of continuity and change mingled freely and which entailed an altogether better relationship with Western powers than that which had marked most of the Guided Democracy period. Domestically the military régime introduced a greater degree of control over political activities which, through diminished popular opportunities directly to affect foreign policy, also gave the new leadership more freedom to follow their chosen policies without having constantly to keep a weary eye on the domestic scene. Much of the initial attention of the New Order régime was focused on restoring the economy of Indonesia to a reasonable state of health after the disasters inflicted on it during the Sukarno years. Given its enormous (by the standards of the day) external debt owed both to the West and the Soviet Union, this was a task which became as much a concern of foreign as domestic policies. The Indonesian ambassador to the United States of the time summed up the predicament of Indonesia at the end of the Sukarno period:

> It has become quite clear that for all our claims to international leadership we ended up with an even greater dependency on foreign credits and with our freedom of action seriously compromised.[14]

Extensive economic reforms were required of which a considerable number were demanded by Indonesia's creditors, led by the United States. One of these was that Indonesia accept an international consortium which would 'set overall aid targets and review Indonesia's economic policies'.[15] The Inter-Governmental Group on Indonesia (IGGI) was established in February 1967 with the United States and Japan as the principal donors and involving experts from the International Monetary Fund and the World Bank.[16] In the following years the IGGI kept up a steady flow of aid to Indonesia's gradually more prosperous economy, with Japan assuming the position of by far the largest donor.[17]

Even during the days when the economic dependence on the IGGI and the United States in particular was at its strongest, Indonesia continued to adhere to its non-aligned policy. The brand of non-alignment it now expounded was, to be sure, in terms of tone, style, and content significantly different from the flamboyant, firebrand and distinctly left-leaning variety of Sukarno's later years. The general tilt of the policies was now towards the West, the departures from and criticism of Western and especially US policies phrased in softer language and conveyed through conventional channels rather than being hurled from temporary platforms at big public gatherings in town and city squares. Although strongly anti-communist by inclination, the régime inveighed against aspects of the US involvement during the war in Indochina such as the military incursions into Cambodia in 1970 and Laos in 1971, but sought at the same time to balance its criticism by condemning all foreign military presence in these two countries. Throughout the Indochina War Indonesia maintained an embassy in Hanoi and even welcomed a mission from the National Liberation Front of South Vietnam.[18] The general thrust of Indonesia's policies under the New Order régime was to try to keep outside influence in the region on as low a level as possible by itself rejecting intimate political and military relations with great powers. Given its economic dependence on the West, the United States in particular and increasingly on Japan, it has not been easy to keep great powers at arm's length. What it prescribed for itself was also not necessarily equally palatable to all its neighbours in the region.

Indonesia's first experiences with the Soviet Union were none to helpful to the development of relations between them. As the other principal protagonist in the bipolar global structure, the Soviet Union too sought to court the non-committed Third World nations. Its initial attitude was almost a mirror image of that to which the US Secretary of State, John Foster Dulles, gave expression when in 1956 he called non-alignment 'an immoral and short-sighted conception'. Before it came around to adjust its policies to better fit the circumstances of the Third World in the late 1940s and early 1950s, the Soviet Union viewed with hostility countries which failed to declare themselves clearly in favour of the cause of socialism.[19] As early as 1948 its relations with Indonesia got off to a poor start when in line with the general policy of fomenting insurrections, it supported the Indonesian Communist Party's (PKI) uprising in the east Javanese town of Maduin.[20] This particular adventure on the part of the PKI was quickly crushed by nationalist forces. The Soviet Union had apparently taken to heart this and other lessons from elsewhere because in the mid-1950s it altered its policies to allow for greater flexibility towards Third World non-alignment.[21] This turned out a rather fortunate change for the Soviet Union coming as it did not long before the Guided Democracy period of Sukarno during which it could be exploited to great advantage. As a consequence, Soviet influence in Indonesia reached a peak never attained since.

The issue which proved the most rewarding to Soviet ambitions was the dispute over Irian Jaya. To the United States this case posed in its starkest form a rather difficult question – how to support non-aligned Indonesia and thereby gain a political and Cold War competitive advantage on the Soviet Union without unduly harming relations with the Netherlands, its close friend and trusted NATO partner? To the Soviet Union, on the other hand, there was no such awkward dilemma involved. Because of the adjustments already made, it could without decisive reservations throw in its lot with Indonesia. Relatively lavish economic and military aid was provided, and the relationship between the Soviet Union and Indonesia blossomed sufficiently to cause serious concern in the United States and make it put pressure on the Netherlands to negotiate over West Irian.[22]

By the time Indonesia's policy of Confrontation with Malaysia was in full flight, however, Soviet influence was waning. Sukarno's increasing radicalism and desire to play a leading role in the Third World led him into a more intimate relationship with China. His ideas of the New Emerging Forces (NEFO), among which Indonesia and China were found, as pitted against the Old Established Forces (OLDEFO), left the Soviet Union on the wrong side of the dominant dividing line. The Soviet Union also felt uneasy about perhaps compromising its position within the Third World by supporting Indonesia in its dispute with another Third World country, Malaysia. Sukarno's gradually greater reliance on the PKI, which in 1963 came out in open support of the Chinese side of the Sino-Soviet split, had a similarly strongly corrosive effect on the relationship.[23]

Although the New Order régime of Suharto had no sympathy for communism as such, it did not fall back on an attitude of undifferentiated hostility towards all communist states. Indonesia's relations with the Soviet Union, however, have remained cool ever since Sukarno's days and are characterised by suspicion of Soviet motives and intentions. The Soviet view of the role of and links with the PKI, experiences gathered in connection with the negotiations about the rescheduling of Indonesia's debt to the Soviet Union left by Sukarno, the Brezhnev Asia collective security proposal of 1969, the growing Soviet naval presence in oceans adjacent to Southeast Asia from the early 1970s, and the Soviet Union's underwriting of the Vietnamese invasion and occupation of Cambodia in late 1978, were all events which did little to improve relations between the two. Nevertheless, a credible adherence to non-alignment required at least 'correct' relations with the Soviet Union after the complete break in 1967 with the other principal communist power, China.[24] Beyond that the Soviet Union has had relatively little to offer Indonesia by way, for instance, of aid and trade, which from the Indonesian perspective would have been the most useful.

Of the relations of Indonesia with the three great powers, none has reached higher peaks of empathy or plunged into deeper troughs of enmity than those with China. The declaration of the People's Republic of China on 1 October 1949 occurred almost contemporaneously with the official birth of the Republic of Indonesia, and the two almost immediately exchanged the 'courtesy' of recognition. During the first few years, however, when each was preoccupied with domestic matters or external events in which the other took no direct or special interest, not much happened in the relations between them. It was only just before and during the Bandung conference of April 1955, which marked a turning point in the emergence of the Non-Aligned Movement, that some energy began to be injected into the relationship. Two factors in particular set the tone of the development which, after some ups and downs, reached its high point during the last couple of years of Sukarno's Guided Democracy period.

The first was a shared outlook of strong hostility towards colonialism. This was mixed with a certain degree of anti-Western feelings to which China was especially partial. Issued with increasing frequency when he was at the pinnacle of the Indonesian power structure, Sukarno's injunctions against what he termed imperialism and neo-colonialism found in the leaders of China a group quite ready to lend him support. The other very important factor was the Chinese minority. Of a community totalling in excess of two and a half millions after the Second World War, about 70 per cent were descendants of earlier immigrants whereas nearly 30 per cent were recent immigrants born in China. Some members of the Chinese community, known to the Indonesians as Peranakans, had a history as residents of Indonesia going back perhaps three hundred years and more. As elsewhere in Southeast Asia the Chinese in Indonesia were mainly involved in commerce, industry and small scale trading in which areas they occupied a dominant position. And as elsewhere this led to much resentment. During colonial times the 'role of the Chinese in many ways resembled that of the Jews in nineteenth century Europe – disliked by the natives, but patronised and used by the ruling class; in Indonesia the latter were the Dutch'.[25]

When Indonesia became independent, the relative economic freedom which the Chinese had enjoyed under the Dutch was restricted by the introduction of laws which also defined their citizenship status. This issue became, in Indonesia as in other countries in Southeast Asia, related to the wider issue of the loyalty of and integration of the Chinese in the country of residence. The Kuomintang government of China had based its policy towards the overseas Chinese on the maxim of *jus sanguinis*, 'the identification of man's nationality by his descent',[26] which made all Chinese, whether born in China or not, citizens of China. This was the view of the matter which the communist government in Peking inherited from its predecessors, and, partly because of its ideological colour, it caused much trouble in the relations between the People's Republic of China and governments in Southeast Asia, including the Indonesian.

The status of the Chinese in Indonesia became an issue of negotiations between the People's Republic and Indonesia in the latter part of 1954. The talks were continued on behalf of China by Chou En-lai at the Bandung conference where an agreement was reached whose most important provision was that China renounced the doctrine of *jus sanguinis*. The agreement was not, however, ratified for many years, and several of its provisions were in fact nullified by legislation passed in Indonesia in 1958 which reduced the Chinese community's position to the discriminatory levels of earlier years.[27] It was not before 1960–61 that the issue receded into the background and ceased to impair the development of other aspects of Indonesia's relations with China. In 1961 a treaty of friendship was signed in Jakarta, and in the shadow of the widening Sino-Soviet rift China saw new opportunities for gaining influence in Indonesia. As the influence of the PKI also grew and Sukarno's policies became more radical, China sought to exploit the situation by making an ally of Indonesia in its struggle with the Soviet Union and perhaps the United States.[28] China supported Indonesia in its Confrontation with Malaysia and applauded Sukarno's repudiation of the United Nations. In a speech on the Indonesian national day in August 1965 Sukarno enthused about the 'anti-imperialist axis, namely the axis Djakarta-Phnom Penh-Hanoi-Peking-Pyongyang'.[29] Only a few days later came the attempted coup which turned out to be the beginning of the end of Sukarno.

The Indonesian military régime which assumed the reins of power after Sukarno, accused China of having actively supported the PKI which it held responsible for the attempted coup.[30] Relations with China deteriorated rapidly over the next couple of years, and in 1967 diplomatic relations between the two were severed. In subsequent years, those within Indonesia who from time to time argued in favour of resumption of relations always came up against strong opposition from within the military, and relations were not restored before 1990.

This brief sketch of the relations between Indonesia, on the one hand, and the United States, the Soviet Union, and China, on the other, brings out some salient features which have a bearing on the subject matter of this enquiry. First, especially after the Bandung conference of Afro-Asian states, all the great powers came to regard Indonesia as a key country and 'an important potential prize'[30] among those which refused to align themselves with one or the other side in the Cold War. As the Sino-Soviet rift burst into the open around 1960, the competition between the three, to which the intricate political scene in Indonesia itself greatly contributed, became very complicated indeed. Each of the great powers has had periods when it exerted greater influence than the others, or at least found its efforts given a less reserved reception. As we have seen, these periods have been of rather short duration as far as the Soviet Union and China are concerned, and not for lack of effort on their part. The outstanding fact to note, however, is that none of the great powers has succeeded in attaining what at one time or another has been their ultimate goal, namely to make of Indonesia a close and lasting member of its own sphere of influence.

Second, the features which made Indonesia a much desired prize – its size and importance – are also among the very features which helped it escape being too warmly embraced by the great powers. Because they made the task of preserving territorial integrity all the harder, its size and geographically widely dispersed territory may have been from a domestic point of view a mixed blessing. From the great powers' point of view these features, coupled with cultural and social heterogeneity, provided also tempting points of access to exploit regional discontent within Indonesia. Yet, a weakness of size of this sort may turn out to be a strength. It would seem at least from the tepidness of the few attempts they made that Indonesia's sheer size, especially when seen in conjunction with the complexity of its domestic political scene, in the end caused the great powers to turn back from the brink of more forceful intervention, however tempted they may have been.

Third, the importance of Indonesia in the eyes of the great powers does not derive from its size only. Its strategic location astride some of the world's most important routes of transportation and trade has also contributed to making it a source of great attraction. In this game, it has been as much a matter of denying Indonesia to one's opponent as a matter of winning it for oneself. Its abundant natural resources of various kinds made it in the eyes of President Kennedy one of the potentially significant nations of Asia. During the Irian Jaya dispute he took diplomatic initiatives whose aim was to find a solution to the dispute lest it should develop into a fully fledged crisis out of which Sukarno perhaps would emerge the loser and the PKI the winner, with obvious international consequences for the prestige and international position of the United States.[31]

Last, and by no means least, successive leaders of Indonesia have shown in their conduct of relations with the great powers a degree of confidence which has roots in historical and cultural factors, and in the awareness that they, despite all present shortcomings and difficulties, are leaders of a potentially very significant state, even from a global perspective. Sukarno – volatile, emotional, romantic and prone to rashness and exaggerations – retained even in his most flirtatious moments with China, enough of the nationalist in himself to keep the Chinese leaders none to certain about their degree of influence on him. Although this 'distance' no doubt also sprang from his colossal vanity, which would not allow him to be anyone's subordinate, it also derived from an awareness of the importance of the country he led.

Suharto's style has been very different from his predecessor, in part perhaps deliberately so. Shunning exhibitionism and publicity seeking of the Sukarno type, Suharto has been sober, 'cautious and somewhat

colourless as a public figure'.[32] Although Indonesia's economic predicament compelled him and the military New Order régime to accept certain
changes in economic policy dictated by the United States and other creditor
nations in return for badly needed aid and external debt rescheduling, the
emphasis on an 'independent and active' foreign policy constituted more
than mere lip service to a course set already before Indonesia gained its
formal independence. The economic dependence on the West no doubt had
an effect on what Indonesia felt it could say and do internationally. Yet, the
adjustments made by Suharto were not all due to this state of affairs but also
to a measured affinity of outlook between Indonesian leaders and the United
States in particular on several international questions which had as its main
source a shared and strong opposition to communism.[33] Though with a
clear tilt towards the West, Indonesia has nevertheless avoided getting
entangled in relations with the United States which would seriously
compromise its non-alignment and 'independent and active' course in
international affairs.

It is worth recalling what was said earlier about the difficulties any
non-aligned country inevitably must experience if it is to chart a course
in foreign policy which is seen by all great powers as non-aligned. When
Indonesia from time to time seems to have veered to this or that side the
cause is as often to be found in changing relations between the great
powers themselves or in great power policies which have been perceived
in Indonesia to lead it into too close relations with this or that great power.
It seems in any event fair to say about Indonesia that its relative success in
staying more or less on the course it set itself in international affairs owes
much both to its own perception of itself as a state of some importance
and to a similar perception on the part of the great powers that Indonesia
is indeed a state of some importance, all its weaknesses notwithstanding.
That alone, of course, does not automatically make it a regional great power.
Its role and standing within the region to which it belongs are also important
ingredients.

Relations with States in the Region

For a state to be regarded the undisputed leader within its own region
requires, on the one hand, outstanding qualities and, on the other, their
ready recognition and acceptance by all other regional states. These are,
of course, very demanding requirements which no state, even the most
powerful, can meet fully. There will always be other states which harbour
ambitions of one sort or another or possess abilities in this or that field to
which it will seek to give vent. To accept fully the superiority of another

state is also a form of surrender and may even imply a denial of the right to be heard on issues of importance to one's own well-being. Furthermore, it goes against the grain of some of the most revered principles of international society, fictitious in part though they may be, such as independence and sovereign equality. Because they stand to lose the most by their disregard, it is precisely the weaker states which are the more prone to insist on the observance of such principles. For these and other reasons then, we cannot demand of regional great power status that it meets the 'ideal' requirements because to do so would simply force us to abandon the search in the real world for anything that could be remotely called a regional great power. This leaves us necessarily with a phenomenon which is very hard to identify, and Indonesia is indeed a case in point.

Indonesia's involvement in regional affairs has developed in almost reverse proportion to its activities on the global scene. Under Sukarno its aspirations, which to a large extent were Sukarno's own, were focused on the world stage and the desire for a leadership role in the Third World and the non-aligned movement, and relatively little attention was paid to regional affairs.[34] One issue did attract its attention though, and that concerned Malaysia. Its involvement in regional cooperation through the almost still-born Maphilindo was little more than a ruse staged as part of its campaign against the formation of Malaysia in 1963 in relation to which it also resorted to more forceful actions.[35] Far then from being the progeny of a commitment to regionalism and rooted in regionalist sentiments, the involvement in Maphilindo and Confrontation (which, of course, was its very own 'creation') was primarily inspired by the yearning for a leading role on the world stage through being seen as a vehement and uncompromising opponent of all vestiges of imperialism and neo-colonialism as defined by Sukarno. The removal of the latter from power placed this particular ambition in at least temporary abeyance and confronted the New Order régime with the arduous task of coping with an economy in deep crisis and repairing Indonesia's extremely tattered image in much of Southeast Asia (and, for that matter, elsewhere too).

The transition from Sukarno to Suharto and the resultant changes in Indonesia's external relations deserve, however, more than a passing mention in this context. They are, indeed, especially revealing because eventful and changing times have a tendency to call into service and to place in sharper relief a country's degree of influence, position, and inherent importance relative to others. Despite the somewhat oblique and gradual manner of the transition from one to the other régime, the significance of the events in Indonesia and their importance to the region at large did not escape notice in other parts of Southeast Asia. The rather feeble attempts at regional cooperation had by 1965–66 come to almost nothing. Maphilindo had barely taken a single breath before all life expired. The Association of Southeast Asia (ASA), formed in 1963 by Malaysia, the Philippines and Thailand, fared a shade better but stranded on the Philippine claim to Sabah and the fact that the Philippines colluded with Indonesia in opposing the formation of Malaysia. The demise of Sukarno and the almost simultaneous shelving of the Sabah claim and the end of Confrontation in 1966 created, however, an altogether more propitious climate for political initiatives with a regional scope and content. When attempts were first made to revive the motionless ASA, the role and place of Indonesia in the new regional political structure was the principal issue. Among those charged with responsibility for creating the regional cooperative structure, it was a shared view that the success of the venture was to a very considerable degree dependent on Indonesia's participation. When, therefore, in August 1967, the Association of Southeast Asian Nations (ASEAN) was formed, it was the culmination of a process which first and foremost had catered to Indonesian desires and sensibilities to which ASA – ill liked by the Indonesians – was sacrificed.[36]

Indonesia itself, on the other hand, was aware of its own importance at least to a degree equal to that found among the other members. The way it gave vent to this awareness, however, was this time around radically different from the methods and style of Sukarno. Apart from insisting on a new rather than accepting a refurbished old framework and taking an active part in the formation of ASEAN, Indonesia was prepared to compromise on virtually all issues of some importance. Its adherence to non-alignment, for example, included of course opposition to formal alliances with great powers and to great power military bases in the region, and in this respect its views went contrary to the policies and practices of all its fellow ASEAN members which, without exception, had entered into security relations of one sort or another with Western powers. To reconcile the different views on security matters consequently turned out to be the most time-consuming and difficult task at the meeting in Bangkok during those August days in 1967. Thus in the ASEAN Declaration's references to security, foreign bases were declared to be temporary because Adam Malik, Indonesia's foreign minister, had made clear that such a statement was necessary to the survival of the New Order régime.[37] Yet, at the same time they fell well short of what the Indonesians originally had wanted, and in this respect reflected a new flexibility and an awareness on the part of Indonesia that more intimate relations with the rest of the region had its price.

The regional political scene which it now wished, and perhaps even was compelled to join in a more complete and constructive manner than before, was not only different but in important ways also more difficult to operate on than had been the world stage on which it had sought a leading role under Sukarno. The practice of manipulation and playing one against the other which Sukarno had used with alacrity and considerable success in the relations with the great powers, would scarcely yield the same rewards in the different setting and could, in any event, only be destructive of the position it now sought in regional affairs. Though they were by temperament very unlike Sukarno and therefore perhaps in any case inclined to behave in a more measured fashion, the new leaders were convinced that Indonesia's position, influence, and reputation in the region required not only a clear break with many past policies but also the cultivation of a different style. Reliance on more conventional diplomatic methods and mores, eschewal of abrasive behaviour, and consciousness of the need to accommodate the interests of its regional partners came in the years which followed to characterise much of Indonesia's involvement in Southeast Asian affairs.[38]

In part designed to allay strongly lingering fears and suspicions of its intentions among neighbours such as Malaysia and Singapore, which had been the targets of the Confrontation policy, the tempered approach to regional affairs, however, stopped well short of being self-effacing. A case in point was the question of an ASEAN central secretariat. No provision had been made for such an institution when ASEAN was formed but already the following year the issue was raised by the Philippines at the Ministerial Meeting in August 1968. Five years went by before a decision was made in 1973 and another year passed before Jakarta was chosen as the site of the new institution. The Filipinos had campaigned hard on behalf of Manila but found themselves in the end compelled to defer to the Indonesian wish to have the Secretariat located in Jakarta. The statement by Foreign Secretary Romulo of the Philippines, in which he withdrew his government's offer of Manila as the site, is indicative of the importance Indonesia attached to the issue and of the weight of Indonesia within ASEAN. The statement read in part, 'In deference to President Suharto's wishes and in the interest of regional unity and harmony, the Philippines hereby withdraws its offer in favor of Indonesia'.[39] It has also been suggested that the powers of initiative and decision conferred on the Secretariat, which only could and indeed did fall well short of being in any way supranational, were additionally circumscribed to prevent Indonesia from adding further to its weight within the organisation by being in an advantageous position to influence the work of a Secretariat located in its own capital.[40] That the question of the Secretariat in any event was a significant issue within the Association is borne out by the United Nations' team of experts which in 1972 submitted a report on the potential for economic cooperation among the ASEAN countries. Referring to the question, the report remarked *inter alia* that the 'problems of institutions are important and delicate'.[41]

When the first Meeting of ASEAN Heads of State and Government took place in February 1976, the Indonesians were given the task of acting as hosts. 'The convening of the first summit in Bali and the location of ASEAN's Secretariat in Jakarta confirmed the understanding that Indonesia was the natural centre of gravity of the Association'.[42] When the next summit was held in 1977 Malaysia acted as host with the Philippines performing the same role in regard to the third summit in 1987. The order in which the summits were held, however, suggested a sequence based on the principle of alphabetical rotation, and by coincidence Indonesia was therefore first in line. The resort to this sort of explanation about the choice of Indonesia as host of the first summit by some officials in ASEAN countries testifies to the need to cope with the tension, which always will be there, between those states which carry less and those which carry more weight, and to the need for rules, practices, and indeed justifications which serve to deflect the full impact of the gap between the more and the less influential.

As far as regional economic cooperation is concerned, the weight and influence of Indonesia on the policies pursued by ASEAN are less easy to assess. This has much to do with the nature of the subject matter itself. Once it was decided that all policies of ASEAN should be the subject of unanimous decision, it could but be the minimum common denominator which determined the pace of the evolution of economic cooperation. Absolute size and power became less influential than real level of economic development. It therefore could have been any but in this case happened to be Indonesia which had the least advanced economy and thus became the pace setter. Yet, overt signs of Indonesia's influence are not wholly absent in this domain either. When the UN team submitted its report on economic cooperation, the recommendations regarding trade liberalisation pandered rather more to the Indonesian preference for an item-by-item lowering of tariffs rather than to the more sweeping across-the-board approach of Singapore and others.[43]

Although a variety of methods of liberalisation existed and were discussed, it was in the end the Indonesian preference which prevailed when ASEAN in the years after 1976 set about the task of trade liberalisation. In general it seems appropriate to say about Indonesia that because of its overall weight and influence but perhaps more importantly because of the decision-making procedures adopted, it set a tempo which meant that internal economic cooperation has evolved only as quickly as the slowest partner – Indonesia – has permitted.

The tension between the desire to observe the principle of sovereign equality and the existence of actual inequality has inspired the adoption of all manner of decision-making procedures in international institutions. The rule of unanimity is better able than most other procedural devices to disguise differences of power and influence. Within ASEAN this has been especially evident in the field of economic cooperation which to develop demands a high degree of harmonisation of policies based on economic laws and principles. In the field of politics and especially in the field of international politics, however, matters are different, more fluid, and dependent on a whole array of factors which obey few, if any, immutable laws of behaviour. International politics is to a considerable degree the realm of the free agent within which, to be sure, there exist 'principles' but of which many are only partially accepted and often tenuously observed. Yet, as a field of operation international politics is certainly not free of constraints, a fact of life with which Indonesia has been repeatedly confronted. And in the realm of regional politics no issue has been as trying on Indonesia's aspirations to regional leadership as the Cambodia question.

No sooner had the strong apprehension with which the ASEAN countries had viewed the communist victories in Indochina abated somewhat, before Vietnam invaded and occupied Cambodia in late 1978. Like no other, this event brought out the extent to which Southeast Asia had become polarised into two opposed camps. When China attacked Vietnam shortly afterwards, in February 1979, with the clear purpose of forcing a Vietnamese withdrawal from Cambodia and failed, considerable anxiety again surfaced in the ASEAN region as to the nature of Vietnam's ultimate intentions. Although the ASEAN states in the years since have, on the whole, been unanimous in their condemnation of Vietnam's role in Cambodia and have on numerous occasions appeared in international fora as a collective entity with a common policy, significantly different views have none the less surfaced among members about how to handle the Cambodia question. None, however, has been as ready to try its own approach as Indonesia.[44]

In some respects Indonesia may be said to have been in a better position than the others to go its own ways. Despite the communist nature of the régime in Hanoi, Indonesian leaders have tended to make an exception of Vietnam which they have viewed with considerable sympathy, especially because of what they see as the similarities between the independence struggle of Vietnam and Indonesia. Emphasis has been put on the nationalist rather than the communist element of the political creed to which Vietnam holds. Unlike Thailand, Indonesia is geographically removed from Indochina and does not carry with it a baggage of historical experiences and memories of past competition for power and influence in its dealings with Vietnam. Furthermore, given historical relations between China and Vietnam, the latter occupies in Indonesian eyes a special position in the region by constituting, as it were, a natural buffer against the interests of China, which to the Indonesians appear as much the greatest long term threat to Southeast Asia.[45] Moreover, the mission Indonesia assumed in the Cambodia question was one which conformed well with the role as leader and principal advocate of the need for 'regional resilience' and regional solutions to regional problems.

In March 1980 Indonesia began what turned out to be a whole string of diplomatic initiatives aimed at finding a negotiated solution to the Cambodia issue. As one attempt petered out without tangible results another would be launched after some time. New attempts were made in mid-1981, in early 1984, during 1985, and in early 1986. Beginning in July 1988 Indonesia sponsored a series of meetings which became known as the Jakarta Informal Meetings (JIM). JIM II took place in February 1989 and JIM III in February 1990. The meeting in 1988 marked the first occasion on which the four Cambodian factions met face to face since the invasion of Cambodia and the installation of the Vietnamese backed régime in January 1979.[46] In August 1989 the Paris International Conference on Cambodia (PICC) was held with France and Indonesia as co-chairmen. In October 1990 yet another meeting was held in Jakarta in preparation for the reconvening of the Paris (PICC) talks which had ended inconclusively the previous year, and which took place the following month.

This almost endless series of meetings (and it is not yet completed since the fighting is still going on) produced at long last a UN sponsored peace plan for Cambodia which, however, still has not been accepted by all parties. Nor is this fleeting summary of meetings in any way complete because it does not mention, among many more, the ASEAN ministerial meetings at which Cambodia has been a principal issue on the agenda. And, of course, Indonesia has not been the only one to act as peacemaker either from inside or from outside the region. Should a lasting and just solution be found to the Cambodia problem, however, there can be no doubt that Indonesia rightfully belongs among the very few who more than others deserve to share the praise and glory. The perseverance and efforts that Indonesia have invested in the search for a solution are of a sort which one would expect to be associated with or indicative of a state which aspires to regional leadership. At the same time its endeavours show clearly the constraints at work, some of which issue directly from the sort of state which Indonesia is, and others from the international environment.

Born of geographical insularity and free from historical experiences, the emotionally 'dispassionate' distance between Indonesia and Indochina may, as mentioned earlier, in one sense have enhanced Indonesia's suitability for the role of intermediary. But in another it clearly curtailed its freedom of action. Molded by a long history of strong rivalry between themselves and the Vietnamese for influence in Cambodia, the lenses through which the Thais saw the conflict were very different from the Indonesian. Though they also in varying degrees were directly affected by the situation in Cambodia, the other members of ASEAN could but early recognise that the interests of Thailand were at stake in a way theirs were not. Quite apart from the weight that Thailand in any event could bring to bear on regional affairs, its exposed position as the 'front line' state in relation to the Cambodia problem gave it a tone-setting influence on ASEAN policies. Time and again Indonesia therefore had to adjust its policies to make them fall in line with the more confrontational approach on which Thailand insisted throughout much of the 1980s.[47] The adjustments Indonesia had to make in these situations were based on many considerations among which the intransigence of Vietnam often was an important ingredient. There was also an element of compulsion involved in the sense that Indonesia realised that its own particular approach could not win the day. Yet, whenever it reverted to the position adopted by the other ASEAN states led by Thailand, it also did so out of a sense of responsibility towards ASEAN as such. At the end of the day there was always the awareness of the need to preserve ASEAN unity and not to resort to methods and courses of action which would too openly split or perhaps even destroy the association. In other words, ASEAN as such was a most important instrument through which regional leadership could be exercised.

What made the search for solutions to the Cambodia conflict all the more difficult was, of course, the fact that the dispute was far from being a purely regional matter. The politically polarised state of affairs in which Southeast Asia found itself after 1975, was reflected in the relations which the states of the region had with the outside world. Each side had its own group of favoured supporters from which they sought help and encouragement of both a material and political kind in their disputes with each other. The Cambodia issue figured in this respect very prominently. Here the Soviet Union acted as the patron of Vietnam, which on its part acted as the chief patron of the régime which it had itself installed in Cambodia. China performed much the same role in relation to the Khmer Rouge, with the United States backing Thailand and the other ASEAN states who in turn supported any group opposed to Vietnam and the Heng Samrin and Hun Sen régime in Cambodia.[48] When discernible progress began to be made on the Cambodia issue this came as a result of changes in the extra-regional environment of which the new policies of the Soviet Union towards Vietnam and the improvement in the relations between the former and China were important turning points. Substantially completed in 1989, the Vietnamese withdrawal from Cambodia further accelerated the search for a solution which was also facilitated by the change in the US attitude towards Vietnam in the middle of 1990. When the latest train of events began to move in 1988, Indonesia's earlier involvement stood it in good stead and it played a major role in the unfolding sequence of meetings, of which it was the convenor of several.

Indonesia's involvement in the Cambodia question clearly demonstrated its 'desire to distinguish [itself] both regionally and internationally',[49] and, one must say, not without a measure of success. Its growing assertiveness, not only regionally but also in international affairs in general, has also found other expressions. Suharto, one of the least internationally travelled leaders in the world, attended his first non-aligned summit in eighteen years in 1989 as a prelude, observers think, to a bid for the leadership of the non-aligned movement when Yugoslavia vacates the position in 1992. Nearer home Indonesia has made its feelings known on many occasions about the prospects for an increased Japanese military role in the general vicinity of Southeast Asia as urged by the United States.[50] Notwithstanding that from time to time it tacitly may have seen a certain utility in a great power (read US) military presence in the region, its general policy of discouraging this should not be seen only as the programmatic expression of non-alignment but also as a realisation that to have the great powers around may curtail its ability to give vent to its own aspirations to regional leadership.

Today Indonesia occupies a more secure position and a more established reputation within ASEAN than ever before. The fact that it is 'the natural centre of gravity' has found expression over the years in many ways and contexts. The importance attached to its participation in regional cooperation and the fact that ASA was dismantled to accommodate Indonesia's wishes in this regard were early indications of the weight it possessed. The location of the ASEAN Secretariat in Jakarta indicates the same. It has, of course, not always gained acceptance for its own preferred solutions to many problems but this would be unreasonable to expect. Because of its 'special' relationship with Vietnam it is also well poised to assume a leading role in the region as a whole, should the ideological cleavage which still marks relations in Southeast Asia one day disappear.

CONCLUSIONS

By what features or qualities shall we recognise a 'regional great power'? I would suggest that the status of regional great power rests on three sorts of consideration. First, a regional great power is endowed with physical attributes which sets it apart from other powers in the region. Its rank on these attributes, whichever they may be, need not be consistently the highest but their combined weight must be seen clearly to be superior to all rivals. Second, these attributes are presumably reflected in the foreign policies pursued and perhaps especially in the way it perceives itself and is perceived by others. In all these respects one would expect a regional great power to be outstanding compared to other powers in the region. Third, the policies and conduct of a regional great power must be reasonably stable and coherent. This does not mean that all powers whose conduct exhibit these qualities are regional great powers. Nor are these requirements absolute in the sense of precluding all change. Not to take account of changing circumstances is as often as not foolish. But there is attached to high position in any hierarchical structure expectations of predictability of which stability and coherence are fortifying – and sudden changes and erratic behaviour corrupting – agents.

How then does Indonesia measure up to these requirements? On most attributes Indonesia's rank is the highest in Southeast Asia. In the field of economic development, however, it ranks among the lower third even when the non-ASEAN states of the region are included. This dimension of regional affairs is especially important because a principal purpose of ASEAN is, after all, the promotion of regional economic cooperation. The relatively underdeveloped state of the Indonesia's economy has not allowed it to play a role in economic cooperation which is commensurate with its position in other regional matters, and it has consequently tended to act as a break on the more ambitious policies of its partners.

In the political arena many of the policies of Indonesia reflect a strong ambition to play a leading role. As we have seen, the attitude and demeanour of the great powers have, if anything, acted as a spur on this ambition. The fact that some great powers have more intimate relations with other regional states does not detract from the status of Indonesia in this respect. When Indonesia has kept a greater distance than most others between itself and the great powers for most of the time, it is the result of a conscious choice. The fact that it has succeeded as well as obtained from the great powers a 'recognition' of this stance, is itself a testimony to its standing. Its standing in the region is also well established although at times somewhat grudgingly accepted. This does not mean that it will on all occasions get its way. But it does mean that on most regional issues of some importance the others will tend to look to it first. Whether one chooses 'first among equals' or 'centre of gravity' as the adage which best describes its standing among its ASEAN partners matters little. However, its position in a region without the divide between non-communist and communist states is a more uncertain quantity.

Two decades and a half of rule by the New Order régime has given to Indonesia's policy a coherence and stability it lacked under Sukarno. The continuity of the leadership itself has clearly been important. Quite apart from the role of Suharto himself, only three persons have occupied the post of minister of foreign affairs in Indonesia during the last twenty-five years. There can be little doubt that this has benefitted Indonesia's general reputation and position in both the region and the world at large. A role as leader requires that the led has some idea on which issues the leader can be trusted to lead. Trust develops neither overnight nor as the result of erratic twists and turns. Indonesia's readiness to tackle the really difficult political issues in the region, with attendant risks, and not to push its own views too far to the obvious detriment of ASEAN, is the mark of regional leadership.

NOTES

1. Michael Banks, 'Systems Analysis and the Study of Regions', *International Studies Quarterly*, XIII (1969): 338.
2. General works on Southeast Asian regionalism include Arnfinn Jørgensen-Dahl, *Regional Organization and Order in South-East Asia* (London: Macmillan, 1982); Alison Broinowski (ed.), *Understanding ASEAN* (New York, NY: St. Martin's Press, 1982); Donald K. Crone, *The ASEAN States. Coping with Dependence* (New York, NY: Praeger, 1983); Michael Leifer, *ASEAN and the Security of Southeast Asia* (London: Routledge, 1989).
3. Keith A. J. Hay, 'ASEAN and the Shifting Tide of Economic Power at the End of the 1980s', *International Journal*, XLIV (1989): 645–47.
4. Iyanatal Islam, 'Socio-Economic Progress in Indonesia under the New Order: An Assessment', in *Southeast Asian Affairs 1984* (Singapore: Institute of Southeast Asian Studies, 1984), pp. 137–50; also Staffan Burenstam Linder, *The Pacific Century. Economic and Political Consequences of Asian-Pacific Dynamism* (Stanford, CA: Stanford University Press, 1986), esp. pp. 57–67; Juwono Sudarsono, 'For Indonesia, a Future of Wealth and Inequity', *International Herald Tribune* (hereafter IHT), 28 September 1990, p. 9.
5. Hildred Geertz, 'Indonesian Culture and Communities', in Ruth

T. McVey (ed.), *Indonesia* (New Haven, MA: HRAF Press, n.d.), p. 24.

6. For example Barbara Crosette, 'Aceh, Barometer of Indonesian Dissent', *IHT*, 13 March 1986, p. 2; reports of armed rebellion in Aceh on Sumatra in *Financial Times* (hereafter *FT*), 24–25 November 1990, p. 3.
7. Michael Leifer, *Indonesia's Foreign Policy* (London: George Allen & Unwin, for the Royal Institute of International Affairs, 1983), pp. 48–51.
8. On the role of Islam, see Leifer, *Indonesia's Foreign Policy*, pp. 136–40 and 176–7. See also his commentary article in *IHT*, 19 September 1990.
9. See Leo Suryadinata, 'Indonesian Policies Toward the Chinese Minority under the New Order', *Asian Survey*, XVI (1976): 770–87. For a report on the role of the Chinese in the economy, see Michael Richardson, 'Unwanted in Indonesia: Rich Chinese', *IHT*, 5 March 1990, p. 1.
10. Harold Crouch, *The Army and Politics in Indonesia* (Ithaca, NY: Cornell University Press, 1978), pp. 344–5.
11. *The Military Balance 1990–1991* (London: The International Institute for Strategic Studies, 1990).
12. Leifer, *Indonesia's Foreign Policy*, pp. 49–51.
13. On Confrontation, see ibid., pp. 75–110.
14. Sudjatmoko quoted ibid., p. 110.
15. See Charles E. Morrison and Astri Suhrke, *Strategies of Survival. The Foreign Policy Dilemmas of Smaller Asian States* (St. Lucia, Queensland: Queensland University Press, 1978), pp. 213–14.
16. On the economic reforms, see Morrison and Suhrke, *Strategies of Survival*, pp. 211–17; Leifer, *Indonesia's Foreign Policy*, pp. 115–17.
17. *FT*, 13 June 1989, p. 8.
18. Leifer, *Indonesia's Foreign Policy*, p. 130.
19. Leszek Buszynski, *Soviet Foreign Policy and Southeast Asia* (London: Croom Helm, 1986), p 11.
20. Ibid., pp. 11–12; Leifer, *Indonesia's Foreign Policy*, pp. 20–1.
21. Buszynski, *Soviet Foreign Policy and Southeast Asia*, p. 13.
22. Ibid., pp. 21–4.
23. Ibid., p. 24.
24. Ibid., esp. pp. 71–4.
25. See C. P. Fitzgerald, *China and Southeast Asia Since 1945* (Camberwell, Victoria: Longman Australia, 1973), pp. 34–5.
26. Ibid., pp 35–45.
27. See J. D. Armstrong, *Revolutionary Diplomacy. Chinese Foreign Policy and the United Front Doctrine* (Berkeley, CA: University of California Press, 1977), p. 149.
28. Leifer, *Indonesia's Foreign Policy*, pp. 104–5.
29. For an argument which casts doubt on the alleged involvement of China, see Fitzgerald, *China and Southeast Asia Since 1945*, esp. pp. 48–53.
30. Morrison and Suhrke, *Strategies of Survival*, p. 202.

31. See Arthur M. Schlesinger Jr., *A Thousand Days. John F. Kennedy in the White House* (New York, NY: Fawcett Crest, March 1967), pp. 492–3.
32. Leifer, *Indonesia's Foreign Policy*, p. 112.
33. Ibid., p. 117–8.
34. Jørgensen-Dahl, *Regional Organization and Order in South-East Asia*, pp. 11–12.
35. For an exhaustive account of Confrontation, see J. A. C. Mackie, *Konfrontasi. The Indonesia-Malaysia Dispute 1963–1966* (Kuala Lumpur: Oxford University Press, 1974).
36. For an account of the process leading to the formation of ASEAN, see Jørgensen-Dahl, *Regional Organization and Order in South-East Asia*, pp. 28–44.
37. Ibid., p 38.
38. See the article by Adam Malik, 'Promise in Indonesia', *Foreign Affairs*, XLVI (1968): 292–303.
39. *10 Years ASEAN* (Jakarta: ASEAN Secretariat, April 1978), p. 276.
40. Jørgensen-Dahl, *Regional Organization and Order in South-East Asia*, p. 186.
41. 'Economic Cooperation Among Member Countries of the Association of Southeast Asian Nations: Report of a United Nations Team', *Journal of Development Planning*, No. 7 (1974), p. 244.
42. Leifer, *ASEAN and the Security of Southeast Asia*, p. 154.
43. Jørgensen-Dahl, *Regional Organization and Order in South-East Asia*, p. 144.
44. For a detailed account of Indonesian initiatives, see Andrew J. MacIntyre, 'Interpreting Indonesian Foreign Policy. The Case of Kampuchea, 1979–1986', *Asian Survey*, XXVII (1987): 515–34.
45. See Leifer, *ASEAN and the Security of Southeast Asia*, pp. 91–2.
46. *Keesing's Record of World Events*, XXXV (1989): 36615.
47. For examples, see MacIntyre, 'Interpreting Indonesian Foreign Policy'.
48. This paragraph is for the most part taken from author's 'Southeast Asia in 1983. Approaching a Turning Point?', in *Southeast Asian Affairs 1984* (Singapore: Institute of Southeast Asian Studies, 1984), p. 14.
49. MacIntyre, 'Interpreting Indonesian Foreign Policy', p. 534.
50. *FT*, 7 September 1989, p. 4.

5 Israel as a Regional Great Power: Paradoxes of Regional Alienation

Nils A. Butenschøn

INTRODUCTION

Israel is a small state with few natural resources, and has no accepted position in the regional, and predominantly Arab, states system. Still, Israel's presence in the region is felt in every corner of the Middle East. It is the 'logic' of Israel's problematic regional relations which is the theme of this chapter.

In the context of this book, the State of Israel is clearly a deviant case. Israel is included because of its dominant role in the Middle Eastern conflict theatre, but otherwise – in terms of regional state interaction – its role as a local great power is highly atypical. It is not self-evident that Israel is related to the rest of the Middle East in a way that qualifies it as a genuine *Middle Eastern* political entity, nor that we can count this tiny state among the *regional great powers* of the world. That depends on how we define the 'Middle East', how we connect Israel to this region and what we mean by a 'regional great power'.

Many studies of the Middle East as a regional system simply exclude Israel. The apparent reason is one of convenience: most generalisations about socio-cultural and institutional patterns in the region would have to be supplemented with ' . . . except in the case of Israel'.[1] Also, if we apply Bruce M. Russett's five criteria for delineating regions – 'social and cultural homogeneity, political attitudes or external behaviour, political institutions, economic interdependence, and geographical proximity' – we do not need much empirical evidence to conclude that Israel is not part of the 'Middle East' (whatever geographical convention of the term we apply), except by geographical chance.[2] As Leonard Fein puts it, though in the region, Israel is not of the region.[3]

Neither does Israel – in contrast to all the other regional great powers discussed in this book – qualify as what Carsten Holbraad calls middle power in the international states system, according to his quantitative criteria.[4] Within his global system approach, the middle powers have an intermediate position in the hierarchy between superpowers and small states. If we follow Holbraad and use Gross National Product as the basic indicator of strength and the conventional six continents as the geographical regions, Israel has no chance of attaining the status of an Asian regional great power.[5] On Holbraad's list of middle powers only Iran is situated in the Middle East.[6]

Still, no scholar would deny that Israel today directly or indirectly has a political-military strength that at least balances its regional Arab contenders and that it plays a role in global politics which is more important than the size and wealth of this country should suggest. Israel is not only the most privileged 'client state' of the United States (in terms of economic and military assistance, strategic cooperation and trade),[7] but is also involved on its own on the African continent from Ethiopia to South Africa as well as in Latin American countries.[8]

Thus, any serious analysis of intra-regional Middle Eastern politics or of trans-regional relations that involves the Middle East would have to include Israel.[9] Our focus is specifically on the regional context: how should we describe and explain Israel's position and influence in the Middle East? What kind of a regional power is Israel? What are the sources of Israel's regional influence? Let us start with a more precise definition of the Middle East as a regional framework for analysis.

The Middle East has no 'natural' boundaries, and there is no conventional or academic consensus as to its precise extension. Like the geographical terms 'Far East' and 'Near East', 'Middle East' is a European invention with reference to British geo-strategic planning at the turn of the century.[10] It is very much a term that was introduced to Europe by officers and correspondents, and its geographical representation has varied over the decades with the changing locations of military headquarters and news agencies. Some scholars, especially Arabists, identify the Middle East as the home region of the 'Arab Nation' and include all member states of the Arab League. Others, such as anthropologists and orientalists, see the Islamic civilisation as the most important common denominator of the region, and include Iran and Turkey in addition to the Arab countries.

Students of international relations tend to view the Middle East as a geo-strategic region delimited by the territories that cojoin the three large continents of Europe, Asia, and Africa. But also within this approach we find a variety of answers to the question of a more precise geographical definition. Some concentrate on the Gulf area, others on the south-eastern Mediterranean countries. This is basically an external approach to the

Middle East with global politics as the frame of reference, and does not take internal identities and socio-cultural characteristics specifically into consideration.

Two conclusions can be drawn from this sketchy discussion. Firstly, while there are almost as many geographical definitions of the region as there are Middle East experts, it is possible to identify a *core* area that is common in most contemporary definitions.[11] This area is the geographical continuum that stretches from Egypt to the west and includes Iraq to the east. Secondly, specific professional identities and research purposes determine the variety of scholarly definitions of the Middle East as a geographical construct. This means that although there exists a general conception, both popular and scholarly, of the Middle East's whereabouts, individual scholars (or professional networks) have to construct, explicitly or implicitly, a 'Middle East' of their own, designed to fit their research purposes.

In our case, it is clear that we cannot apply any definition that is based on socio-cultural continuities to connect Israel to the Middle East. Israel is not part of this continuity, and would consequently have to be regarded more as an extra-regional entity than as a regional power in this respect. An external geo-political definition would clearly include Israel and be relevant if our purpose were to study Israel's role in global politics.

The only analytical approach that makes Israel part of the Middle East is one that looks at what kinds of regional interaction Israel is involved in. The answer is rather simple; practically none, apart from conflict-related exchanges. Like White South Africa, but in contrast to other regional great powers, Israel's relations with neighbouring states are characterised by socio-cultural alienation and basic enmity. Israel's regional position is not that of a 'big brother' who, hated or loved (or both) by its regional underdogs, unquestionably shares and usually represents the centre of the collective regional identity. Egypt's position as a leading power in the Arab world, controversial and changing as it has been over the last forty years, is a telling contrast to the character of Israel's dominance in the same region since the war in 1967. Following the Camp David agreement in 1978 between Israel, Egypt, and the USA, president Sadat's Egypt was condemned by most Arab countries in the region as 'apostate' and 'treacherous' and consequently expelled from the League of Arab States. This was, however, a quarrel within the family. The Egyptian state and society will always be a geo-cultural and geo-political centre of the Arab world, no matter what régime rules the country at any given time. Israel, in contrast, is perceived by the dominant regional culture as 'the enemy', a bridgehead of colonialism and an agent of an alien civilisation, violently implanted into the heart of the Arab world. This image, rooted in the collective Arab political culture, has, with an exception being made for Iraq, hardly been 'operational' for many years on the official Arab level. However, as demonstrated during the Gulf war, it still prevails under the surface.

Thus, as a political, economical and cultural entity Israel is basically not functionally integrated into the Middle Eastern region. The Jewish State is not a member of any of the regional cooperative organisations; it dominates its regional surroundings from a negative position of strength.

To conclude the discussion of approach: the most relevant field of interaction that can serve as a framework for analysing Israel's influence in the Middle East is the Arab-Israeli conflict. More specifically, in the present study the core area of this region includes – in addition to Israel – Syria, Iraq, Jordan, and Egypt, a group of countries that according to Aluoph Hareven, a prominent Israeli security expert, is the most extended of probable 'Arab war coalitions' under the present geo-strategic conditions.[12]

Where the question of Israel's relative strength is concerned, there is a lack of correspondence between capabilities and power. There are parallels between Israel's and South Africa's relations to their respective regional surroundings. Still, what makes Israel's position unique as a dominant regional actor is its mini-state size (20 700 km^2),[13] with a moderate GNP – at US\$ 45 billion, it is slightly more than Egypt's and about half of Algeria's),[14] and a small population of 4.5 million.[15] Israel does not control natural resources and infrastructures (such as transportation networks) vital to the economic survival of neighbouring countries.[16]

Israel's economy is separated from the region at large with two exceptions: limited economic cooperation with Egypt since 1979, and exploitation of the territories which Israel occupies or controls – that is, the West Bank and Gaza Strip, the Golan Heights, and the Israeli 'security zone' in South Lebanon.

Still, Israel is a powerful state in the Middle East, since 1967 indeed the most powerful. At several critical moments it has proven its ability to impose its will on the region. The war in June 1967, when Israel destroyed the offensive military capacity of Egypt, Syria and Jordan within a week, is but the most spectacular example. Israel's ability to take the initiative and strike back after the initial combined surprise attack by Egypt and Syria in 1973 also indicates a relative military superiority. Israel's invasions of Lebanon in 1978 and 1982, which included the bombing of Beirut, an Arab capital, were not countered significantly by the Arab side. In both the latter cases, Egypt was diplomatically pacified through the Camp David process and politically isolated in the Arab world, Syria was not prepared to confront Israel directly, and Lebanon itself had practically no military capabilities as a state and was deeply split by destructive civil war. The PLO fought stubbornly back from its positions in South Lebanon and its headquarters in Beirut, but was no match in the long run for the Israeli Defence Forces (IDF). Such individual Israeli operations as the bombing of the Iraqi nuclear reactor not far from Baghdad in 1981 and of the PLO headquarters in Tunisia in 1985, again with practically no more than oral reactions from the Arab capitals, gave further evidence of Israel's relative strength in the region. Finally, Israel's ability to hold onto the occupied territories since 1967, to expand the Israeli-Jewish society into these areas through ambitious settlement programmes condemned by the world at large as illegal, its *de jure* annexation of East Jerusalem, *de facto* annexation of the Golan Heights, and the continued *de facto* occupation of a 'security zone' in South Lebanon since 1982, all add to the picture of Israel as a regional power with a large degree of *action indépendence*, both in the short and long term perspectives.

How should one explain Israel's action independence on the regional level? From what has already been said, it is clear that Israel's position as a regional great power is not based on its *greatness* in terms of size, population, GDP, and so on, but rather on its *power*, especially its military capabilities. And indeed, if we look at the military variable, it is the only quantitative indicator of national strength which tells us that Israel is not an ordinary small state. Israel's military expenditure as a percentage of GDP is approximately seven times that of Spain's, which has a GDP only slightly smaller than Israel's. *Numerically*, Israel is not a dominating military power in the Middle East. Alosuph Haraven estimates this balance as follows: 'with the IDF deploying against a coalition of Egypt, Jordan, Iraq, and Syria, the quantitative . . . ratio will be approximately 1:4. Without Egypt, this is reduced to about 1:3, and without Iraq, to about 1:2. With only Syria, the numerical balance of forces is reduced to about 1:1'.[17]

Israel's numerical inferiority relative to the possible Arab war coalitions is compensated by elements of *qualitative* military strength. These include highly trained and qualified soldiers, an effective system of military mobilisation for half a million soldiers, and an economy organised to serve the security needs of the state and bear the high costs of a military system that keeps a large part of the working force away from production. Moreover, the West has in numerous ways supplied Israel with modern technology and strategic goods. The Israelis now have a technological capacity to produce weapon systems with an impressive technological standard and great destructive power. Israel's military industry, with Israel Aircraft

Industries in the forefront, has developed the Kfir aircraft fighter, the Arrow anti-tactical ballistic missile, and a spy satellite programme. Israel does not officially admit posession of nuclear weapons, but its capacity in this respect is taken for granted by military experts.[18] The fact that Israel is the most important foreign partner in the American SDI-program can also be seen as an indication of technological capacity and direction of strategic planning.

The significance of these qualitative aspects of the Israeli military for the strategic balance between Israel and potential Arab war coalitions are difficult to measure. The Arab countries have over the last twenty years invested enormously to modernise and improve the quality of their military systems and are undoubtedly narrowing the gap. Iraq under Saddam Hussein has been leading the race on the Arab side for developing and managing high-technology weapons. The Gulf War did, however, demonstrate a basic Arab inferiority when engaged in advanced technological warfare. The war was a fatal blow to Iraq's regional ambitions and probably to any Arab hope in the forseeable future for parity with Israel in terms of military offensive capacity.

When judging Israel's regional behaviour, what is surprising is not so much its numerous and aggressive interventions, but that the Israelis – given their limited resource base – have the ability to operate as a regional boss *and get away with it*. Israel often acts contrary to universally accepted norms and rules for state behaviour, but is seldom confronted with regional or international resistance that could effectively deter such behaviour. Israel's military capabilities alone can hardly explain the freedom of action that it has demonstrated in the Middle East. Even if this freedom is demonstrated most clearly in military behaviour, it is not necessarily only military in *character*. In order to explain Israel's regional strength we have to search for other sources of power, both within the Israeli system and in its relations with the outside world.

REGIONAL PROFILE

An isolated mapping of a state's power resources will tell us very little about its relative strength within its region. The question is whether these power resources can be converted to actual strength in concrete contexts. Power in one context can be powerlessness in another. A striking example is how the Israelis effectively have organised their resources in the conflict with the quantitatively superior neighbouring states, whilst they appear to stand 'powerless' in the face of the Palestinian civilian unarmed uprising in the occupied territories (the *intifada*, which started in December 1987). A closer look at the resources available, how they are organised and utilised, and how the balance of power is fixed in actual interactive patterns are needed in order to explain the constraints and possibilities of the use of power.

The conclusion of the introductary section was that there is no correlation between Israel's regional position of power and the country's non-military quantitative resource base (size, population, economy). Other sources of power must be sought in order to explain Israel's special role in regional and international politics. Two such sources that are not too easily measurable and that demand a more qualitative approach to the question are functionality and legitimacy.

By *functionality* we think of a state's integrative strength politically, socially and economically in relation to other states. In the case of Israel this factor is especially significant given a unique combination of two models of state-building, one settler-colonial and one socialist. As a settler-colonial structure – with security guarantees from Great Powers, European know-how, capital and organisational efficiency – the pre-1948 Zionist state-building movement in Palestine was basically stronger than its underdeveloped, partly pre-modern and politically divided Arab surroundings. In addition, the movement had a national and social emancipatory programme linked especially to the conquering of Palestine. This laid the foundations for a determined, collective utilisation of human resources that was much better suited to modern state-building strategies than clan-based Arab society. These patterns have been sustained after the creation of the State of Israel in 1948.

A country's *legitimacy* in a regional system is an important power resource in deciding the normative basis for the surrounding region's level of tolerance (for example, threshold for use of sanctions) of the country in question. In our context the concept refers to the power-potential state A can be supplied with or deprived of through other countries' view of A's natural position in a state-system. The American hegemony attained in the West after the Second World War was not only achieved through the use of superior force, but was built on the other western states' acceptance of the USA as a leader – a leader that could bring prosperity to and defend 'the Free World' in a cooperative system.[19] However, a lack of legitimacy may paradoxically, in certain situations, also be a source of power. One could call such power 'negative normative power'. Israel is a state without established legitimacy in its regional system, but is nevertheless a dominating factor in the regional balance of power. Israel's regional dominance has not, arguably, been achieved in spite of a lack of legitimacy, but to a certain extent *because of* the lack of legitimacy. A lack of legitimacy, epitomised in the Arab negation of a separate Jewish state in Palestine, implies a fundamental lack of security. This has been compensated by means of extraordinary security repercussions, plans for worst-case scenarios, external security guarantees, and a policy of suspicion and defensive aggressiveness towards neighbouring countries. In an extra-regional context, especially in the West, the Arab rejection of the Jewish State has been the basis for the politico-moral support given to Israel. 'Israel's right to exist' has been the undiscussable doctrine on which most Western nations have based their Middle East policy. The normative strength of this doctrine is derived from the West's understanding of the State of Israel as the Jews' legitimate acquisition after Holocaust. In this picture the establishment of Israel is a manifestation of the victory over Nazi-Germany and a moral pillar of the post-war political order. The Arab rejection of Israel has thus been an important source of normative power for the Israelis to exploit.

Zionist Patterns of State-Building

A starting point for a further discussion of the State of Israel's power base in terms of functionality and legitimacy could be that its foundation is structurally similar to earlier cases of European settler-colonialism. For example, the American historians Howard Lamar and Leonard Thompson, in a comparative study of the 'frontier' societies in North America and Southern Africa, write that:

> Probably the nearest contemporary approach to the kind of frontier dealt with in this book, where rival societies compete for control of the land, is to be found in Israel. There, despite the complex earlier history of Jewish-Arab relations, the contemporary situation is in essence the product of modern Jewish immigration into a territory that had been dominated by Arabs for many centuries. It is a frontier situation with many charateristics that will be familiar to readers of this book: settlement by people with a technology superior to that of the 'indigenous' inhabitants and with access to the skills, products, and capital of the industrilized West; their creation of a bridgehead behind the shelter of colonialism; their control of a postcolonial state; and their victories in frontier wars, followed by the incorporation and settlement of conquered territory, the expulsion of many of the indigenous people, and the subjugation and segregation of those remaining. The Israeli frontier is still 'open', with raids and counterraids taking place across

its contested boundaries; and it remains to be seen whether it will have been ephemeral, like the white settlements in tropical Africa.[20]

This perspective throws up a historical framework which illuminates the modern interaction pattern discussed here. The conflict in the Middle East can not be fully understood as a conflict between established states, neither can it be regarded as a conflict between an established state and a people who did not get a state (the Palestinian problem). The conflict is about a state-building project, the Zionist one, which at its outset was organised, financed and imposed on the Middle East by extra-regional actors. This project is still not complete. It is still in an 'open' phase of expansion, without finally stipulated borders, a constitutional organisation and a defined population. The State of Israel can perhaps best be understood as an organisation that has the completion of the state-building project as its constant first priority.

The relative strengths of rivalling civilisations have most likely never been so overwhelmingly unequal as it was in the encounter between European settlers and the indigenous population in the period between the sixteenth and the twentieth centuries. This inequality reached its peak in the last half of the nineteenth century, when the West was able to utilise its superior industrialised technology to further their imperialist aims. The European powers could struggle between themselves for control and influence in other parts of the world without giving much thought to how the non-Europeans perceived these matters. The indigenous populations were either expelled, massacred, died of epidemics or were subjugated to colonial rule.

There are, however, great variations within this framework. In Australia around 300 000 Aboriginies lived without fixed settlements and social superstructures. The population was exceedingly vulnerable to changes in the physical environment, and was not able to produce any sort of resistance to European settlers. On the North American continent the indigenous population was far better equipped and organised. The Indians were gradually able to use firearms and organise effective attacks against the white trespassers. When they eventually had to give up resistance in 1890 they had left their mark on the conscience of American history. In South Africa the conditions were not so advantageous for white immigration and settlement. Moreover, on account of traditional contacts with other peoples, the indigenous population was more immune to new sources of infection than were the Indians. The black tribes would not let themselves be driven out or be broken down physically, but they did not have the capacity to prevent European expansion and establishment of control in the area. They too produced efficient military resistance, but were weakened in internal struggles and were vulnerable to divide-and-rule tactics. Gradually the black population was incorporated into a white economic-political hegemonic system, giving rise to the system of Apartheid in South Africa.

Does the State of Israel fit into this picture? In many ways no, but in a fundamental sense yes, especially concerning mechanisms of conflict in the relationship between settler-colonial societies and the indigenous population. Here the 'indigenous population' basically refers to the Arabs of Palestine. But in a wider context the whole of the Arab Middle East could be included, since the establishment of a Zionist polity in the area was from the outset a regional concern. It was perceived by the Arabs at large as an intruding system imposed on them by colonial powers and designed to preserve colonial influence in the region. Within this broad approach it is possible to regard the Arab world as a 'continent' with established, traditional societies (resembling Black Africa, the Indian North America), and the Zionist movement as a trespassing system with its beginnings in modern Europe. The frontier perspective is concerned with what is happening in the encounter between these two systems. Which interactive patterns arise, and how can these explain the character of the political systems which become the historical product? An important part of the explanation of the State of Israel's faculty for regional dominance lies probably in its characteristics as a 'frontier-state'.[21]

Israel as Historically Atypical

Few systematic attempts have been made to interpret the Arab-Israeli conflict as part of a frontier-perspective.[22] One reason for this may be that this approach, like the more radical anti-imperialist approach,[23] is easily perceived as 'anti-Zionist' and so by implication delegitimises the State of Israel. Another reason could be that Israel is in many ways atypical as a settler-colonial enterprise. Firstly, the Zionist colonising of Palestine started at a time when the rest of the European settler-colonising was over. The classic frontier conflict belongs to the time of colonialism, not to post-colonialism. Secondly, the Zionists could link themselves with a Jewish cultural and political tradition in Palestine, a historical rights argument which gave the Zionist movement a nationalist and religious legitimation, especially in the West. Thirdly, the Zionists were not settler-colonialists in the traditional European sense of the word; they did not settle the country in order to exploit its labour and resources or otherwise defend imperial interests. The Zionists were nationalist state-builders on behalf of their own tribe, and on the ground in Palestine a socialist movement was leading the pioneers.

However, these are distinctive features of the Zionist colonialisation which do not invalidiate the settler-colonial perspective. Rather, these unique features become more visible and easier to evaluate in comparison to other cases of settler colonialism. The perspective seems useful for highlighting the general and the distinctive features of the modern Jewish state-building in Palestine. Regardless of how the State of Israel is interpretated as a historical phenomenon, the Zionists unavoidably faced an Arab region that *rejected* them. This necessitated a strategy of survival that implied both conquest and dominance.

As colonisers the Zionists did not meet isolated indigenous tribal societies with no knowledge of the modern world, but a culturally and politically self-conscious region with century-old traditions of political organisation, as well as with experience of contacts and conflict with the West. The Arabs too aspired for membership in the family of modern nation-states. The colonisation of Palestine occurred *concurrently* with the growth of Arab nationalism. The idea of national political organisation was totally unknown to the indigenous societies in earlier cases of European settler-colonisation. Moreover, a special challenge for the Zionists was the fact that the idea of national self-determination made its normative breakthrough in international society after the First World War. On the one hand, this principle could be used to justify Jewish demands for their own state; on the other, the 84 000 Jews made up only some 11 per cent of the population in Palestine when the League of Nations made the territory a British mandate in 1922. Based on the idea of national rights advocated by Woodrow Wilson and others, legitimising the formation of a Jewish State in a territory where almost 90 per cent of the population was non-Jews was a somewhat problematic task.

Moreover, the Zionists were subjected to restrictions concerning the handling of Arab opposition and the campaign for an expansion of the Jewish colony in Palestine. Through the British Balfour Declaration of 1917 and the League of Nations' mandate they had achieved security guarantees and international legitimacy. But the Zionists did not have a sufficiently independent power base on their own. The support of the great powers was given on condition that the building of the 'Jewish national home' would not take place at the expense of the 'civil and political rights' of the indigenous population. How should this be interpreted? The British grappled with this question throughout the 26 years of the mandate period. They attempted to restrict the Zionists' eagerness for expansion, whilst at the same time suppressing Arab opposition to the mandate which included 'the first Palestinian revolution' of 1936–39. Finally, right up to the 1930s, the Zionists had problems recruiting colonisers, especially to the strategically important agricultural colonies.[24]

In relation to other European settler populations the Zionists had a number of disadvantages, related to the beginnings of an organised and self-conscious world outside of Europe, the lack of a European mother country which among other things could have represented a possibility for retreat, and the growth of local nationalism. Despite all these problems the Zionists managed during the mandate period to build an infrastructure that withstood the Arab attack in 1948. They were able to take over government in Palestine from the British at short notice and reorganise the economy after more than half of the population disappeared as refugees. It is symptomatic that it was the Palestinian population and not the Jewish newcomers who were driven to flight during the war in 1947–49.[25] The Jewish society emerged from the war stronger and more coherent, whereas the Palestinian population disintegrated in its traditional form.

The 'Zionist revolution' of which David Ben-Gurion became the undisputed leader did not only aim to procure 'a country without people for a people without a country'. It was just as important to bring the Jews into the family of modern nations, liberated from societies ridden by religious prejudice and aristocratic privilege. Ben-Gurion wanted to build a new Jewish workers' state, based on principles of collective ownership, on Jewish work in agriculture and industry, and with the Jewish State as the uniting focus of identity. Thus, Zionism was a strategy of modernisation with a clear base in the European ideologies of the nineteenth and twentieth centuries.[26]

The Zionist Labour Organisation Histadrut was the chief instrument of state-building in the mandate period. The organisation covered the majority of the institutional needs of economic and social character that the settlers had, and was based on principles of central planning, ethnic segregation and maximal exploitation of human resources. Histadrut became the largest employer in the Jewish society, a position it still holds. Hagana, the Jewish defence organisation in Palestine (and the basis for the Israeli Defence Forces), was also organised with its basis in Histadrut. Thus Histadrut not only became a state-building instrument, but also a nation-building one. It was a 'meltingpot' that could gather different fragments of the Jewish immigrants in a collective, determined effort.[27]

The *yishuv*'s (the Jewish community in Palestine) character as representative of the modern civilisation in the Middle East is important in our context not only because it gives information about a gap in development levels between the Jewish colonial society and the surrounding Arab clan society.[28] This role as 'modernising agent' also became the Zionists' central card in negotiations with Arabs, locally and regionally. The Jewish immigrants formed a direct bridgehead to the most powerful economic and political centres of the world – London, Paris, New York. Zionist leaders, from the founder Theodore Herzl onwards, claimed that a Jewish state in Palestine would be in the Arabs' own interest. Such a state would create development, well-being and modernity in the area, and represent a connecting link with the power centres of the West. On the basis of such perspectives many Arabs, especially outside of Palestine, wished the Zionists welcome to the Middle East.[29] But the organisation of the Jewish economy and the nationalist conflict did not create the type of positive consequences some had hoped for. Through the Jewish National Fund and other channels the settler society in Palestine was supplied with considerable capital from the outside Jewish world. This capital was subject to political control, and was seldom invested in work-intensive production based on a native, non-Jewish workforce. Therefore, the indigenous population of Palestine was not integrated into the settler economy on a broad scale, as was the rule in other cases of European settler-colonialism. The implication was a low degree of economic and functional interdependence between the two groups in Palestine.

This fact also explains why the general economic boycott of the new State of Israel instigated by the Arab States had no dramatic consequences for the Israeli economy; it was already on the outset functionally separated from the surrounding region. The boycott became rather an incentive for further modernisation of the Jewish economic sector in Palestine. There was a strong dependence on adjustment to the markets in Western Europe and the United States, both in order to attract investments and to be able to compete in these markets. Today, Israel has an economical-technological capacity that is equal to the average of the West European Mediterranean countries measured in GNP per capita. Compared with the Arab economies Israel has a staggering level of development with a GNP per capita of over thirteen times that of Egypt.

This structural inequality has been dramatically illustrated in the encounter between the Israeli and Palestinian economies in the occupied areas. The Israeli expert Meron Benevisti comments that,

> The Israeli occupation did not create the territories' economic malaise. It only aggravated it. The fragmented, non-viable, dependent, under-developed nature of its economic branches became more visible as a result of the tremendous disparity between them and the Israeli

economic sectors. Instead of being subservient and auxiliary to the less-developed Jordanian economy, the territories were sucked into the highly developed Israeli system. The outcome was inevitable: the economy of the West Bank and Gaza was fully integrated with that of Israel.[30]

EXTERNAL AND INTERNAL CONSTRAINTS

In recent years the majority of Arab states has given clear signals that it is ready to accept a political arrangement with Israel which could stabilise the Middle East politically and economically. In 1979 Israel and Egypt signed a peace treaty based on the Camp David Agreements from 1978, the first in the history of the Arab-Israeli conflict. A breakthrough for Arab recognition of the State of Israel came in November 1988 at a meeting of the Palestine National Congress (PNC). With reference to the United Nation Partition Plan for Palestine (resolution 181 of 1947) the PNC – which is the Palestinian parliament in exile and PLO's supreme authority – recognised the principle of dividing Palestine into a Jewish and a Palestinian state. This was an important event in the history of the conflict. The PNC also accepted the Security Council's resolutions 242 (1967) and 338 (1973). Practically, this meant that the PLO, as the basis for a solution, accepted the borders as they were before the war in 1967 (that is, the armistice lines of 1949). In this way, moreover, the United States' main conditions for accepting the PLO as a 'discussion partner' were also met.

These developments represent a fundamental shift in the Arab political approach towards Israel. A united Arab world had rejected the *principle* of a Jewish state in the region ever since the Balfour Declaration was issued in 1917. In it, the British government declared its sympathy with the idea of establishing a 'Jewish National Home' in Palestine. This British support for a Zionist programme of Jewish nation-building in Palestine was accepted by the other Western powers at the time, and incorporated into the text of the League of Nations' mandate for Palestine in 1922. Historically, the Middle East conflict has revolved around whether, and if so on what terms, an independent Jewish state should be integrated into Palestine and the Middle East. The Arab side is now in the process of recognising the legitimacy of a separate Jewish state, and direct the attention more specifically to the terms under which such a recognition can be formally institutionalised. These terms relate basically to the territorial extension of Israel and the framework for Palestinian national self-determination. What does this basic change in Arab attitudes towards Israel mean for Israel's regional position?

Compatibility of Israel's Political-Military Doctrine and Arab Perceptions

From the Israeli point of view this development is not unambiguously positive. The Arab compliance, especially that on the part of PLO leader Yasir Arafat, has not been celebrated as a victory in Israel. Rather it has created uncertainty, a widening political split between 'hawks' and 'doves', and a feeling of political paralysis. It has been difficult for the Israelis to match the Arab, and particulary the Palestinian, initiative in the peace process. Israeli security thinking has been based on, and is suited to, a presupposition that there is an Arab annihilation motive – with reference to the traditional Arab rejection of the Jewish state's legitimacy. It is this premise more than anything else that has justified the build-up of Israeli military superiority in the region, that has given Israel a motive for regional dominance. Israel has lacked the kind of national security which lies in recognition by its neighbours, but has compensated for this lack by a formidable military strength, external guarantees, and a strategy of regional activism directed against Arab build-up that could threaten Israeli superiority.

These basic elements in established Israeli strategic thinking are reflected in what has been called *Israel's political-military doctrine*[31] as formulated by among others the Israeli political scientist M. I. Handel.

– The basic assumption underlying the Israeli political-military doctrine is the understanding that the *central aim of the Arab countries is to destroy the State of Israel whenever they feel able to do so*, while doing everything to harass and disturb its peaceful life.
– Israel is militarily and, to a lesser extent, politically isolated from the rest of the world; it is not a member of any political or military alliance and *must* ultimately *rely completely on its own power in case of emergency.*
– Israel is a Jewish state desiring to continue to maintain its national character.
– The IDF will undertake *a pre-emptive (interceptive) attack if the security of the state is endangered*. The political and military intention is defensive, but the strategy is offensive.
– The IDF has to build up and develop its forces and design its strategic plans according to the assumption that it would have to face *a combined*

and coordinated military effort by all neighboring Arab armies at the same time.[32]

To sum up: As long as the Israelis insist on maintaining their Jewish State and as long as the Arabs do not regard that state as a legitimate part of the Middle East, it is in the nature of things that Israel alone must stand as strongly or even stronger than the Arab states taken together.

This doctrine is now challenged by an active Arab willingness to seek political reconciliation, and to give Israel legitimacy as a state. This represents a dramatic challenge for Israel.[33] If the change in Arab attitudes is genuine, it pulls the rug from under established Israeli security policy. In fact, the whole fabric of the Israeli infrastructure is modelled on the assumption of an operational Arab annihilation motive: patterns of settlement, the communication network, water supply, agricultural policy, central industrial structures, educational and scientific programmes, and so on. Now the Israelis are being bombarded with Arab assurances of the willingness to conciliate and recognise. For two reasons, this emerging regional legitimacy can undermine Israel's strength as a state.

Firstly, Israel is not prepared for the new situation. There is a natural inertia in the country's security perceptions and defence systems which relates to fundamental principles for the organisation of collective resources. Israel is not adapted to peaceful surroundings. The Jewish-Israeli society is always on the alert, prepared to meet a surprise attack from whatever corner of the Arab world. It should not be surprising, then, if the Israelis have difficulties in relating to an Arab world that appears conciliatory, and if the Israelis in the near future will experience a good deal of uncertainty and internal conflicts in relation to national aims and the use of defence resources.

Secondly, Israel's position *vis-à-vis* the international community has already been affected by this development, and is as a result bound to grow more complicated. When neighbours open their doors to negotiations, it is more difficult for Israel to obtain international sympathy and political and economic support for its traditional security concepts and individual acts of aggression in the region – justified as 'self defence'. In other words, with increasing Arab moderation and willingness to negotiate, Israel's established action-independence in the region is weakened. However, as seen by many Israelis, this is the price Israel must pay for peace.

The impact of the Gulf War in this context is difficult to predict because the signals from the Arab world towards Israel were so ambigious. On the one hand, the popular support expressed in most Arab countries for Saddam Hussein and his attempts to involve Israel in a military confrontation indicated a latent hostility towards Israel of considerable intensity. On the other hand, no Arab government supported Iraq's attacks on Israel. Indeed, the most important of these countries, Egypt, Syria and Saudi Arabia, stayed firmly within the US-led coalition throughout the war, and would probably not have changed sides even if Israel had retaliated. Israel's most ardent enemies – pan-Arab militants, Islamic fundamentalists and Palestinian nationalists – lost the Gulf War. With Iraq out of any Arab war coalition for years to come, with the PLO weakened and discredited and with the US as the only superpower deeply involved in Middle Eastern affairs, Israel's geo-strategic position was clearly strengthened by the war. However, the new US role in the Middle East includes efforts to coordinate policies with the leading Arab governments much more closely than before. Combined with Israel's dependence on America for security guarantees and economic assistance, the net effect of the war might be that considerable constraints will be imposed on Israel's action independence in the future.

'Unilateral Security' and 'National Existence'

Israel's argument when confronted with Arab peace initiatives is that they are conditional and uncertain: how can we be certain that the Arabs do not return to their traditional goal of 'liberating the whole of Palestine'? Is not the new Arab moderation precisely contingent upon Israel's crushing military power? What will happen if Israel reduces its power capabilities? What if a new Saddam Hussein takes power in Egypt? As the majority of Israelis see it, there is, within the Arab-Israeli constellation, a built-in threat towards Israel's existence as a state. Israel cannot base its security on Arab declarations at any given time. A friendly régime today may be an enemy tomorrow.

Reasoning of this sort is the basis for Israel's demands for 'unilateral security'. As opposed to reciprocal security, this implies that one does not grant the opponent the same right of security against attack as one demands for oneself. As Shlomo Gazit, former chief of Israeli Army Intelligence, and others view this, Israel must – also *after* a comprehensive peace agreement with the Arab states – secure its regional dominance.[34] For Israel it is not sufficient that the Arabs recognise the Jewish state, they must also recognise Israel's need for unilateral security.[35]

This demanding quest for security must further be related to the more fundamental Israeli concept of 'national existence'. The established Israeli concept of *nation* is connected to an *ethno-religious* community (world Jewry), not to a *territorially* defined community (of Jews and non-Jews). Territorial conquests and the struggle for secure borders is important only to the extent that it gives the Jewish nation a territorial basis for survival and further development in the modern world. A fundamental motive in Israeli strategic thought is to defend the integrity and autonomy of the *yishuv* no matter what territorial framework this defence will require. Confronted with regional surroundings which traditionally deny the *yishuv's* political legitimacy, and which therefore may be thought of as a motive for 'annihilating' this community, Israel can, it is argued, to an even lesser extent than other states, accept the risk of military defeat. Such a defeat, if it implied an Arab 'liberation of the whole of Palestine', would not only put an end to the Jewish State. As seen by the Israelis, it would threaten the physical existence of the Jewish community in the country despite Arab assurances to the contrary.

Since approximately 1920 institutional defence systems have been built up around the *yishuv* on different levels. Locally (within the borders of the state of Israel), this now takes the form of an *ethnocracy*, an ethnic hegemony which secures Jewish control over the most important positions and institutional structures in society. As long as the 'non-Jewish', that is Palestinian, share of the population is small, Palestinians can – as in present-day Israel (excluding the occupied territories) – be granted political rights without this posing a threat to the State's Jewish character. But the larger this share of the population becomes, the more difficult it is to combine the ethnocratic principle with democratic political structures. If the majority of Palestinians had not fled or been driven out in the period 1947–49, they would have constituted a clear majority in the Jewish State. This also explains the strong Israeli resistance to the Palestinian refugees' right to return. A special commission appointed by the first Israeli government concluded that the non-Jewish share of the population in a democratic Jewish state should not exceed 15 per cent.[36] Legal measures would have had to be introduced to control non-Jewish influence if this limit was exeeded. One notes that today, the Palestinians constitute about 18 per cent of the population in the internationally recognised territory of Israel. This 'demographic problem' also comes to the fore in the debate on the future of the occupied territories and their possible integration into Israel. An annexation of the areas will bring the share of Palestinians in Israel to about 40 per cent. Israeli demographers calculate that by the turn of the century that share may rise to 46 per cent as a result of high Palestinian fertility rates.[37]

On the regional level, 'national existence' is secured through the principle of unilateral security and strategic superiority. On a global level, it is first and foremost security guarantees from external powers that are central agents in the defence of the Jewish State.

Israel in a Regional Arms Race

The Israeli political-military doctrine implies an obvious dilemma: it sets off a regional arms race which Israel already has great problems financing and mastering politically. A clear sign of this was the fact that Israel in 1987 had to shelve plans to produce the advanced fighter plane Lavi, a project that had already swallowed enormous development costs. When the numerically superior Arab countries develop their military forces qualitatively, the relative cost to Israel of securing superiority will be enormous. After the October War in 1973, and especially after the Camp David agreement in 1978, the United States met a substantial part of these costs. In 1979 the United States' aid to Israel was more than 5 billion dollars. Since then it has been around 3 billion dollars annually. Israel is the country which receives most help from the United States, followed by Egypt. Together the two countries receive approximately one third of the United States' total budget for foreign aid. However, such transfers of funds from the United States are dependent upon a strongly pro-Israeli Congress. The United States' enormous deficit in the balance of payments is one aspect that could threaten future transfers. Israel, therefore, has to apply several strategies for reducing the costs of maintaining its security doctrine. The four most important of these are preventing a qualitative build-up of arms on the Arab side, diplomatic strategies, borrowing power and preventing Arab Unity.

One alternative to developing increasingly advanced defence systems is *to prevent one's opponents from improving his military technology.* This was the rationale behind the Israeli bombing of an atomic reactor near Baghdad in 1981. Likewise, Israel has directed attacks against Syrian missile bases in Lebanon, and threatened action against Saudi Arabia's long-range missiles and Libya's chemical weapons. Yet, in the long run, Israel cannot bomb every Arab industrial plant that has the potential to produce weapon types that Israel regards as unacceptable, or other military installations that could represent a threat. Neither can Israel count on continued American military activism of the type that was demonstrated in the Gulf war. This illustrates the dilemma inherent in Israel's demand for unilateral security. If Israel is to prevent the Arabs from producing sophisticated offensive weapons, it must in fact have the capacity to block further technological-industrial development in the Arab world – or at least hold a hidden 'veto power' in this respect.

Secondly, *active diplomacy* is also a possible method of reducing the costs attached to maintaining military superiority. Israel has for example for many years mobilised its diplomacy to influence western weapon-exporting countries to prevent export of weapons to Arab countries that could change the regional balance of power in Israel's disfavour. The powerful pro-Israeli lobby in the American Congress has on many occasions had such a strong influence on decisions concerning such export that it has been commonplace to ask whether it is Israel's or the United States' national interests that decide the United States' policies in this field. The exposure of Israeli espionage directed at American military intelligence and illegal and inhumane policies in the occupied territories do not appear to have clearly weakened Israel's position in the Congress, and any possible damage was possibly more than corrected in the course of the Gulf war.

A third strategy, and a continuation of the preceding one, is for Israel to gamble on *borrowed power* from the United States, which implies linking US global security interests to the maintenance of Israel's regional dominance. Israel has counted on this, especially after 1981, when Menahem Begin came to power for the second time. In December 1981 Israel and the United States signed a 'memorandum of understanding' concerning strategic cooperation. The agreement was aimed at the Soviet Union and 'Soviet-controlled forces' in the Middle East, but was not formalised in the form of an alliance.[38] The 'Special Relationship' between the United States and Israel has had its ups and downs, but on a higher interactive level than before 1981. The United States has on a number of occasions, in the Arab-Israeli context and in the conflicts in Lebanon and the Gulf, proved willing to intervene. And on all such occasions the coordination with Israel has been an important element, witness for example Israel's controversial role in the so-called Iran-Contras Scandal. Israel has been able to benefit from robust American security guarantees, not least through the presence of American Marines in the region.

Finally, Israel can attempt *to prevent Arab war coalitions*. The more extended such a coalition is, the more costly it will be to match it. The Peace Agreement with Egypt in 1979 implied that Israel's potentially strongest Arab opponent veered away from the Arab course of confrontation. Israel could concentrate its forces towards the East and the North. The character and political orientations of the different Arab régimes greatly effect Israel's security. This situation gives the Israelis a motive for closely watching and even intervening in internal Arab politics. It is especially important for Israel to prevent pan-Arab radicalisation of the neighbouring Arab states. Israel's part in the Suez campaign against president Nasser in 1956 and its efforts to influence Lebanese politics in connection with its invasion of the country in 1982 must, among other things, be seen in this context.

Summing up this section, the fact that the State of Israel was forced on the Arab world against its wishes defines the logic and political premises of Israel's role as regional power. To survive in this area, Israel had to be defended by means of power that could meet or deter *every conceivable attack* occurring from the region. It follows from this that Israel had to develop a capacity for regional dominance. If one accepts the Jewish State's legitimacy, and acknowledges the Arab resistance to this principle, one will also have to acknowledge the Jewish State's right to 'unilateral security', a guaranteed strategic superiority in the region. This train of thought has caught western governments in a political trap because 'Israel's right to exist' has been the undisputed doctrine of their approach to Middle East politics. Furthermore, this has produced political guarantees and military and economic support sufficient to defend Israel as a Jewish ethnocracy in the Middle East.

However, a state's demand for unilateral security creates a very unstable situation. It may start a regional arms race, with the impending dangers of war. In recent years it has been clear that the Arabs, both the PLO and the Arab governments, have reconsidered their original aims in the conflict with Israel because they perceive the realisation of these aims to have become too costly. The Arabs are now prepared for a political reconciliation that implies recognition of Israel under certain conditions. For Israel, the Arab rejection has been the *raison d'être* for a build-up of state capabilities which has involved Israeli society as an organic entity. The adjustment to a situation of Arab recognition is problematic for Israel, partly because there is uncertainty associated with the changes in Arab political positions, and partly because Israel now will need new ways to justify regional strategic superiority and action independence. Up to now, Israel's military freedom of action has been tolerated by its western supporters. The new attitudes in the Arab world can threaten the West's patience towards irregular Israeli behaviour such as the violation of international law in the occupied territories. In this way it may be politically and economically more expensive for the Israelis to maintain their present regional strength.

CONCLUSION

Israel's position as a regional great power was created under exceptional historical circumstances. There are basically two sources of strength that can explain Israel's dominant position and action independence in the Middle East. One is to be found in the patterns of Zionist state-building in Palestine. We have here both the last effort in the general course of European expansion in the non-European world, where the gap in techno-logical skills and development has been dramatic, and also an emancipatory social-nationalist movement based on the modernising doctrines of European ideologies of the nineteenth and twentieth centuries, characterised by determined mobilisation and utilisation of collective resources.

The second source of strength is implied in the conflict dynamics created by the imposition of the Jewish state on the Arab world. From the outset, Israel had no legitimacy as part of the regional states system, and, due to its tiny size and limited resources, had consequently to rely on external political, economical and military guarantees for its basic security. Israel's central security doctrine has always been that it should be capable of resisting every conceivable regional threat. Given the Arab rejection of Israel's legitimacy, this doctrine has been accepted by Israel's main supporters among the Western powers, and has proved the normative basis of their own Middle East policies. Paradoxically, then, Israel's lack of political legitimacy in the Middle East is at the same time a condition that Israel can refer to in order to justify its position as a dominant military power in the region, and an argument for external support to uphold this position.

However, with the new signals of Arab willingness to recognise Israel, as demonstrated by the peace diplomacy over the last few years, the basis for an Arab acceptance of a separate Jewish state in their midst has been laid. Logically, this process undermines the justification for Israel's regional dominance, which economically, militarily and politically is exceedingly expensive to uphold. Thus, the question now is how the Israelis will meet the challenge of Arab recognition. If they accept a political arrangement which is compatible with established minimum conditions on the Arab side, a regional security system, guaranteed by the international community and with a defined and recognised place for Israel, would most probably be the outcome. This would, however, require a qualitatively new Israeli approach to its regional surroundings as well as reduced ambitions, both in terms of military capabilities and territorial control. It is more likely that Israel will stick to its established political-military doctrine and demand a clearcut Arab recognition of Israel's concept of unilateral security and a right to intervene militarily whenever there is a regional threat to its security. In that case, Israel may remain a regional great power in the foreseeable future.

NOTES

1. The following quotation gives one reason for excluding Israel from studies of the Middle East: ' . . . [F]or the present, official Judaism, European cultural affinities, the political strength of the Ashkenazis

[Jews of European extraction], and the intimate connection with the United States make Israel unique in, and thus different from, the region. As a result, we define The Middle East as excluding Israel, but including eigtheen Arab states, Iran, and Turkey.' J. P. Piscatori and R. K. Ramazani, 'The Middle East', in W. J. Feld and G. Boyd (eds), *Comparative Regional Systems* (New York, NY: Pergamon Press, 1980), p. 275.

2. B. M. Russett, *International Regions and the International System* (Chicago: Rand McNally, 1967), p. 11.

3. L. J. Fein, *Politics in Israel* (Boston: Little, Brown, 1967), p. 65.

4. Carsten Holbraad, *Middle Power in International Politics* (London: Macmillan, 1984).

5. *Ibid.*, p. 79.

6. The other middle powers in Holbraad's list are (according to rank, based on figures from 1980): Japan, West Germany, France, Great Britain, Italy, China, Brazil, Canada, Spain, India, Mexico, Australia, Poland, Nigeria, South Africa, Argentina, Indonesia; *Middle Power in International Politics*, p. 222.

7. There are numerous works covering different aspects of the 'Special Relationship' between Israel and USA, see for example N. Chomsky, *The Fateful Triangle. The United States, Israel and the Palestinians* (London and Sidney: Pluto, 1983); B. Reich, *The United States and Israel. Influence in the Special Relationship* (New York, NY: Praeger, 1984); N. Safran, *Israel. The Embattled Ally* (Cambridge, MA: Harvard University Press, 1978).

8. One important source of information that covers Israel's relations (mostly military) with extra-regional régimes from a critical point of view is the monthly bulletin *Israeli Foreign Affairs*, published in the USA.

9. This conclusion is clearly validated by D. E. Lampert in his study 'Patterns of Transregional Relations' in W. J. Feld and G. Boyd, *Comparative Regional Systems*, pp. 459–62.

10. 'The Middle East' was apparently first applied by the American naval strategist A. T. Mahan in a study from 1902 about British maritime strategy. R. H. Davidson, 'Where is the Middle East?', *Foreign Affairs*, XXXVIII (1960): 665–75.

11. This is consistent with B. M. Russett's conclusion that there exist distinctive core areas that are representative of international regions with extended, but loosely defined boundaries. B. M. Russett, *International Regions and the International System*, p. 182.

12. A. Hareven, 'Is Another Arab War Coalition Possible?', *The Jerusalem Quarterly*, No. 49 (1989). Judging from the experiences of the recent Gulf war, it is unlikely that these four Arab states will join forces in a conflict with Israel in the forseeable future.

13. The borders of this area is often referred to as Israel's 'pre-1967 borders' or 'the Green Line', that is, the ceasefire lines of 1949, recognised as international borders when the State of Israel became a member of the

United Nations the same year. (The territory within these borders are also called 'Israel Proper'). If we add the present occupied Palestinian territories (the West Bank with East Jerusalem and the Gaza Strip) we get pre-1948 Palestine (under British mandatory government since 1922), a total area of 27 090 km^2. The whole of Palestine is thus presently under effective Israeli control, and represents Israel's *de facto* territorial power base. In addition come the Syrian Golan Hights (1760 km^2), occupied in 1967 and included in the extended Israeli civil jurisdiction – though not formally annexed as happened with East Jerusalem – in 1981, and Israel's 'security zone' in South Lebanon. The territorial base of the (potential) State of Palestine, proclaimed by the Palestine National Congress in 1988, is limited to the West Bank with East Jerusalem and Gaza Strip and adds up to a mere 6400 km^2.

14. If we look at GNP *per capita*, however, the picture is different. In 1988 they were: Israel, US$ 8650; Egypt, US$ 650; Algeria, US$ 2360.

15. As of 31 December 1988. Included in this figure are the predominantly non-Jewish populations of occupied East Jerusalem annexed *de jure* by Israel in 1967, confirmed in 1980 and the Golan Hights (cf. note 13). About 18% of the population in this territory are Palestinians. See *The Middle East and North Africa 1991* (London: Europe Publications Ltd, 1990), p. 525.

16. South Africa (1 122 037 km^2) has what Israel lacks in this respect, and is clearly an economic superpower relative to its regional neighbouring states, some of which are among the poorest in the world. This centre-periphery relationship with its corresponding semi-feudal structure of interaction gives South Africa strategic assets in its hegemonic policy of regional control, specifically in terms of regional destabiliization.

17. A. Hareven, 'Is Another Arab War Coalition Possible?', p. 107.

18. *The Military Balance 1990–91* (London: The International Institute for Strategic Studies, 1990) reckons that Israel has about 100 nuclear warheads, among them neutron weapons.

19. See Robert O. Keohane, *After Hegemony. Cooperation and Discord in the World Political Economy* (Princeton, NJ: Princeton University Press, 1984), especially Chapter 8.

20. H. Lamar and L. Thompson, *The Frontier in History* (New Haven, CN and London: Yale University Press, 1981) p. 312.

21. For a more detailed discussion of this concept, see N. A. Butenschøn, 'The Frontier State at Work: Patterns of Contemporary Israeli State-Building', *Chair in International Conflict Studies, Working Papers*, No. 9 (1988) (Oslo: University of Oslo, Institute of Political Science).

22. There are some exceptions; see B. Kimmerling, 'Boundaries and Frontiers of the Israeli Control System: Analytical Conclusions' in B. Kimmerling (ed.), *The Israeli State and Society. Boundaries and Frontiers* (New York, NY: State University of New York Press, 1989) and G. Shafir, 'Changing Nationalism and Israel's 'Open Frontier' on the West Bank', *Theory and Society*, XIII (1984).

23. The French historian Maxime Rodinson is a well-known representative of this school, see for instance his *Israel: A Colonial-Settler State?* (New York, NY: Monad Press, 1973).

24. As late as 1925, 43 years after the first Zionist 'wave of immigration', the Zionist organisation had only established 42 such settlements with a total of 4353 inhabitants (the rest of the Jewish population lived in towns or Jewish settlements outside of the Zionist movement's control). See A. Ruppin, *The Agricultural Colonization of the Zionist Organisation in Palestine* (Westport, CN: Hyperion Press, [1926] 1976) p. 78.

25. The most comprehensive account of the Palestinian mass exudos is given by the Israeli historian and journalist Benny Morris, *The Birth of the Palestinian Refugee Problem, 1947–1949* (London: Cambridge University Press, 1988).

26. Cf. for example S. Avineri, *The Making of Modern Zionism* (New York, NY: Basic Books, 1981). Vladimir (Ze'ev) Jabotinsky was just as dominant a figure on the Zionist Right as Ben-Gurion was on the Left. Jabotinsky's movement, The Revisionist Party, had Italian Fascism as one of its most important sources of inspiration.

27. The Israeli sociologist S. N. Eisenstadt has written extensively on these matters, see for instance his classical work *Israeli Society* (London: Weidenfeld and Nicolson, 1967) especially Chapter 4.

28. See Rosmary Sayigh, *Palestinians: From Peasants to Revolutionaries* (London: Zed Press, 1979) for an analysis of the class structure of the Palestinian society and how it has been effected by the conflict with the Jewish settlers.

29. This was for instance expressed in the well-known talks between the Zionist leader (and later president of Israel) Chaim Weizmann and Feisal ibn Hussein (son of the Sharif of Mekka and later king of Iraq). See W. Laqueur and B. Rubin (eds), *The Israel-Arab Reader* (London: Penguin Books, 1984), p. 18–22.

30. Meron Benvinisti, *The West Bank Data Base Project. A Survey of Israel's Policies* (Washington and London: American Enterprise Institute for Public Policy Research, 1984) p. 9.

31. This does not refer to an official declaration (like the Truman doctrine etc.), but to fundamental elements in Israeli security policy as interpreted by observers.

32. Emphasis in the original. M. I. Handel, *Israel's Political-Military Doctrine*, Occasional Papers in International Affairs No. 30, Harvard University Center for International Affairs (Cambridge, MA, 1973), pp. 64–68. Handel mentions several other points, but they are chiefly amplifications and explanations of the points I have included. A similar formulation of Israel's security doctrine, quoted in *Middle East International*, 22 February 1991, occurs in S. C. Pelletiere, D. V. Johnson and L. R. Rosenberger, *Iraqi Power and US Security in the Middle East*, published by the Strategic Studies Institute of the US Army War College in 1990.

6 Poland as a Regional Great Power: the Inter-war Heritage

Iver B. Neumann

INTRODUCTION

The third partition of Poland in 1795 wiped a great power off the map of Europe. In its heyday, the Polish-Lithuanian kingdom had stretched from the Baltic in the north to the Black Sea in the south, and Poland had been known as the land between the seas. In the system of states that existed around the Baltic until it was finally submerged into an all-European system during the Thirty Years War, the Polish-Lithuanian kingdom was a centrally placed great power.[1] In 1683, the forces which stopped the Ottoman empire's penetration into Europe at the gates of Vienna were led by a Pole. At this time, however, Poland-Lithuania was already in decline. At the end of the eighteenth century, as a result of three partitions, the formerly Polish lands were incorporated into Prussia and the Russian and Habsburg empires.

Even though the Polish state thus ceased to exist, what was called the Polish nation still remained. The Polish nation was the *szlachta*, that is, the Polish gentry. This group made up around eight per cent of the population, and was ethnically diverse. During the nineteenth century, influenced by the new ideas of a nation as an imagined community arising west of the areas where Polish was spoken, the *szlachta* was able to transform itself into the Polish *społeczeństwo*. *Społeczeństwo* may be translated as society, but it 'signified, in fact, the more complex notion of the organized, politicized, albeit still stateless, community of all Poles, led now by an intelligentsia that preserved, at the same time as it modified, the values and the style of the old szlachta'.[2] In lieu of a Polish state, the Polish intelligentsia took it upon themselves to furnish the cultural leadership of the Polish nation, which since the 1870s they saw in organic terms. One may speculate that the intelligentsia's role as a predecessor of the *szlachta* did not only imbibe it with state-bearing aspirations, but also with some of that social group's belief in military power as a problem solver. Whereas in Western Europe and also in Czechoslovakia the bourgeoisie played an important part in the nation-building processes, the Polish experience was very different. The three main foci of the nation building process were the Polish language, catholicism, and a shared and glorious history. Polish belongs to the Slavonic language group, which makes it immediately distinct from German. Catholicism made the Poles culturally distinct from their Slavonic-speaking Russian neighbours. Polish history up to 1795 is from the earliest times rife with episodes of Polish-German and Polish-Russian skirmishes, from which the Poles often emerged victorious. The nation builders did not suffer from a dearth of historical material which could be utilised in the making of the Polish nation.

The Polish national romantic poet, Adam Mickiewicz, had called on the Polish patriots to 'measure your powers by your purpose, not your purposes by your powers'. Heeding his advise, they attempted to re-establish a Polish state in 1830 and 1863. When this failed, a number of Poles started to believe that sovereign Polish statehood was predicated on a change in the relative distribution of power in the international system. While waiting for the change in international relations to happen, they concentrated on strengthening the community of Polish-speaking people by strengthening *all* aspects of social life within what to them had now become the living organism of the Polish nation. In this way, Poles could aspire in their everyday work to surpass the other, albeit state-bearing nations amongst which they lived.[3]

With the coming of the First World War and the October revolution, the international system underwent a drastic change, and a possibility for re-establishing a Polish state did indeed emerge. Polish soldiers who had served in various armies combined under commanders like Józef Piłsudski and took advantage of the power vacuum left by the collapsing Austrian, German and Russian war efforts to seize the initiative. At the same time, the American President Woodrow Wilson saw the re-establishment of a Polish state as a vital part of a new European order based on the principle of national self-determination. Thus, the shape and character of the new Polish state were to be defined both militarily on the ground, and in negotiations between the great powers at Versailles, where Poland's traditional opponents Germany and Russia were not present.

Given the historical setting and the contemporary weakness of Germany and Russia, it comes as no surprise that most Poles saw the new Poland as a great power. First, the precedent for such a role was readily available, and not too far removed historically. Secondly, the cultural hegemony in Poland was still held by an élite that understood itself and legitimated its leading role as the successor of the *szlachta* of the old kingdom, which had been a great power. Thirdly, Poland was located between Germany in the West and Soviet Russia in the east. These state formations were the historical successors to two of the three states that had partitioned Poland between themselves, and they were both great powers. There seems to have existed a Polish psychological need to feel on a par with its former colonisers, which would imply perceiving Poland too as a great power. Fourthly, as a result of lost wars and internal upheavals, both German and Soviet Russian capabilities were temporarily weakened, and both states were having trouble projecting their great power image on their surroundings. The dip in German and Russian prestige following their First World War losses and the October revolution made it easier for the Poles to have their psychological need fulfilled: Poland could stand up to comparisons with these two great powers, and so Poland, too, had to be a great power. Even when the German and Russian weakness proved to be ephemeral, an overwhelming number of Poles stuck to the perception that Poland was a great power. Characteristically, as late as in 1939, the former Polish ambassador to Moscow and Paris published a book programmatically entitled *Polska jest mocarstwem* – Poland is a great power.[4]

The reason why the new Polish state was from the very beginning perceived as a great power by an overwhelming number of Poles has, not surprisingly, to be sought in the Polish collective memory rather than in a sober assessment of the contemporary political facts. Although Poland's great power *history* was undoubted in all quarters at home and abroad, the new state was in many ways a precarious creation. By size and population, Poland was a factor to be reckoned with. With a population of around 30 million and a standing army of over 250 000 men, Poland did not lag hopelessly behind a great power like France (see Table 6.1). Because of its weak economy, however, Poland could ill afford to keep an army of this size. In the 1930s, defence costs reached as much as 27.5 per cent of government expenditure, which was high even by contemporary high standards.[5] Polish territory, which had belonged to three different political units for well over one hundred years, lacked a common infrastructure. The northwestmost part of Polish territory, the so-called Polish Corridor (Pomerelia), gave Poland access to the sea, but at the same time split Germany in two. Polish territory, ravaged by warfare, included few industrialised patches, and what economic life there was, was often shorn of its previous context and so not necessarily complementary. John Maynard Keynes even characterised the new Poland as 'an economic impossibility whose only industry is Jew-baiting'.[6]

TABLE 6.1   *Perceived population in millions
and size of armed forces*

	Population			Size of armed forces		
	1922	1937	1990	1922	1937	1990
Poland	27	32	38	255 000	265 000	313 000
Czechoslovakia	13	13	16	150 000	165 000	170 000
Lithuania	5	2.5	3.7	50 000	22 000	—
France[1]	39	42	56	390 000	485 000	447 000
Germany	60	66	77	100 000	555 000	446 000
USSR	131[2]	166[2]	200[3]	5 300 000	1 300 000	3 063 000

[1] Metropolitan forces only
[2] Given as European Russia, i.e. west of the Urals.
[3] Estimate of figure compatible with the figures given for 1922 amd 1938. The total population of the USSR according to the 1989 census was 286 million.

SOURCES: *The Statesman's Yearbooks*, 1922 & 1937 (London, Macmillan, 1922, 1938); *The Military Balance 1990–1991* (London: Brassey's, The International Institute for Strategic Studies, 1990); Ann Sheehy, 'Russian Share of Soviet Population down to 50.8 per cent', *Report on the USSR*, 20 October 1989.

Keynes's remark pinpoints the two main problems of Polish inter-war history – economy and ethnic friction. When Poland's borders were consolidated, there was a Ukrainian minority of around 5 million, a Jewish minority 2 750 000 strong, a Belorussian minority numbering around 1.5 million, and a German minority of around 750 000. With a total population of some 30 million, that makes for a heavily multiethnic state.[7] This had immediate repercussions both for the question of what it was to be Polish, and for foreign policy. The Polish polity could not agree between itself about what the shape and character of the state should be and, as an integral part of this, what its regional profile should be. The foreign policy consensus stopped at the idea of Poland as a great power, whose destiny it was to play a leading role in the region between the German and Russian state formations.

One crucial question presents itself immediately: Did the Central European region really exist, i.e. was the existence of a region between Germany and Russia a working reality for foreign policy decision makers in the relevant European states during the inter-war period? From Warsaw, it certainly looked like such a region existed. One of the stories told below is how Poland tried to institutionalise this region politically, so that it should be able to withstand the pressure from the neighbouring great powers. Indeed, the immediate focus not only for Polish foreign policy, but for all the governments of the successor states to the Habsburg and

Russian empires, was the area consisting of those very states. To the states in what one may call Central Europe itself, then, the region was a reality. As to the great powers, Germany and the Soviet Union certainly perceived this area to be a region, and a region where they should have special great power privilege due to their geographical proximity. To France, a more relevant category may have been 'states to the East of Germany', including the Soviet Union. However, to the extent that the Soviet Union and the other states (Poland, the powers of the Little Entente, and so on) were mutually exclusive candidates as allies against Germany, the Central European region was a reality to France. Great Britain, and to an even greater extent the United States, tended to treat continental Europe as one region, which indeed goes a long way to explain why London's policy in this area of 'faraway countries' was hardly refined. It is also interesting that it was the League Powers, France and Great Britain, which were the least prone to acknowledge the existence of a Central European region in the inter-war period.

Where the borders of the Central European region should end, and what the ethnic composition of Poland itself should be, had been hotly debated among Polish patriots ever since 1795. This question loomed at the top of the Polish political agenda throughout the inter-war period.

POLAND'S SELF-PERCEPTION AND REGIONAL PROFILE

In the tumultuous situation that existed in Central Europe in 1919, neither the borders of the new Polish state nor the nature of the balance of power in the region had yet been fixed. A number of political groupings with a variety of political programmes wanted a say in what the new Polish state should look like. On the Polish side, two groups stood out, one clustering around Józef Piłsudski, the other around Roman Dmowski. To both of them, and indeed to almost any Pole, it was clear that between Germany and Russia there was no place for a small and weak buffer state.[8] Poland had to be a power. On the question of how this could best be achieved, however, they parted ways.

Piłsudski thought in terms of state building, and to him, the only possible point of departure was pre-partition Poland. The Poland that had been carved up in 1772 had been a multiethnic empire. Since nobody thought in terms of ethnic nations at the time, the multiethnic character of the state and of the *szlachta* had not been a problem. Since then, however, the main body of the *szlachta* had transformed itself into a national Polish leadership, and some of its members had joined the smaller nascent national movements based wholly or partly within the old Polish lands. The best organised of these groups were probably the Lithuanians. As late as in the 1860s, 'Lithuanian' was more a territorial designation than an ethnic one.[9] Beginning at this time, however, a Lithuanian nationalism was forged by a handful of Polish-speaking intellectuals, and in 1919, this group wanted its own national state. Similar ideas existed among Ukrainian-speaking groups, and to some faint extent also among Belorussian-speaking groups. The drawing of the border between Poland and Germany had also, inevitably, left a German irredenta within Poland. Some of the Jews in the area were zionists intent on leaving for Israel, while others wanted some degree of autonomy for their ethnic group. Responding to this situation, Piłsudski wanted some kind of federation of the lands of the old Polish kingdom.

Dmowski, on the other hand, thought in terms of nation building. As a nationalist, he also harked back to the pre-1772 period and the glorious history of the Polish nation. To him, however, it was the nation of Poles defined in terms of modern ethnic and cultural criteria, and not the territorial entity called Poland, that was now coming into its own. His idea of the Polish state was not the Jagiellonian idea of a Polish-Lithuanian multiethnic kingdom so dear to Piłsudski, but rather the mediaeval Piastian period of Polish history, when the state formation was much more ethnically homogenous. While Piłsudski had insisted on Polish independent statehood all through his politically active life, Dmowski spent most of the First World War working for some arrangement whereby the Polish nation could be brought together within one single political entity, if need be under Russian tutelage. Where Piłsudski's personal and political history pitted him against the Russians, Dmowski's *bête noir* was the Germans.[10]

These differences in ideas had immediate repercussions for the foreign policy programme of the two camps. Piłsudski gave priority to a campaign in the East in order to secure pre-1772 territory for the new Poland. This brought him into direct conflict with the Soviet Russians, who had designs on the same territory. In the West, Piłsudski wanted a low Polish profile at the Paris Peace Conference. Following his own military exploits in the East, he held diplomatic reticence to be the best strategy for Poland in the West. When France and Great Britain had settled its Western border, Poland 'would become a first-rate force in the East with which everyone not excluding the Entente would have to reckon'.[11]

Dmowski thought differently. The old areas in the East did not have a Polish ethnic majority any more. Some Polish landlords remained, but the bulk of the peasantry was Lithuanian, Belorussian and Ukrainian. Furthermore, to Dmowski these peoples of the Russian empire were 'not mature enough' to form their own nation states.[12] Therefore, it was best that they remain within Russia. Instead of clamouring to seize these areas with force of arms, Dmowski held that the energy of the Polish state should be used politically *vis-à-vis* France in order to incorporate ethnically Polish people of Upper Silesia and other formerly Prussian areas in the West into the new Poland.

The re-establishment of Poland's borders as a source of regional conflict

The borders of the Polish state were fixed during the period 1919 to 1921.[13] However, the sources of tension between Poland and its neighbours regarding the drawing of borders were not eliminated. As a matter of fact, problems remained on all sides: to the northeast, to the south, and to the west. The ethnically diverse character of the region made any lasting settlement along nationalist lines very difficult.

In the northeast, Poland claimed the ethnically Polish city of Vilna on ethnic grounds; the city was undoubtedly Polish-Jewish ethnically, linguistically, and culturally.[14] However, although in the all-Russian census of 1897 only 2 per cent of the population identified themselves as Lithuanians, the Lithuanian nationalists claimed the city and its surroundings on historical grounds. Vilna had been the capital of the old Lithuania that had been united with Poland in 1386, and so it should be the capital of the newly established Lithuanian state, they argued. In August 1919, local Poles rose and took over the city in a coup orchestrated by Piłsudski. In 1920, the Russian bolsheviks captured it, and upon withdrawing later that same year left the city in Lithuanian hands. On 9 October, however, a Polish general, again following Piłsudski's covert lead, rose against the Lithuanians and secured the city for the Poles. Because of the situation in Vilna, Lithuania decided against opening diplomatic relations with Poland. When the Conference of Ambassadors gave Vilna to the Poles, Lithuania refused to accept the verdict of the great powers acting in concert.

What happened in Vilna was part of a greater game between Poland and Russia about the borderlands. The old rivalries dating back to the beginning of the 16th century between Russian and Polish state formations were entering yet another phase. Poland's great power status before its decline and fall had among other things rested on the mastery of the area surrounding the Pripet marshes and the people living there. That mastery had always been contested by Russian state formations. In the wake of the Brest-Litovsk peace between the Russian bolsheviks and the Germans, Belorussians and Ukrainians tried to establish separate state formations in the area. The Russian bolsheviks pressed for the inclusion of these state formations in a union of Soviet republics, while Poland tried to enrol them together with Lithuania in a federation under Polish leadership, built on the historical model of the Polish-Lithuanian kingdom. The war they fought over this did not solve the issue one way or the other; the Polish border was neither drawn between the Russians and all the other national groups as Piłsudski had wanted, nor was it drawn between Poland and all the others, with Poland ending up as a Soviet republic, as was the aim of the bolsheviks. After the war, the immediate Polish federalist programme was no longer a viable one.[15] Neither did it have much support left in the Sejm.

In the south, there was the problem of Teschen. The dutchy of Teschen had a mixed Polish-Czech population, with Poles being in a solid majority. The Czechs, however, claimed the area mainly on economic grounds, insisting that the local industry and coal mines were indispensible to the national economy. They also noted that Teschen throughout history had several times changed hands between Poland and the mediaeval kingdom of Bohemia. During the First World War, Polish and Czech exile groups discussed the problem several times and reached a general understanding that the problem would be solved, but did not make any headway on the actual details. The Czechs did not wait for the Paris Peace Conference to umpire the conflict, but occupied Teschen in January 1919. In June 1919, the Czechs needed to mass their troops in order to deter Hungarian bolsheviks under Bela Kun, and so they pulled troops out of the area contested by the Poles. Local Polish troops actually seized the opportunity to fill the vacuum, but Piłsudski urged restraint. In July 1920, the Conference of Ambassadors gave Czechoslovakia the major part of Teschen.

In the west, as a result of peasant migrations, Polish-speaking groups made up a majority in areas that had been part of German state formations since the middle ages. At the Paris Peace Conference, Poland was given Upper Silesia, and Danzig with its predominantly German population was made a free city. The Poles challenged only the Conference's decisions concerning Danzig, Allenstein and Marienwerder, the latter being two districts on the southern confines of East Prussia. In the plebiscites held here in 1920, no less than 96.5 per cent of the population opted to remain part of Germany.[16] At no point in the inter-war period did Germany accept the permanence of the border with Poland as it had been laid down by the Paris Peace Conference. This was due not only to ethnic, but also to geostrategic reasons. The Polish Corridor (Pomerelia), jutting up through formerly German territory and, together with the Free State of Danzig, thus cutting East Prussia off from the rest of Germany, made Germany the only landbased non-contiguous state in Europe. It is hard to imagine a more striking way of continuously reminding a state about a lost war. The Corridor's negative impact on German-Polish relations in particular can hardly be overrated.[17]

In 1921, then, Poland's borders were fixed. Still, of its five neighbours, the only ones with which Poland had no outstanding territorial questions were the two weakest ones: Romania and Latvia.

Poland's relations with the Great Powers

The preceding section brings out the prominence of Polish military power in the history of the border settlements. However, the great power committee of the Paris Peace Conference, the Conference of Ambassadors, also played an important role. The partitions of Poland had been the work of the three great powers Austria, Prussia, and Russia. Now, three other great powers, France, Great Britain, and the United States, contributed to the re-establishment of the state.

As noted above, before the war many analysts of Polish political life had postulated a *prymat polityki zewnętrznej*, or primacy of external relations, and meant that the re-establishment of a Polish state was dependent on developments outside the community of Polish speakers. With the return of a Polish state, this turn of speech was still widely used, but now signified that Poland and Polish foreign policy were in an unusual degree confined by the configuration of forces in the international system as a whole.

That configuration was changing throughout the inter-war period. As predicted by Piłsudski, the result of the Great War was that Germany beat Russia, only to be beaten by France and Great Britain. At the beginning of the inter-war period, then, Germany and Soviet Russia were temporarily weakened. As mentioned above, this made it easier for Poland to take an inflated view of its own role in the European system. That was so especially after the conclusion of the Russo-Polish war in 1921. Poles conveniently tended to forget that they had beaten Russia at a time when it was, as it were, as weak as a lobster shedding its old shell for a new one; 'the experience of singlehandedly fighting a successful war against Soviet Russia and at the same time successfully maintaining a posture of hostility toward Germany led to the false and dangerous conclusion that she could long endure the simultaneous enmity of both.'[18]

Moreover, it meant that Germany and Soviet Russia as the two beaten, revisionistic, great powers had a general interest in cooperating against what the Germans saw as the victors' league and the Russians as the robbers' league, in other words the League of Nations and its two leading members, Britain and France. When Russia came out of its international isolation in

1921, it seized the opportunity to initiate cooperation with Germany. This cooperation between its two great power antagonists could not but spell problems for Poland, and also made it more dependent on France and Great Britain.

Whereas the losers at the Paris Peace Conference (Russia was not present and Germany did not participate in its proceedings) found a common cause in attacking the results of the Conference, the recreation of the Polish state among them, the victors did not see eye to eye on the question of the future shape of political Europe. France was the only great power advocating a status quo, where Germany was kept weak, with its neighbours sticking together to assure that it stayed that way. Britain, on the other hand, wanted to return to the status quo ante, where France, Germany and the other continental powers balanced each other, and Britain could sit on the sidelines holding the balance.[19]

These differences, which persisted throughout the inter-war period, had indeed surfaced at an early stage of the Paris Peace Conference. In the very first memorandum from the Quai d'Orsay to the conference, it was clearly said that France wanted 'a strong Poland as rapidly as possible', including Eastern Galicia and in union with Lithuania. Five reasons were given. First, 'Germany will not be really defeated unless she loses her Polish provinces'; second, French security on the Rhine depended on a strong power on the other side of Germany; third, 'the more we aggrandize Poland at Germany's expence, the more certain shall we be that she will remain her enemy'; fourth, Poland would constitute 'the necessary barrier between Russian Bolshevism and a German revolution', and, lastly, an active support in favour of the victors.[20]

Britain, on the other hand, was not willing to let its relations with Germany deteriorate too significantly over Poland. Therefore, Britain held back when France wanted to strengthen Poland territorially at Germany's expense. In the upshot, the Conferance never determined what constituted Polish territories in the east, but left the situation to straighten itself out.

Against this backdrop of events, it was hardly surprising that Poland and France felt that their bilateral relations needed a stronger foundation than what they could obtain within the multilateral framework of the League of Nations, and so they signed an alliance treaty in February 1921. The two states had shared interests *vis-à-vis* what they expected to become a resurgent Germany; also, cooperation was facilitated by historical and cultural bonds extending back to the Napoleonic era and beyond. However, France's relative isolation in Europe meant that its foreign policy came under considerable strain in the inter-war period, and that strain could not but affect its ally Poland as well.

France's situation after the First World War was unenviable, and placed it in dire need of allies like Poland. Although Germany had been defeated in war, its power potential was hardly impaired. Demographically and economically, Germany's growth exceeded that of France. Germany's intent of playing the leading role in European affairs was also intact. In 1923, France reacted to this general challenge, in the specific form of German unwillingness to pay wartime reparations, by intervening militarily in the Rhineland. Poland was immediately caught up in the Ruhr crisis, since the Soviet Union seized the opportunity to revive its pressure on the Polish borderlands, and tried to establish itself as mediator in the continuous Polish-Lithuanian conflict. The crisis clearly brought out how dependent Poland was on the general balance of power between Europe's great powers.

Germany's reaction to the French military intervention in the Ruhr was to finance civil disobedience in the area. After a stalemate lasting close to a year, France decided to change tack. Whereas the overall strategic goal remained the same, that is, to contain Germany, France now decided to engage Germany in a web of international agreements, and so give Berlin a stake in the system and thereby bind it to it. Again, this great-power rapprochement was to have immediate implications for Poland's standing as a European power.

France's initial idea was to make an arrangement whereby Germany's new borders in the west and in the east were recognised and guaranteed by Germany, its neighbours, and also the great powers Britain and Italy. Britain, however, refused even to discuss a guarantee for Poland. When France tried to pressure the Germans to give the same guarantees to Poland as to France itself, the German foreign minister Stresemann refused. France gave in, and the Locarno treaties proper were confined to Germany's western border.

To Poland and also Czechoslovakia, whose foreign ministers were present at Locarno but did not, to their humiliation, take part in the main negotiations, Locarno was a disaster. By guaranteeing Germany's borders in the west, but not in the east, the western great powers had created a situation whereby German revisionism in the east was greatly facilitated. Although it was not of course proclaimed at the time, in addition to being accepted yet again as a great power on a par with France and Britain, the point of Locarno was to Stresemann 'above all an instrument to achieve a revision of the Eastern boundaries'. Later, he would claim that 'I never thought more about the East than during the time I was looking for an understanding in the West.'[21]

Within the wider Locarno system, Poland had to sign a security treaty with France. This treaty weakened the treaty of 1921 by subordinating automatic mutual assistance to League of Nations procedures.[22] Stresemann went so far as to say that a Franco-Polish alliance did not exist any more.[23] Since the main point of the treaty was to deter Germany, the changed German perception of it added gravely to Poland's problems.

The losers at Locarno were the states east of Germany.[24] The Soviet Union had tried to keep Germany from entering into cooperation with the Western powers, but had been thwarted. Soviet attempts at compensating for the relative loss of influence over Germany involved in the Locarno process by trying to obtain a nonaggression treaty with Poland was, moreover, not taken up by Warsaw.[25]

If Locarno was a shock to Polish security, it was even more of a shock to Polish great power ambitions. Locarno had exposed the Polish aspirations to sit at table with the great powers as an equal power as mere wishful thinking. Nevertheless, nearly all Poles clung to their perceptions of Poland as a great power with unimpaired tenacity. If Locarno had been a tragedy for Polish foreign policy, the tug of war which followed it at the League's headquarters in Geneva was a farce. As part of Locarno, Germany would re-enter the League of Nations, and, as a great power, it had been promised a permanent seat on the League's Council. Warsaw reacted by demanding that Poland, too, should be given a permanent seat.[26] In the upshot, Poland was refused a permanent seat. However, in a move which confirms our assumption that the great powers perceived some kind of Central European region between Germany and Russia to exist, Czechoslovakia was made to give up its temporary seat, and the Assembly was asked to give it to Poland instead. It was understood that Poland would expect to hang onto its temporary seat on a quasi-permanent basis. This half-baked solution to the question of Poland's standing in the main international organisation of the day indicates that Poland as a regional great power was able to get some concessions from the great powers at the expence of neighbouring Czechoslovakia, but that it was a far cry from inhabiting great power status.

Although Locarno was a rude shock to Polish security and Polish great power sensibilities, Warsaw was not prepared to compensate for the added pressure from the west by tying itself closer to its eastern neighbour. To the contrary, when Piłsudski seized power by a *coup d'état* against the democratically elected government in May, 1926, he told his foreign minister August Zaleski that 'Poland must maintain the strictest neutrality between Germany and Russia, so that these two states could be absolutely certain that Poland would not go with one against the other'.[27] Indeed, this principle of a policy of balance, meaning equidistance to the two great power neighbours, became the cornerstone of Polish foreign policy in the years to come.

Nevertheless, Piłsudski significantly held that Poland's borders were already perhaps too stretched. Therefore, he started to put out feelers to both neighbouring great powers. Unfortunately, he had very few concessions to make, and so the balancing act was bound to be a precarious one. Poland signed a non-aggression pact with the Soviet Union in 1932, and one with Germany in 1934. Since Poland also weakened its ties with France and played down the importance of the League, however, it is hard to see where Warsaw thought it was heading.[28]

The picture painted above brings out Poland's constant aspirations to great powerhood, but it also brings out that the policies designed to carry out those aspirations varied with the changes in the general balance of power in Europe. In the years immediately after the First World War, with Germany and Russia temporarily weakened, Poland tried to go it alone. When Germany and Russia again came in the ascendent, Poland looked to France and tried to prod Quai d'Orsay into taking a strong line against those two states. When that policy proved unsuccessful, Poland once again tried to go it alone by distancing itself from Germany and Russia in equal measure, and also from France and the League.

However, as Poland's aspirations to great powerhood remained constant, so did an integral part of that policy, in other words the aspiration to play the role of a regional great power. Throughout the inter-war period, in order to boost its security and underline its stature, Poland was trying to establish regional alliances under Polish leadership.

Poland's relations with other regional states

Perhaps Poland expected the pressure generated by Locarno on the states situated to the east of Germany, to facilitate this quest for a leading role in the region between Germany and Russia. It was part and parcel of Poland's great power aspirations to insist on a leading regional role, in the Baltic as well as in Central Europe generally. Warsaw pursued this goal by presenting ever new schemes for Baltic and Central European groupings, or, ideally, for a grouping of all the states lying between Germany and Russia. The obstacles were to prove insurmountable. Not only did Germany and Russia strongly resent the formation of regional groupings where they were not themselves members: there were also the problems arising from the border quarrels with Lithuania over Vilna in the Baltics, and with Czechoslovakia over Teschen in the south. Partly because of these struggles, and partly out of scepticism about Polish motives, throughout the period Kaunas and

Prague tended to take another and more positive view than Poland where relations with Russia and Germany were concerned.

At the League of Nations conference on reparations in Genoa in 1922, Poland had actually been able to play a leading role among the breakaway successor states to Tsarist Russia. The reason for this could, however, be traced back to the common economic interest of these states in not having to meet a share of the old Tsarist debts. With that common interest gone, Poland failed to interest Lithuania in its project to organise a Baltic League later on in the same year, and Lithuania's absence contributed heavily to the idea's downfall. Although Poland, Estonia, Latvia and Finland actually signed a convention, Finland failed to ratify it, and so the scheme came to naught. When, in 1924, a 'small' Baltic conference comprising Estonia, Latvia, and Lithuania was held in Kaunas, this was widely interpreted as a further dent to the Polish leadership of the successor states. Undeterred, after Piłsudski's *coup d'état* Poland tried to bypass Lithuania again. Enrolling Western support, Warsaw tried to build a four power Baltic alliance with Finland, Estonia and Latvia, which would act as a bloc *vis-à-vis* the Soviet Union. At the same time, the Soviet Union, supported by the Lithuanians, tried to initiate separate agreements with each of the four powers. Later in the year, both Latvia and Finland followed Lithuania's lead and turned to Moscow for bilateral talks.

Indeed, Lithuania proved to be an insurmountable obstacle to Polish aspirations in the Baltic. One could go so far as to claim that 'Anti-Polonism was the touchstone of Lithuanian nationalism'.[29] Kaunas's short-sighted policy has to take much of the blame for what was to happen a decade later. In 1927, the Lithuanian dictator Voldemaras answered the anxieties of the visiting Latvian foreign minister about German and Russian intentions by insisting that Poland was the greater threat.[30] Again, in May 1928, Voldemaras told an inquiring Chamberlain that Lithuania would join no Baltic bloc, asserting that the 'Russian peril' was 'purely theoretical,' whereas 'the Polish peril is entirely real'.[31] In 1934, and again in 1938, the Polish foreign minister visited Estonia and Latvia in order to forge a common defence against the dangers that lurked from Germany and the Soviet Union. At the later occasion, in an attempt to widen the prospective group of collaborators, he also visited Sweden and Norway. The Polish attempts were not crowned with success. Instead of hanging together, the countries between Germany and Russia were soon to hang separately.

In the south, too, Polish attempts at forging a Central European organisation all folded. During the First World War, Beneš had found cooperation with the Poles to be 'systematic, sincere, and rather successful'.[32] However, as noted above, Teschen soon made cooperation between the two states difficult.[33] When, in 1920–21, what came to be known as the Little Entente between Czechoslovakia, Romania, and Yugoslavia was forged, it was a setback for Poland. Warsaw, rightly, saw it as an obstacle to the formation of a Polish-led Central European anti-bolshevik front. It was particularly irking to Poland that Romania, which shared with Poland an ingrained scepticism of Russian bolshevism, now gave priority to the defence against Hungarian revanchism and teamed up with Prague. (In 1921, Bucharest also signed a non-aggression treaty with Warsaw). This also meant that Polish efforts to bring about a Romanian-Hungarian rapprochement in order to secure Central Europe's eastern border had been scuppered over the issue of Transylvania, located in Central Europe itself. Regional solidarity ran low, and Poland was in this sense correct in condemning the Little Entente as an inferior alternative to all-regional cooperation. Given the level of hostility between Warsaw and Prague, however, all-regional cooperation did not seem to be a workable option. Romania's adherence to a Little Entente was thus dictated by a sober assessment of the situation, and the Polish allegations that the Little Entente was anti-Polish were clearly exaggerated. Rather, the setting up of the Little Entente was a blatant defiance of the Polish aspirations to regional leadership. Nevertheless, the Poles persisted in their quest.

When Konstanty Skirmunt became Polish foreign minister in 1921, Polish-Czechoslovak relations experienced a minor thaw. Skirmunt was aware that Warsaw had acquired an imperialist reputation as a result of the post-war upheavals. Whereas he held this to have been inevitable, he now thought the time had come to work for a settlement of differences. To Skirmunt, relations with Prague were the key to reverse this trend, and his work to improve them actually met with some success. When, however, in 1922 Czechoslovakia aborted a goodwill scheme to return the village of Jaworzyna with its 400 Polish-speaking inhabitants to Poland, the thaw in relations proved to have been ephemeral.

One may question whether the course steered by Prague gave an optimum of security for Czechoslovakia and Central Europe as a whole. To Piotr Wandycz, that seems not to have been the case. 'If Prague had realized that the risk of an alliance with Poland was preferable to the less immediate risk of isolation – the Little Alliance was of no use against an aggressive great power – she might have helped to create a united bloc of forty million people or more in East Central Europe. Such a bloc would perhaps have been able to put greater pressure on France and draw her away from Locarno and subsequent dependence on England.'[34]

With the event of Locarno, Warsaw felt that the matter of regional cooperation was more urgent than ever. In late 1925, the Polish MP

Jan Dąbski initiated a campaign for economic union and perhaps even a customs union between Poland and Czechoslovakia. In Poland, the idea received a mixed reaction, and the Czechoslovak foreign minister Beneš intimated to a British diplomat that Prague would find such a suggestion quite embarrassing, and would not know how to respond.[35] Nevertheless, the Poles would not let go of the idea of a regional bloc. When Warsaw floated an official Polish initiative for some kind of a political bloc again in 1926, it did not meet with an enthusiastic Czech reaction. In the year of Piłsudski's coup, Czech reticence added to Polish isolation.[36] When, in 1927, Warsaw presented a plan for an 'Eastern Locarno', it had to act on its own, and the initiative proved fruitless.

In 1934, plans for an 'Eastern Pact' were being prepared within the framework provided by the League Covenant. The Eastern Pact would consist of a regional mutual assistance pact, a Franco-Soviet guarantee pact, and a general treaty signed by all participants. France would be the guarantor, and the Soviet Union would assume obligations towards France as if it were a signatory of Locarno. The pact needed Polish support to be realised. However, Beck regarded it as a 'form of a big concern, this time Russo-French, to push Poland down'.[37] To Warsaw, the Eastern Pact clearly showed that France attached less value to the bilateral alliance with Poland than to relations with Prague and the Little Entente. Moreover, accepting the Pact would mean bowing to the revived Russo-French combination, and writing off the idea of regional cooperation under Polish leadership once and for all. This Warsaw would not like to do, and the Polish position contributed crucially to the downfall of the Pact. Plans for a Danubian Pact centering on Austria also folded. Nevertheless, under the heading of 'Third Europe', Beck in 1937 produced a new plan for the setting up of a neutral bloc between Germany and Russia.[38]

Poland's foreign policy towards its smaller neighbours in the inter-war period was a failure. Two episodes at the end of the period graphically illustrated how Polish diplomacy was unable to reach results by peaceful means: following the 1938 *Anschluss*, Poland presented Lithuania with an ultimatum, and was only this way able to establish diplomatic relations with Kaunas. And following the German intervention in Sudetenland, Beck, thinking that Czechoslovakia was dispensable, seized the opportunity to take Teschen by force of arms.[39]

Whereas Poland insisted that the small states between Germany and Russia had to cooperate, under Polish leadership, Lithuania and Czechoslovakia judged the danger of and the price for cooperating under Polish leadership too great to justify the effort. Since Poland's other smaller neighbours were neither willing nor able to achieve cooperation without Lithuanian or Czechoslovak participation, and since Poland because of its great power aspirations was not willing to submerge regional cooperation in a broader framework including two or more great powers, Poland remained isolated within the region throughout the inter-war period. Especially after Locarno, when international relations to the east of Germany were to a certain degree cut off from those to the west of Germany, this situation was untenable not only for Poland, but for Central Europe as a whole. When, in September 1939, Germany and the Soviet Union split the region between themselves, the inter-regional squabbles were put in a sombre perspective.

EXTERNAL CONSTRAINTS ON POLAND

In its quest for great powerhood, Poland was constrained by other states' perceptions, and by the climate and structure of the international system.

Incidentally, a number of academics hold that Poland made it to regional great power, but not to great power. Already in 1920, the French historian Louis Eisenmann held that 'It was a tragedy for Poland to have been reborn too weak to be a power, and strong enough to aspire to more than the status of a small state.'[40] Carsten Holbraad, in his attempt to range powers mechanically, without regard to their immediate regional surroundings, takes up a similar position by including Poland in his category of 'middle powers' in the international system.[41] Anton DePorte holds that the main actors in the inter-war system perceived Poland to be ' . . . almost a great power'.[42] Josef Korbel even claims that from 1934 onwards, following the Declaration of Non-Aggression and Understanding with Germany and Hitler's view that Poland was 'a bastion toward Asia', Poland's ' . . . ambition was fulfilled – she was recognized as a big power'.[43]

Whereas Eisenmann's observation is a shrewd one, it could be questioned to what extent these generalisations are valid. Korbel's is certainly an overstatement. Indeed, the account above indicates that there exists no persistent pattern in the policies of the great powers towards Poland and its neighbouring states which can sustain the view that Poland was always singled out for particular concern. Even France, the most accomodating of the great powers, did not persistently give priority to its relations with Poland over its relations with the Little Entente (and certainly not over relations with the Soviet Union). Nor, as shown above, did Czechoslovakia and Lithuania recognise Poland's claim to regional great powerhood. Moreover, they were repeatedly able to thwart Polish regional designs. The other Central European states, especially Estonia, Latvia, and Romania, did not recognise Poland's claim to great powerhood, but were more ready than were Czechoslovakia and Lithuania to give Polish interests and priorities a more privileged place in the formulation of their own foreign policies than that allotted to other powers in the region. However, because of the lack of consensus in the region, they held themselves unable to act on their perceptions, as a result of which their perceptions did not help Poland's standing very much.

Even in their rhetoric, the great powers were at one in not perceiving Poland as a great power. The Soviet Union would at most hint that Poland was almost a great power: in 1926, Chicherin remarked to Stresemann that 'once Lithuania was swallowed by Poland, Poland would become a big power'.[44] However, as Soviet power itself grew, so the Soviet leadership grew more contemptuous. That observation holds for Germany as well. As long as Germany's armed forces were constrained by the Versailles treaty, and also during the first years of Hitler's reign, Poland was perceived as a regional great power.

One might have expected France to show a tendency to overrate an ally. However, during the inter-war period the French seemed never quite to stop longing for the time when it had been allied to Russia. Moreover, France was not willing to give up its good relations with Czechoslovakia and the Little Entente. Both tendencies seem to suggest that France perceived Poland as a regional great power *manquée*. As to Britain, Austen Chamberlain's oft-quoted remark from 1925 that 'for the Polish corridor no British Government ever will or ever can risk the bones of a British grenadier' seems to reflect a widespread perception of Poland in its entirety which held good well into the 1930s.[45]

In addition to lacking recognition of its claim to great powerhood, Poland also found itself constrained by the international system and the international climate of the day. The re-establishment of the Polish state owed a lot to the universalisation of the principle of national self-determination suggested by Woodrow Wilson. However, this principle also worked against Poland's aspirations to a leading regional role. Lithuania and Czechoslovakia had just broken away from multinational empires, and their ethnically Lituanian and Czech leaderships and populations jealously guarded their newly won nation states. A logical outcome of cooperation with Poland might easily have been the forging of a union of states under Polish leadership, as had indeed happened to a Lithuanian state formation once before. To the new élites in Kaunas and Prague, once again to play a subordinate role in a union of states was not a tempting option. In the upshot, cooperation with Poland was ruled out altogether. The Polish argument, which was mainly predicated on a reading of the international structure in Europe which held that the states of Central Europe would have to stand together against both Soviet and German pressures, was brushed aside. In a situation where the nation state was about to become the new hegemonic state form in international relations, the international climate favoured Czechoslovak and Lithuanian national aspirations over Polish aspirations for regional leadership. Nevertheless, the Polish perspective was vindicated when Lithuania, Estonia, and Latvia lost their statehood in 1940, and when Czechoslovakia, together with most other states in the area, had their sovereignty penetrated by the Soviet Union after the Second World War.

CONCLUSIONS

Poland's quest for regional leadership in Central Europe in the inter-war period invites some tentative generalisations. The importance of shared regional perceptions of the great powers seems to be of more than idiographic concern. The Central European states followed different strategies *vis-à-vis* the great powers, because they perceived the dangers lurking from each of them differently. However, the importance of this point should not be exaggerated. There were periods before 1926 when the Polish government consisted of political forces close to Dmowski, and whose perceptions of Germany and Russia were more in line with those of the Czechoslovak and Lithuanian governments than with Piłsudski's. Nonetheless, Poland did not make more headway towards regional leadership under one leadership than under another.

Although Poland was clearly the largest state in Central Europe in terms of territory and population, the state of the Polish economy was not good. Poland did not possess that whole range of political tools which comes from having a strong economy, and a strong military potential. Warsaw simply could not afford to enter into economic diplomacy at any scale that would make a difference. In this regard they differed from Czechoslovakia, which could use its well-developed industry to curry favours with neighbouring states, including its allies in the Little Entente. Moreover, the difference in economic capability had immediate military consequences. Poland had more men under arms than had Czechoslovakia (see Table 6.1), and most estimates of mobilisation potential focused on manpower. In 1925 Sir Frederick Maurice held that Poland's mobilisation potential was 550 000, to Czechoslovakia's 300 000, whereas Jan Ciałowycz, writing in 1970, estimated that the Polish inter-war army in case of war could be expanded to include over one million men.[46] According to an estimate which takes economic potential into consideration, however, Poland was in 1927 able to finance and field 20 divisions. Czechoslovakia, on the other hand, although beginning with fewer men, could nevertheless outdo Poland by mobilising 38 divisions![47] This is only one possible illustration of how Poland's advantage in population size could be challenged by a smaller but economically ebullient Czechoslovakia.

A third possible generalisation concerns the contending claims of would-be regional great powers and constraining great powers. In the case at hand, two great powers bordered on the region. Both had a clear strategic interest in penetrating the region, and both had ideologies at hand with which to boost their strategic interests. To the Soviet Union, the region generally, and Poland especially, presented itself as a springboard from which it could carry out its claimed historical mission of supporting proletarian revolutions in Western Europe, as well as a *cordon sanitaire* against capitalist encroachment. To Germany, the region was a candidate for industrial expansion and domination ('*Mitteleuropa*'), and, later on, a natural conduit for racialist expansion ('*Lebensraum*'). For an aspiring regional great power, there is a difference between being constrained by geographically distant great powers with an abstract interest in regional balance, or by immediately neighbouring great powers with specific hegemonic interests and aspirations. Poland was exposed to the latter experience, and could actually count two great powers among its regional challengers. The historically unique situation which arose after the First World War, when Germany and Russia were weak and internationally constrained at the same time, combined with Poland's historical great power heritage to muddle Warsaw's perceptions of regional potential. To an aspiring regional great power it may not be enough to analyse the regional dynamics at hand; *la longue durée* may reveal factors which should also be considered.

Poland's inter-war heritage today

When Germany and the Soviet Union divided Central Europe between themselves in September 1939, it marked the beginning of a war which transformed the international system, and started a fifty year interlude in Polish history. In a move parallel to that of France and Great Britain, from October 1939 onwards Poland and Czechoslovakia initiated negotiations in order to form a confederation after the war. However, not even the extreme strain to which the two states were exposed at this time proved enough to bring them together, and negotiations petered out in 1942. At Yalta, despite talk about dividing influence between the Western Allies and the Soviet Union on a 50/50 basis, the great power concert laid Poland open to

Soviet penetration. It soon became clear that Poland's regional role would be severely circumscribed: In the standing instruction of 1946 from the Canadian administration, the Canadian delegates to the UN were asked to 'establish a working relationship with the other middle powers: Brazil, Mexico, the Netherlands, Belgium, Czechoslovakia, Australia, India (and Poland if it secures reasonable freedom of action)'.[48] The parentheses and the caveat were well chosen. Although the Polish government came up with some proposals during the postwar years, notably the Rapacki plan, Poland was generally much too penetrated by the Soviet Union to be in the running for regional great powerhood. Specifically, in order to fend off the forging of regional alliances the Soviet Union conducted a policy which minimised bilateral contacts between its European allies.

With that constraint on bilateral relations gone, in the late 1980s the Silesian University in Katowice was allowed to establish a branch in Czechoslovak Teschen. Given Teschen's place in the history of Polish-Czech relations, this was an important event, and a harbinger of things to come.

Developments in Poland, Czechoslovakia and the other European states allied to the Soviet Union in the autumn of 1989, as well as developments in Estonia, Latvia and Lithuania, have shown the communist period in the region to have been historically parenthetical. Central Europe is again 'the lands between' Germany and Russia. With the relaxation of tensions and the rise of a new climate of cooperation in Europe, the question of Poland's role in the international system has once again come to the fore. It may be useful to conclude this chapter by taking a look at how the situation today compares with the one existing in the inter-war period.

Some may have heard a faint echo of that period in the Polish-German squabbling over the Oder-Neisse border between the two states in early 1990. When Poland at Potsdam was moved geographically to the west, as the Soviet Union took over the contested Russo-Polish borderlands and compensated Poland by former German territories, Poland was in effect condemned to look to the east for protection against any German attempts at retrieving the lost territory. When, in 1989, German cultural and economic reunification went ahead, and political reunification soon followed, Polish anxieties were quick to surface. In October 1989, president Jaruzelski remarked that 'It would be the biggest misfortune, and not only to us, if there were some kind of anschluss' (ostensibly between the two Germanies), and added that Poland was the only European country with a disputed border.[49] In November 1989, Adam Michnik, while bowing to the inevitability of German reunification, held that 'I may sound too categorical, but anyone who speaks of redrawing national boundaries is either a fool or a troublemaker'.[50] In January 1990, prime minister Tadeusz Mazowiecki went before the Council of Europe's parliamentary assembly and demanded guarantees from Germany and all interested parties of Poland's western frontier. Although the GDR accepted the Oder-Neisse line in 1950, and the FRG in 1970 recognised that 'the existing boundary constitutes the western frontier of the Polish People's Republic', Poland obviously perceived the issue of its Western border to be very much alive. When the decision had been taken at Potsdam, it was agreed that final delimitation should await the peace settlement. Such an official settlement never saw the light of day, and it had therefore been argued that the case was still legally open. Moreover, it had been argued that the pledges of the FRG could not be binding on a reunified Germany. This position was actually recorded in an amendment to the 1970 agreement with Poland, thus making that agreement an ambiguous one. However, as part of the 2 plus 4 negotiations on German reunification and following considerable Polish pressure, the Germanies at last gave in and guaranteed the border. The formal drawing up of the treaty between Poland and Germany took place shortly after the advent of German reunification. This notwithstanding, Poland will still have a potential border problem in the West, with potential minority squabbles to match.[51] Polish-German relations are also certain to be riddled by problems arising from asymmetries in economic capabilities, as was the case in the inter-war period. Although Poland seems eager for German loans and a planned bilateral economic agreement, voices warning against German economic domination can already be heard.

Although the Soviet Union no longer demands the right to lay down the shape of Polish domestic politics, Poland will still have an Eastern great power neighbour with extensive interests in Polish foreign policy. One may remark that any weakening of Russia following the ongoing régime change may, once again, prove to be ephemeral, and that Poland will probably keep this in mind. Janusz Onyszkiewicz, Poland's Deputy Minister of Defence, seemed to give vent to such feelings, and to a certain anxiety about the future as well, when he remarked that 'Poland is now being squeezed between two major areas of change, the Germanies and the Soviet Union . . . and no one knows what will happen there'.[52] Asked by the Polish press agency PAP in October 1989 how the new conditions would influence Soviet-Polish relations, Soviet foreign minister Eduard Shevardnadze answered that the two strongest European member states of the Warsaw Pact should cooperate in the construction of the Common European Home.[53] This answer highlights two things: the Soviet Union hopes for a privileged partnership with Poland compared to other great powers (whether within some predecessor to the Warsaw Pact or by some other means). However, at the same time the Soviet Union fully accepts that with the relaxation of tensions in Europe, Poland will also play an individual role in all-European relations. The Polish government was quick to adjust to the new situation. As part of the campaign mentioned above to get a border guarantee from the Germanies, Prime Minister Mazowiecki at one point declared that he would not ask Soviet troops to leave before the guarantee was forthcoming. This is not likely to be the last time when Poland attempts to play Russian and German state formations against each other.

Echoes of the inter-war period are clearly resounding in Polish-French relations. During a visit to France in July 1990, the Polish Foreign Minister Krzystof Skubiszewski repeatedly called that country Poland's 'most important political partner', and mentioned the possibility of a treaty of friendship between the two countries. Moreover, he explicitly suggested that such a treaty would be a continuation of the inter-war treaty relationship, and took note of an atmosphere in Paris whereby Poland was treated as a prodigal son.[54] A treaty was indeed concluded in April 1991.

However, on the same occasion Skubiszewski underlined the differences between the political situation in the inter-war years and now, highlighting the positive role played by the European Community in bringing Germany and France together. Indeed, Polish Western policy has so far revolved around its relationship with the EC. Poland has pressed for an explicit membership option beyond an association agreement. President Mitterrand and others have suggested that some kind of organisation comprising the EC and the Central European countries should be established. Jaruzelski gave support to President Mitterrand's idea of a Europeanwide Confederation, and wanted to develop the Helsinki Final Act into a fully fledged international treaty.[55] Similar policies are being pursued under President Wałęsa. Certainly, this kind of setting will provide Poland with the possibility of conducting a European-wide foreign policy which should have a greater potential than the policy it conducted within the League of Nations.

Where Poland's relations with its smaller neighbours are concerned, Lithuanian anti-Polish sentiment is still strong. For example, in a fairly representative article printed in Vilnius in May 1989, entitled 'Can Lithuanians trust Poles?', Edita Degutiene seemed to be answering in the negative. The article included comments on the 'unhealthy cult' of Vilnius in Poland, and on Polish 'inflated feeling of national pride'.[56] Some 260 000 Poles live in Lithuania, comprising some 7 per cent of the total population (there are also some 7500 Lithuanians in Poland). Poles in Lithuania have been worried by the rising tide of Lithuanian nationalism. When Lithuanian was made the official language of the republic in January 1989, the Poles responded by demanding the right to use their own language in education, and administratively on district (*rayon*) level. During the autumn of 1989, the Vilnius and Šalčininkai districts in Lithuania declared themselves to be autonomous Polish districts. This was strongly opposed by Lithuanians across the political spectrum, who held that Lithuania was indivisible. Beginning in October 1989, Lithuania limited the number of visits from 'citizens of CMEA countries' to one per year, and introduced forced exchange of hard currency. The Lithuanian Communications Ministry was instructed to intercept parcels from Lithuania to Poland.[57] Warsaw perceived these moves as discriminatory to Poles on either side of the border. Nevertheless, the Poles have officially offered their services as negotiators in the ongoing conflict between Moscow and Vilnius, and have drawn up a draft for a declaration on bilateral cooperation. The Lithuanian foreign minister has by spring 1991 taken up five invitations to visit Warsaw. Skubiszewski, his opposite number who has yet to be invited for a return visit, commented in January 1991 that 'I would like to see the Lithuanian side looking at our relations more broadly, with more vision, and not – to be forthright – nationalistically. If these nationalistic elements do not disappear, our relations will not be good'.[58] On the whole, Lithuania seems to persist in the anti-Polish foreign policy conducted in the inter-war period, the disastrous consequences of that policy for Lithuania itself notwithstanding.

In the inter-war period, Polish-Ukrainian relations were rife with problems. This seems to be changing. In September 1989, Adam Michnik was invited to address the founding congress of the Popular Movement of Ukraine for Perestroyka (Rukh), and he did so by hailing a 'free Ukraine'. At the congress, a motion from the floor suggested making 17 September a national Ukrainian holiday. That was the day when the Red Army invaded Poland in 1939, and, to the mover, the day when Ukraine was united. 'Luckily', Michnik commented afterwards, 'it didn't pass. I say luckily because no one in Poland would understand this . . . the Ukrainians are right in their belief that this was their land, but not their state. And the Poles are right because the Polish state had existed on this land for 500 years.' Furthermore, Michnik recognised this as a bone of contention in Polish-Ukrainian affairs, and held that Stalinist forces would exploit these differences for their own ends. However, history shows that a third party has always gained from Polish-Ukrainian conflicts, Michnik warned. Rather, the two peoples should think of the other as enriching its culture; having Ukrainians, Belorussians and Lithuanians living in Poland enriches Polish culture and public discourse, and 'leads to our becoming spiritually richer than we would be without it'.[59] By giving vent to the idea that a political unit comprising more ethnic groups than one is normatively better than a nation state, Michnik places himself squarely in the Jagiellonian, federalist tradition in Polish politics discussed above. Since a number of Poles, notably Lech Wałęsa, seem to be leaning towards a new Polish nationalism, the inter-war debate about Polish identity and the Polish national role is making a speedy comeback. Although Poland has been fairly successful in pursuing their dualistic approach to relations with the Soviet centre on the one hand, and with Ukraine, Lithuania and White Russia on the other, the problems inherent in this approach should not be underestimated. Still, the signing of a friendship treaty with Ukraine in October 1990 and the repeated attempts to reach similar arrangements with Lithuania and a decidedly reticent White Russia indicate that this element of a traditional Polish federalist programme will continue to be a central ingredient in Polish foreign policy.

Polish relations with the Czech and Slovak Federation seem to be excellent. The new élites that have risen to power in the two countries share a number of political ideas, including the concept of 'Central Europe' and a strong European orientation generally. On 25 January 1990, President Havel went before the Polish parliament and proposed a 'political forma- tion' of Czechoslovakia, Hungary and Poland.[60] On 15 February 1991, a broad summit meeting between the three states took place in Visegrád. Although important as a goodwill scheme, this meeting saw no attempts at following up on the initial ideas for institutionalised cooperation, and an immediate breakthrough for such ideas seems unlikely.

One could argue that a faint echo of the inter-war period resounded through the initial pairing off of Central European states following the end of the Cold War. Poland's inter-war attempts at regional cooperation broke down due to the existence of limited groupings to the North and South of it, revolving around Lituania and Czechoslovakia. Today, with a number of regional cooperation concepts floating about, the two which have so far been most successful have been Baltic cooperation *vis-à-vis* Moscow to the North, and the Pentagonale group consisting of Austria, the Czech and Slovak Federation, Hungary, Italy and Yugoslavia to the South. The declared main priority of the latter group is mutual aid and support in order to obtain EC membership. Success for a Pentagonal grouping excluding Poland might have resulted in the latter's isolation. However, Poland responded by putting out feelers to join the Pentagonale, and was accepted in the summer of 1991. Thus, this particular echo of the inter-war period was in a considerable degree muffled, at least for the time being.

Despite all these caveats, Warsaw stands to reap great profits from the ongoing transformation of international relations in Europe. The Poles seem to have a much more realistic understanding of their proper place in the system than they did in the inter-war period. Poland's territorial integrity is incomparably better now than it was during the inter-war period. However, one of the basic dilemmas of that period remains: population and territory rank Poland much higher in the order of European states than does economy. Nevertheless, despite constraints imposed by German and Russian, and also Czechoslovak and Lithuanian, ambitions, Poland's possibilities for playing a major role in the Central European region, as well as in Europe at large, seem to be better now than at any time since 1919.

NOTES

I would like to thank Drs Marian Grzybowski, Olav F. Knudsen, Geir Lundestad, John Vincent and Jonathan Wright as well as Thomas Hylland Eriksen and my fellow contributors for their comments on earlier drafts of this chapter.

1. Adam Watson, 'European International Society and Its Expansion', in Hedley Bull and Adam Watson (eds), *The Expansion of International Society* (Oxford: Clarendon, 1985), pp. 13–32, on p. 17.
2. Joseph Rothschild, *East Central Europe between the Two World Wars* (Seattle, WA: A History of East Central Europe, IX, University of Washington Press, 1974).
3. Piotr S. Wandycz, *The Lands of Partitioned Poland, 1795–1918* (Seattle, WA: A History of East Central Europe, VII, University of Wisconsin Press, 1974), p. 263.
4. Hans Roos, *Polen und Europa. Studien zur Polnischen Aussenpolitik 1931–1939* (Tübingen: J. C. B. Mohr, Tübinger Studien zur Geschichte und Politik, 7, 1957), p. 240.
5. Norman Davies, *God's Playground. A History of Poland*, vol. II (Oxford: Clarendon Press, 1981), p. 416.
6. Quoted in Davies, *God's Playground*, p. 393.
7. Quoted in Josef Korbel, *Poland between East and West. Soviet and German Diplomacy toward Poland, 1919–1933* (Princeton, NJ: Princeton University Press, 1963), p. 101.
8. Piotr S. Wandycz, *Soviet-Polish Relations, 1917–1921* (Cambridge, MA: Harvard University Press, 1969), p. 94. Also Norman Davies, *Heart of Europe. A Short History of Poland* (Oxford: Oxford University Press, 1986), pp. 129–48.
9. Albert Erich Senn, *The Great Powers, Lithuania, and the Vilna Question, 1920–1928* (Leiden: E. J. Brill, Studien zur Geschichte Osteuropas XI, 1966), p. 3.
10. Dmowski, who thought that Poland might 'grow to be one of the greatest nations in Europe', feared that under German tutelage it might dwindle

to a '*narodek*', a disparaging term for a little people alluding to the nineteenth century idea of non-historic nations; Piotr S. Wandycz, 'Poland's Place in Europe in the Concepts of Piłsudski and Dmowski', *East European Politics and Societies*, IV (1990): 451–69.

11. Quoted in Wandycz, *Soviet-Polish Relations, 1917–1921*, p. 121.

12. Kay Lundgreen-Nielsen, *The Polish Problem at the Paris Peace Conference. A Study of the Politics of the Great Powers and the Poles 1918–1919* (Odense: Odense University Press, 1979), p. 35.

13. That is, for the inter-war period. Cf. Davies, *God's Playground*, pp. 492–535.

14. Senn, *The Great Powers, Lithuania, and the Vilna Question, 1920–1928* pp. 1–45, p. 118 *et passim*.

15. Indeed, the war had convinced Piłsudski of the intensity of the new nationalisms: 'The principle of federation cannot be applied to these lands. Surely we enter them with weapons in our hands which is contrary to the principles of federation. Besides I did not see people there who would want to join such a federation'. Wandycz, *Soviet-Polish Relations, 1917–1921*, p. 99. In a broader sense, however, Piłsudski's federalism was built on the premise that the newly liberated countries of Eastern and Central Europe needed each other more than they needed sovereignty. That belief survives in Polish political culture to this day. Cf. below and M. K. Dziewanowski, *Joseph Pilsudski. A European Federalist, 1918–22* (Stanford, CA: Hoover Institution Press, 1969), p. 350.

16. Davies, *God's Playground*, p. 498.

17. Christoph M. Kimmich, *The Free City. Danzig and German Foreign Policy 1919–1934* (New Haven, CN: Yale University Press, 1968).

18. Korbel, *Poland between East and West*, p. 93. It must also be said, however, that the Russo-Polish war itself was crucial to the configuration of power in Europe; 'Trotsky wrote: "The counterrevolutionary significance of the Riga treaty for the fate of Europe can be best understood if you picture the situation in 1923 [the time of the Ruhr occupation and the crisis in Germany] under the supposition that we had had a common frontier with Germany". Nothing could be more clear. The settlement of 1921 stopped the Soviet westward advance, stabilised the situation in Eastern Europe – and indeed in Europe – and excluded Russia from international politics for at least sixteen years. This was a breakdown of the Bolshevik revolutionary program. It opened the new period of "Socialism in one country" and the New Economic Policy.' Wandycz, *Soviet-Polish Relations, 1917–1921*, p. 286.

19. The classical debate between these two main views is to be found in John Maynard Keynes, *The Economic Consequences of the Peace* (London: Macmillan, 1920) and Etienne Mantoux, *The Carthagenian Peace. The Economic Consequences of Mr. Keynes* (Oxford: Oxford University Press, 1946).

20. Piotr S. Wandycz, *France and Her Eastern Allies 1919–1925. French*

Czechoslovak-Polish Relations from the Paris Peace Conference to Locarno (Minneapolis, MI: University of Minnesota Press, 1962), p. 22.

21. Korbel, *Poland between East and West*, on p. 168 and p. 212, respectively.

22. Roman Debicki, *Foreign Policy of Poland 1919–1939. From the Rebirth of the Polish Republic to World War II* (London: Pall Mall Press, 1962) p. 57. However, the pact noted the right to act in self-defence even if the League Council was not agreed.

23. Korbel, *Poland between East and West*, p. 180. Of course, Stresemann's reason for saying this was probably the need to overcome domestic nationalist opposition to the Locarno treaties.

24. Western contemporary analysts and earlier generations of historians were inclined to interpret Locarno as a genuine European rapprochement. However, new analyses such as Sally Marks, *The Illusion of Peace. International Relations in Europe 1918–1933* (London: Macmillan, 1976) esp. pp. 55–74 and Jon Jakobson, 'Is There a New International History of the 1920s?', *American History Review*, CLXXXVIII (1983): 617–45, are now bringing general Western historiography closer to the bleak picture which arises when one looks at Locarno from the Polish angle.

25. Germany did make a treaty of non-aggression (the so-called Berlin treaty) with the Soviet Union in April 1926, though.

26. This 'in defiance of the old idea that such seats should be reserved for the great Powers', F. S. Northedge, *The League of Nations. Its Life and Times 1920–1946* (Leicester: Leicester University Press, 1988), p. 102. Brazil and Spain promptly came to the fore with demands of their own. Brazil actually left the organisation when its wish was not fulfilled.

27. Piotr S. Wandycz, *The Twilight of French Eastern Alliances, 1926–1936. French-Czechoslovak-Polish Relations from Locarno to the Remilitarization of the Rhineland* (Princeton, NJ: Princeton University Press, 1988), p. 50.

28. Korbel, *Poland between East and West*, p. 206. One sign of the latter was that Poland withdrew from the League's minority right scheme, and refused to comply with it until such a time when all other European states also did so.

29. Senn, *The Great Powers, Lithuania, and the Vilna Question, 1920–1928*, p. 199.

30. On this occasion, the Latvian minister in Kaunas, A. Balodis, remarked to his minister, Felikss Cielens: 'Now you hear for yourself what I write in my reports to Riga . . . Lithuanians, especially their Dictator, are arrogant and stubborn.' Senn, *The Great Powers, Lithuania, and the Vilna Question, 1920–1928*, p. 189.

31. Quoted ibid. p. 215.

32. Wandycz, *France and Her Eastern Allies 1919–1925*, p. 14.

33. There were, of course also other reasons, ranging from national character

to the perception of the Soviet Union. Interestingly, Sarah Meiklejohn Terry, *Poland's Place in Europe. General Sikorski and the Origin of the Oder-Neisse Line, 1939–1943* (Princeton, NJ: Princeton University Press, 1983), on p. 26 maintains that since a wedge of German Silesian land came to separate the Polish and Czech indiustrial districts, and since the Poles did not obtain full control over Danzig, the prospects for economic gains from cooperation were substantially diminished.

34. Wandycz, *France and Her Eastern Allies 1919–1925*, p. 388.
35. Wandycz, *The Twilight of French Eastern Alliances, 1926–1936*, pp. 43–4.
36. It should be mentioned that Masaryk in 1927 suggested to Briand that a Central European grouping should be established. However, 'Masaryk's mention of Poland as a member of the planned Central Eureopean grouping could have been hardly serious', Wandycz, *The Twilight of French Eastern Alliances, 1926–1936*, comments on p. 89.
37. Ibid. p. 362.
38. Roos, *Polen und Europa*, pp. 273–397.
39. Although she discusses this episode under the heading 'The Czechoslovak crisis: The betrayal and its consequences', Anna M. Cienciala, *Poland and the Western Powers 1938–1939. A Study in the Interdependence of Eastern and Western Europe* (London: Routledge & Kegan Paul, 1968) on p. 148 (cf. also p. 256) points out that 'it was not only the lack of direct aid but the obvious reluctance of France and Britain even to threaten Germany with an attack in the West which ultimately decided the course of Beck's policy towards Czechoslovakia'; and indeed, France at one point during the crisis even exerted pressure on Beneš to cede Teschen in return for Polish neutrality.
40. Wandycz, *France and Her Eastern Allies 1919–1925*, p. 383.
41. Carsten Holbraad, *Middle Powers in International Politics* (London: Macmillan, 1984).
42. Anton W. DePorte, *Europe between the Superpowers. The Enduring Balance* (New Haven, CT: Yale University Press, 1979), p. 31.
43. Korbel, *Poland between East and West*, p. 287.
44. Ibid., p. 229. The instrumental reasons for such a statement are, however, obvious.
45. Christopher Thorne, *The Approach of War 1938–39* (London: Macmillan, 1967), p. 129.
46. Wandycz, *The Twilight of French Eastern Alliances, 1926–1936*, pp. 35–6, note 69.
47. Estimate by Kostrba-Skalicky. In 1937, he puts the corresponding figures

at 24 and 42, respectively. France could equip 200 divisions in 1929, but only 160 in 1937. For Germany, the corresponding figures were 250 and 260 respectively; Wandycz, *The Twilight of French Eastern Alliances, 1926–1936*, p. 449. Wandycz himself on p. 474 holds that 'Territory and population placed Poland among the leading states of Europe; underdeveloped economy pulled it back to a much inferior rank.' One notes the discrepancy between these estimates and contemporary estimates given in Table 6.1.

48. Bernard Wood, *Middle Powers and the General Interest* (Ottawa: The North-South Institute, Middle Powers in the International System, 1988), p. iii.
49. Flora Lewis, 'A Smile in Poland, Between Two Worlds', *International Herald Tribune*, 19 October 1989.
50. Interview with the Soviet weekly *New Times*, 28 November, 1989.
51. There is also the problem of the German minority in Poland, which is now a problem that may be discussed openly in the Polish press; cf. 'Gibt es eine deutsche Minderheit in Polen?', *Osteuropa*, XL, 1, 1990, pp. A25–A33. It is hard to say how many Germans are left in Poland; however, an organiser in Opole, Herr Johann Krauss, claims to have gathered 250 000 signatures supporting the creation of a German cultural society.
52. Jan B. de Weydenthal, 'Poland and the Soviet Alliance System', *Report on Eastern Europe*, 29 June 1990.
53. *Pravda*, 20 October 1989.
54. Interview with *Le Monde*, 21 July 1990.
55. *Le Monde*, 2 January 1990; *Polytika*, 20 January 1990. The Helsinki Final Act guarantees Europe's borders against changes by other than peaceful means.
56. *Literatura ir Menas*, translated in *Foreign Broadcast Information Service*, The Soviet Union, 18 October 1989.
57. *Foreign Broadcast Information Service*, 24 October 1989.
58. Anna Sabbat-Swidlicka, 'Polish Reactions to the Lithuanian Crisis', *Report on Eastern Europe*, 8 February 1991.
59. Roman Solchanyk, 'Ukraine and Poland: An Interview with Adam Michnik', *Report on the USSR*, 5 January 1990.
60. *Agence Europe*, 29–30 January 1990.

7 South Africa as a Regional Great Power

Samuel M. Makinda

INTRODUCTION

South Africa is the wealthiest, most populous and militarily the strongest state in southern Africa. There is no clinical definition of the southern Africa region, but it generally consists of 10 countries: South Africa and its former colony, Namibia; former Portuguese colonies of Angola and Mozambique; former British High Commission territories of Botswana, Lesotho and Swaziland; and former Central African Federation members, Malawi, Zambia and Zimbabwe. The region is basically a geographic unit, but it also contains states which have historically maintained a network of commercial, political or communications links with South Africa. Tanzania, as one of the Frontline states, may be thought to be a southern African state, but in my view, it does not fit in the region either geographically or historically. With a population of about 37 million, South Africa accounts for about 40 per cent of the region's total population. It has about 26 million blacks, six million whites, four million 'coloureds' and one million Asians. In spite of international economic sanctions, and a severe recession in 1991, South Africa's economy has remained buoyant in comparison with those of neighbouring states, with the exception of perhaps Botswana and Zimbabwe.[1] With a GDP in 1989 of more than US\$ 90 billion, South Africa accounted for more than 80 per cent of the GDP of the 10 countries of the region taken together. It has a strong industrial base and is self-sufficient in most goods. It does not have oil reserves, but has the technology to convert coal into oil.

South Africa's economic power stems partly from its possession of a large variety of mineral resources, and partly from a higher level of industrialisation which, in turn, has depended on the exploitation of cheap labour and a ready market in the surrounding region. It possesses large reserves of gold, uranium, platinum, diamonds, manganese, coal, iron ore, antimony, asbestos, chromite and vanadium. Indeed, it has a greater variety of minerals than any other country, except perhaps Australia and the Soviet Union. It is these minerals that form the backbone of South

151

Africa's economy. But, because of price fluctuations of most raw materials, South Africa, like most countries which depend on raw materials, has been vulnerable to the vicissitudes of the world market. South Africa's minerals also provide jobs to many migrant workers from neighbouring states, who are paid more poorly than indigenous South Africans. In the past, however, the South African government has occasionally threatened to expel migrant workers as a sanction against some neighbouring states.

As a military power, South Africa's strength is comparable to that of Israel *vis-à-vis* its neighbours. In sheer numbers of personnel and equipment, South Africa has the biggest military force in sub-Saharan Africa. Its total armed forces of more than 103 000, with a reserve force of more than 425 000, is bigger than those of the Frontline African states of Angola, Botswana, Mozambique, Tanzania, Zambia and Zimbabwe combined. In armaments, South Africa has the best-equipped and most mechanised military force on the African continent. The 1963 UN voluntary arms embargo, followed by a mandatory one in 1977, forced South Africa to develop an indigenous arms industry, and that has placed it in a comparatively stronger military position than its neighbours. The arms embargo and the establishment of an indigenous arms industry interacted with other internal and regional dynamics to give the South African military an increased role in national politics.[2]

South Africa established the Armaments Corporation (ARMSCOR), the state arms manufacturing and procuring agency, in 1968. By 1981, ARMSCOR had reached self-sufficiency in some of the most essential categories of weapons systems. By the late 1980s, South Africa was self-sufficient in artillery systems, arms and munition, short-range guided missiles, mines, armoured and mine-resistant vehicles, and tactical telecommunications equipment. The South African Air Force, which has always been better-equipped than the air forces of neighbouring states, had, *inter alia*, 317 combat aircraft, including 27 *Cheetah* aircraft (a locally modified *Mirage*) in service in 1990. South Africa also successfully tested in the late 1980s the booster stage of a rocket, thought to be part of the development of an Intermediate-range Ballistic Missile (IRBM), possibly in cooperation with Israel. The country's defence budget was also increased substantially in the 1980s; defence spending grew by 9 per cent in 1988 and by 8 per cent in 1989, in real terms.

The only white-ruled country on the African continent, South Africa's political system of apartheid discriminates against non-whites, especially the majority black population, which had no vote by 1991. The apartheid system, which euphemistically means separate development for different races, in practice means the exploitation of the black population by the whites.[3] It was introduced in 1948 following the victory of the Afrikaner-dominated Nationalist Party and has since remained the focus of opposition both from within and outside. The Afrikaner leaders have in the past argued that it has been because of South Africa's internal social and political system that it has reached its present level of economic prosperity; but it is also because of apartheid that international economic sanctions have been imposed on the country, thus restricting further growth.

By 1990, the apartheid system was beginning to crumble. Starting with the limited political reforms to remove petty-apartheid in the mid-1980s, introduced by former State President P. W. Botha, most of the pillars on which apartheid was based have been shaken. The South African whites have been deeply divided about the nature and pace of reform, because some whites fear to lose the privileges they have taken for granted for so long. The current ideological splits among the Afrikaners first occurred in the early 1980s, leading to the formation of the Conservative Party, led by Dr. Andries Treurnicht, and other right-wing organisations, including the neo-Nazi AWB. These splits, which reveal the deeply ingrained fear of losing identity and security, have reduced the importance of ethnic identity as a source of party affiliation among the whites.[4]

The schisms among Afrikaners also reflect the changed economic circumstances of the Afrikaners which, in turn, has led to a convergence of perceptions and perspectives between some urbanised Afrikaners and English-speaking whites. Some of these have been inspired by the liberalist conception of the state and a belief in market forces. The Nationalist Party, which initially represented rural and blue-collar Afrikaner interests, now represent a largely white-collar constituency embracing both English-speaking whites and increasingly liberalist Afrikaners. The Afrikaners who have refused to accept change, have sought refuge in extremist organisations.

One of the most important issues which divided the Afrikaners was the role of blacks in the political process. Accustomed to defining social, political and economic issues in racial terms, some Afrikaners were at a loss as to what a new South Africa would mean. The release of Nelson Mandela and the unbanning of the African National Congress (ANC) and other opposition movements in February 1990, dramatically changed the complexion of South African politics, and also consolidated the divisions among whites. De Klerk might have expected to use Mandela's release to co-opt some influential blacks into the system and to reduce pressure on his government, but hardly any blacks proved willing to be co-opted, and resistance to apartheid intensified. The black population remained deeply divided along ideological and ethnic lines, and these splits were exploited by various groups. The most publicised division between the Zulu and other ethnic groups, which has existed for some years, was refueled by security forces and other groups determined to delay the assumption of power by blacks. But, it has also been manipulated by some black leaders from various sides in the course of their power struggles. [5]

Within the region, South Africa has maintained vital links with most southern African states which can be traced back to the colonial period. The independent states of Angola, Botswana, Lesotho, Mozambique, Namibia, Swaziland and Zimbabwe, which have borders with South Africa, are economically poorer and militarily weaker than South Africa.[6] Ever since the mid-1960s, when J. B. Vorster became prime minister, South Africa has sought to deal with its neighbours at two levels: dialogue, which presupposes tolerance of apartheid; and economic and military pressure. Its regional policy, which has in the past included the use of its economic and military power to intimidate and destabilise the neighbouring states, has largely been determined by the imperatives of the apartheid system. This policy has thrived on the military and economic weaknesses of South Africa's neighbours, but it has also been justified as a response to what has been perceived as a national security threat caused by the decisions of these countries to provide sanctuary to South African liberation fighters. The exception has been Namibia, formerly Southwest Africa, which South Africa continued to occupy illegally until March 1990.[7] The South African régime had, until 1990, portrayed the opponents of apartheid as Communist surrogates in an effort to make its regional policy more acceptable to the Western powers. But, in actual fact, the policy has stemmed from economic as well as political and strategic motives.

REGIONAL PROFILE

Owing to the nature of the apartheid system, the South African government's perceptions reflect the views of a white minority and ignore completely the views of 85 per cent of the population. South Africa's self-perception, therefore, refers to the perceptions of the Afrikaner (Dutch descendants), who are dominant within the white minority. The Afrikaners' self-perception is based on the deep-rooted view of themselves as a beleagured nation facing the black peril.

Self-Perception

Until the 1980s, most Afrikaners believed that they alone stood for order against chaos, for civilisation against barbarism, and for development against misery. They argued that South Africa was not one nation, but many, and that they required firm Afrikaner control to prevent civil strife. They have sometimes portrayed themselves as the exclusive agents of a divine and enlightened mission, and the Dutch Reformed Church, the main Afrikaner church, held this view until the 1980s. To protect their social, economic and political privileges, they introduced apartheid with a view to maintaining the total separation of races – physically, socially, economically and politically. As an analyst has observed: 'Without a privileged position a "pure" and separate white race could not survive; without a "pure" and separate white race a privileged position could not be maintained'.[8]

South Africa's regional policy, and especially its eagerness to assert its role as a regional great power, is partly a reflection of the Afrikaners' excessive concern for their security and the fear of losing privileges. South Africa has often acted aggressively towards its neighbours, in attempts to discourage them from threatening white privileges. The Afrikaner ambition to control blacks extends beyond South Africa's borders.

Pretoria's policy in southern Africa has vacillated over the years, depending on several factors: the inclination or personal characteristics of the prime minister or state president; the level of domestic political support for the government and the intensity of internal resistance by non-whites; the strengths or weaknesses of regional anti-apartheid forces; and the nature of the international political climate. J. B. Vorster, who was prime minister from 1966 to 1978, occasionally preferred quiet and subtle diplomacy within the region. During much of the Vorster era, South Africa's main regional objective was to establish a working relationship in which neighbouring states would tolerate apartheid in return for economic aid.[9]

Vorster's successor, P. W. Botha, who ruled between 1978 and 1989 after having served as defence minister for 14 years, often applied military power to try to cow South Africa's neighbours into submission.[10] He also centralised state power and initiated a rapid militarisation of society and the emergence of a military-bureaucratic régime. One of the key institutions established in the new centralised system is the State Security Council, through which the South African Defence Force (SADF) and other security agencies have increased their influence on the decision-making process. The SADF has a preponderance in the SSC through the inclusion of military personnel as primary or coopted members, through the military's control of the SSC secretariat, and through the control which the Directorate of Military Intelligence exercises over the SSC's 'total strategy branch'.[11]

Under Vorster, the government had been reluctant to accede to some of the demands of the military. Vorster, a former police minister, took advice mostly from the Bureau of State Security (BOSS) rather than from the military. This situation was reversed under Botha, who proceeded to appoint the chief of the defence force, General Magnus Malan, defence minister. Botha moved with his military advisers to the prime minister's office, and in the following decade their influence on government decisions was substantial. It was the military chiefs who helped to plan Botha's rationalisation and concentration of power and reorganisation of decision-making [12] He readily embraced the military doctrine of 'total strategy', which included plans to invade neighbouring states. It was also Botha who put forward the proposal for a 'constellation of southern African states' in the late 1970s, with a view to establishing a regional economic grouping controlled by Pretoria.

Botha's successor, F. W. de Klerk, appears more inclined to use diplomatic means to settle differences with opponents both within and outside the country. It is reasonable to argue that Vorster, Botha and de Klerk took different approaches to regional domination partly because of their personal inclinations, but their policies have also to be understood against the background of the nature of domestic forces. Among the domestic forces, the increased activities of anti-apartheid groups compelled many foreign companies to close down their businesses. The Dutch Reformed Church, for many years the main moral force behind apartheid, withdrew its support for apartheid in the 1980s, partly as a result of pressure from the mother-church in Holland. These factors, in conjunction with the regional anti-apartheid forces and the changing international climate, had recognisable effects on Botha's and de Klerk's policies.

Regional Political and Military Objectives

The primary objective of the Nationalist Party since it came to power in 1948 has been to maintain white rule in South Africa. In pursuit of that goal, the Sough African régime has utilised political, economic, diplomatic and military instrumentalities. South Africa's domestic and regional policies, and especially the role of the South African Defence Force, have been geared towards the buttressing of white rule. Central to South Africa's calculations in its dealings with neighbouring states was, until 1990, the desire to discourage or prevent them from hosting the ANC and the South West African People's Organisation (SWAPO) which was fighting for Namibia's independence. In other words, Pretoria tried to use all available means to protect white rule internally and to prolong its illegal occupation of Namibia.

South Africa has no regional challenger of comparable economic and military power, but the Frontline states, as a group, have presented a challenge by aiding liberation fighters. In turn, South Africa has persistently used its military power to coerce and punish them for providing sanctuary to ANC and SWAPO guerrillas, which they did until 1990. It has also recruited and helped rebel forces against these countries.[13] Angola, Botswana, Lesotho, Mozambique, Swaziland, Zambia and Zimbabwe – and the Indian Ocean islands of Seychelles, the Comoros and Mauritius – have all been punished or threatened by the South African military. In the majority of cases, South African military power has been deployed not to deter external aggression, but to *compel* neighbouring states to adopt policies considered desirable by Pretoria.

From the late 1970s to the late 1980s, coercive diplomacy became South Africa's main instrument of regional policy, and was used persistently against most southern African states, but especially against Angola and Mozambique, following their independence in 1975. The Angolan civil war of 1975–76 had led to a re-evaluation of South Africa's military doctrine and an unprecedented military build-up. As Zimbabwe achieved independence in 1980, one of the important links in South Africa's *cordon sanitaire* was removed, after which Pretoria was more determined than ever to use its military and economic muscle to defend apartheid.

From about 1980 until 1988, South Africa's regional policy was pugnacious and militaristic. By this time, the Botha régime had swept away the apparent subtle, behind-the-scenes diplomacy that had characterised previous dealings with African countries during the Vorster era. It launched a systematic policy of destabilisation and undertook raids into Angola, Botswana, Lesotho, Mozambique, Swaziland and Zimbabwe, aimed at alleged ANC bases. It also disrupted oil supplies and attacked railways providing import and export routes of these countries in attempts to cripple them economically.[14] At the same time, South African security agencies increased their support and encouragement to dissident movements in Angola, Lesotho, Mozambique and Zimbabwe. Its agents even tried to assassinate the prime ministers of Lesotho and Zimbabwe. Pretoria was determined to pursue a forward defence of the *status quo*, either by assisting dissident elements hostile to neighbouring régimes or by mounting direct incursions by regular or irregular units of the SADF and ancillary security forces.

South Africa's aims in these efforts were quite clear. First, it sought to weaken and, if possible, destroy the ANC and SWAPO. The weakening of SWAPO would have facilitated Pretoria's search for a new government in Namibia that would have posed no threat to its interests. Second, South Africa sought to intimidate and subvert the neighbouring states, thereby eroding their social order and morale. Third, it hoped to strengthen its military, political and economic hegemony over the region. In the midst of violent incursions, there were tentative overtures and gestures of conciliation. Pretoria's thrust was, however, uncompromising, and the black governments were made to bend.[15] But, the turning point in South Africa's military strategy came about in 1988, following a four-month engagement at Cuito Cuanavale in southern Angola, at which SADF and UNITA guerrillas were humiliated by the Angolan forces, supported by Cuban troops.[16]

It is difficult to pinpoint a specific decision taken by the South African government or agencies to destabilise states in the region. As one analyst has observed, it is 'hard to find any masterplan behind the many paradoxes and elements' of Pretoria's regional policy.[17] But a number of policy lines, some of them opportunistic and often clumsy, and their cumulative impact, point to a determination by the South African régime to destabilise neighbouring states. Although government rhetoric stressed peaceful coexistence, constellation and non-intervention as hallmarks of South African regional policy, actual policy included an extensive record of large-scale open and clandestine raids into neighbouring states, the effects of which were to heighten insecurities in those countries. At first sight, South Africa's incursions into nearby nations might appear to be unrelated *ad hoc* responses to diverse issues. But, in actual fact, they constitute a recognisable pattern of coercive hostility towards governments already inclined to be hostile to Pretoria.[18]

By taking firm action and developing a strong military potential, the SADF created what appeared like a successful strategy of intimidation. Without the SADF, coupled with persistent economic pressure, the negotiations that led to the cease-fires and to non-aggression pacts with neighbouring states could not have been initiated. Swaziland was pressured to conclude a non-aggression pact with South Africa in 1982, but it was not publicly known until 1984, following similar pacts with Angola and Mozambique. Eventually, what appeared like peace in southern Africa in the 1980s was not peace but a regional Pax Pretoriana based on strength and coercion, at least until Cuito Cuanavale showed the limits of SADF's prowess. South Africa had adopted a disruptive doctrine of pre-emptive intervention, which had previously been justified as the exercise of the traditional right of self-defence. Military raids were also rationalised as a form of counter-intervention, that is, intervention to redress a balance of force that has been disrupted by another country's outside intervention.

The doctrine of hot pursuit, well established in international law, has also occasionally been used by SADF. But, South Africa has been hard-pressed to adopt that line in most cases, since cross-border operations are hardly spontaneous hot pursuit. Instead, Pretoria, utilising a full array of resources available, including mobilisation up to a wartime level, has engaged in a form of anticipation defence. According to this political doctrine of pre-emptive intervention, the inherent right of self-defence justifies the use of pre-emptive intervention if a neighbouring government is hostile or is unwilling or unable to curb the activities of anti-apartheid forces.

While all southern African states have been threatened and subverted by South Africa, Angola has endured more pressure than any other country in the region. Angola had maintained friendly relations with South Africa as a Portuguese colony, but from the time it gained independence in 1975, relations between the two states became hostile. South Africa's Angola policy was hinged on three factors: Pretoria's support for UNITA (*União Nacional para a Independencia Total de Angola*) forces fighting a guerrilla war against the Luanda government; the presence, until 1989, of Cuban troops in Angola; and the presence in southern Angola, of SWAPO guerrillas fighting for Namibian independence. South Africa used these issues as a basis for intimidating the Angolan government and asserting its own role as a regional great power in the late 1970s and 1980s.

UNITA, which by the mid-1970s was strongly anti-Western and the most nativist, even racist, liberation movement in Angola, was fighting a losing battle for political supremacy against the better organised MPLA (*Movimento Popular de Libertacião de Angola*). It was formed in 1966 by a breakaway faction from the FNLA (*Frente Nacional de Libertacão de Angola*), and has since been headed by Jonas Savimbi; its main support has come from the Ovimbundu ethnic group, which comprises about 40 per cent of Angola's population. The MPLA, led by Agostinho Neto until his death in the late 1970s, was the most Westernised (but not pro-Western) of the Angolan liberation movements, with a European Marxist-Leninist ideology. Its greatest domestic support was among the educated, the *mulattos* and the Portuguese-speaking Angolans. The third group, the FNLA, led by Holden Roberto, received support from the United States and China. In the civil war that preceded Angola's independence in November 1975, the MPLA defeated the other two groups, took Luanda, the national capital, and formed a government that was recognised by the majority of independent African states and admitted to the Organisation of African Unity (OAU).[19]

In the meantime, South Africa had swung its support behind UNITA, prompting the MPLA to seek Soviet and Cuban help. From the late 1975, the MPLA increasingly looked towards the Eastern bloc for support to maintain its hold on power; Cuba despatched more than 10 000 troops to Angola. The FNLA disintegrated in the late 1970s, with some of its forces joining the MPLA government while others aligned themselves with UNITA. At the same time, UNITA increasingly looked to South Africa and the West for assistance to dislodge the MPLA from power.[20]

Although UNITA is not in any way more democratic than the MPLA, South Africa and some Western powers, including the UNited States during the Reagan era, portrayed it as a democratic force fighting a Marxist government.[21] By supporting UNITA, South Africa's main goal was to install a pliant régime in Angola. But, it also sought to use UNITA to destroy SWAPO guerrilla bases in southern Angola. The UNITA card became very useful to Pretoria, especially in the late 1970s and early 1980s as international pressure increased for South Africa to disengage from Namibia. If UNITA could be used to reduce the effectiveness of SWAPO, South Africa would transfer power to Namibia to a group more friendly to Pretoria. Accordingly, South Africa made strenuous efforts to circumvent the implementation of UN security Council Resolution 435 of 1978, setting forth procedures for Namibia's transition to independence.[22]

In the 1980s, South Africa combined dialogue and military force in its dealings with Angola. In the years 1980–87, SADF occupied extensive territory in southern Angola. Ostensibly, SADF acted against Angola to prevent SWAPO incursions southward and its defence of Namibia was perceived as a forward defence in depth. The SADF's occupation of southern Angola in the 1980s resembled Israel's occupation of southern Lebanon during the same period. It ensured that the first phase of negotiations between Angola and South Africa would centre on military disengagement. But, at every stage of negotiations, the three main issues – Cuban troops, UNITA and Namibia's independence – appeared linked. For instance, in February 1984, South Africa and Angola agreed to a disengagement pact in Lusaka, ostensibly brokered by the United States. A cease-fire to end the fighting in both Angola and Namibia was to be monitored by a Joint Monitoring Commission which consisted of five senior officers and three companies of soldiers from each side. South Africa agreed to a five-phase disengagement of its forces provided that neither Angola nor the SWAPO guerrillas took advantage of the withdrawal.

South Africa promptly carried out four of the five planned phases of disengagement before the 30 March 1984 deadline. But it halted at Ngiva, just 40 kilometres north of the Angola-Namibia border. According to Pretoria, SWAPO fighters were still crossing into Namibia, and the Angolans had not yet agreed to a joint policing of the border. Angola, on the other hand, argued that it could agree only if South Africa set a date for Namibian independence. In response, South Africa, with encouragement from the Reagan Administration, refused to make such a commitment until the Cubans left Angola. The Cuban troops in Angola thus provided a standing alibi, enabling Pretoria to vindicate its refusal to come to terms with the MPLA or with SWAPO or to abandon UNITA.

The apparent obstruction to a settlement in the early 1980s was the South African precondition that Cuban forces must be withdrawn from Angola before Namibia could gain independence. The complexity of the South African-Angolan problem was that threats perceived by various parties kept reinforcing each other. Angola had invited the Cubans because of its perceived threat from South Africa; Pretoria, with support from Washington, insisted that the Cuban military presence was a threat to regional security and started to put greater pressure on Luanda. Angola also felt especially vulnerable to combined SADF-UNITA attacks and insisted that South Africa must first end its assistance to UNITA, before the Cubans would be allowed to go. The linking of the date for Namibia's independence to the departure of Cuban troops, was one extra card in the Reagan Administration's crusade against what it portrayed as Soviet aggression and expansionism. But, the departure of Cuban troops was, in turn, dependent on the termination of South African support for UNITA.

Using Lusaka and the Cape Verde Islands as venues for negotiation, South Africa tried to arrange a Namibian settlement that would assure a role for its government alternative, the so-called Multi-Party Conference (MPC), which included diverse groups. But, in due course, the MPC lost standing as key member organisations drifted out of the MPC and towards SWAPO. The South Africans were left with no viable black conservative group to head an independent Namibia. The stalemate in negotiations for Namibia's independence was partly sustained by the fact that SWAPO, the South African and Angolan governments, UNITA, and local Namibian parties insisted on roles beyond their political-military means.[23]

The situation, however, changed dramatically from 1987. In the fierce fighting of August 1987 to May 1988, the SADF used more than 4000 regular troops, in addition to more than 30 000 UNITA units and 2000 troops from the Southwest African Territorial Force. But it still lost the battle at Cuito Cuanavale. By this time also, the white electorate was already seriously questioning the cost of the war both in human and financial terms. Most of them did not see why their sons should be killed in Angola. They also saw Namibia as a lost cause.[24]

After the SADF's defeat at Cuito Cuanavale, Pretoria sought the way out of Angola, and was more willing to negotiate a Namibian settlement. Following the December 1988 agreements between Angola, Cuba and South Africa in New York, two of the major issues were resolved: Cuba agreed to withdraw its troops from Angola, and South Africa opened the way for Namibia's independence. These measures immediately undercut South Africa's reasons for undermining Angola, as Namibia moved to independence under a SWAPO government in March 1990. These developments have led to a reorganisation of SADF to ease President de Klerk's attempt to address the country's economic problems. But South Africa's relations with Angola remained uneasy because of the UNITA factor.

Another nation in southern Africa which has been subverted persistently by Pretoria is Mozambique. Not only has the SADF carried out commando raids at alleged ANC offices in Maputo, the Mozambican capital, but far more damaging has been South Africa's sponsorship of the MNR (*Resistencia Nacional Mocambican*, sometimes called Renamo). The MNR was established by Rhodesian intelligence agencies in the mid-1970s to try to destabilise Mozambique in retaliation for its support for Zimbabwean liberation fighters. When Rhodesia/Zimbabwe gained independence in 1980, the South African intelligence took over the sponsorship of MNR. South Africa has provided the MNR with sanctuary, arms, supplies, training and logistical support. The Mozambican economy, especially food distribution, has been disrupted, and sabotage and war have been widespread. As a result, Mozambique's government − controlled by the former guerrilla movement Frelimo (*Frente de Liberta cão de Mocambique*) − came perilously close to collapse in the early 1980s. In Mozambique, as elsewhere in the region, South Africa's military action created economic havoc which, in turn, tended to foster disaffection with the existing régimes.

Regional Economic Ambitions

South Africa's ambition has been to dominate Southern Africa politically, militarily and economically. Whether economic domination or survival of white rule has been the *primary* objective is open to debate. There is, however, no doubt that Pretoria has encouraged a variety of regional cooperation schemes to advance its own economic growth, stratus and security. The initiative for a constellation of southern African states in the late 1970s was designed to formalise South Africa's economic domination of the region. The constellation idea never got off the ground as Zimbabwe achieved independence and the regional states launched the Southern African Development Coordination Conference (SADDC) in 1980. Through the 'constellation', Pretoria had hoped to secure a measure of acceptance in Africa and in the West, reduce economic pressures from abroad, permit South African industries to enlarge their fields of activity, and enmesh neighbouring countries in an economic web too profitable and too complex to risk endangering through political adventures against apartheid.

Nevertheless, the South African-controlled set of relations within the region includes trade, capital, labour, energy, water and several forms of communications. South Africa dominates the economies of Botswana, Lesotho, Swaziland. It is also the main trading partner for Malawi and Zimbabwe, and Zambia's main source of imports.[25] During the colonial period, the British treated South Africa as the centre of the periphery and concentrated most of the development there. Other states in the area, especially Botswana, Lesotho and Swaziland, were neglected and treated as labour reserves for South Africa. They naturally became dependent on South Africa's industries, mines and other physical infrastructures, and it is not, therefore, surprising that these states are more economically dependent on South Africa than their larger neighbours. They continue to send large numbers of migrant workers to South Africa, and depend heavily on South African ports and railways for access to the outside world. In fact, Lesotho is an enclave within South Africa and relies entirely on Pretoria's goodwill for access to the outside world.

The three states also belong to an important regional grouping which South Africa has continued to influence, namely the Southern African Customs Union (SACU). The Customs Union was established before Botswana, Lesotho and Swaziland achieved independence in the 1960s and was based on a common colonial experience. South Africa had found the markets in these countries so crucial for its own development that it sought to incorporate them in the early 1960s, but it failed. The Customs Union has now evolved to reflect the imperatives of independence, its terms having been renegotiated several times since the 1960s. But it has also served to reinforce inequalities between South Africa and the other three countries. Their attempts to break from the South African economic web have not been successful, a situation that has meant that their industrial development is significantly contrained by the dominance of South Africa. Although Botswana, Lesotho and Swaziland have their own currencies, the South African rand is the dominant form of exchange within the SACU.

Zimbabwe, the second richest of southern African states, is not a member of SACU, but its economy and transport system are closely linked to those of SACU members. A land-locked country, Zimbabwe has relied on South Africa's transport system for its trade, and in recent years Pretoria has frequently tried to put pressure on it through these links. From the mid-1960s to the late 1970s, when international economic sanctions were imposed on Rhodesia/Zimbabwe following the unilateral declaration of independence (UDI) by Ian Smith in 1965, South Africa became Rhodesia's main trading partner. Under a special agreement, Rhodesia was allowed access to South Africa's protected market at reduced duties. After Zimbabwe achieved formal independence under Prime Minister Robert Mugabe in 1980, it refused to have formal diplomatic and ministerial contacts with South Africa.[26] That was when South Africa moved against Zimbabwe's economy, manipulating the special links the two states had established during the UDI period. It cut back on trade, disrupted the transport network and withdrew some migrant labour concessions.[27] South Africa used economic pressure to try to obtain Zimbabwe's recognition of the apartheid government.

One clear case where South Africa used its economic muscle to realise some of its strategic goals was the non-aggression pact with Mozambique, signed at the border town of Nkomati on 16 March 1984. The two implacable foes agreed not to attack one another and to halt their aid to the dissident groups that each harboured against the other, but it is quite clear that Mozambique did so because of economic need and after considerable arm-twisting by South Africa.

Until 1974, Mozambique, then a Portuguese colony, was on very friendly terms with South Africa. The two countries started to part company following the April 1974 coup in Portugal and the subsequent decision by the new government to grant Mozambique and other Portuguese colonies independence. Mozambique moved to independence in 1975 under a Frelimo government, and that caused concern to South Africa in three ways: first, a neighbouring state, which had for long served as a buffer against radical independent states, was coming under a Marxist government; second, there was a possibility that the ANC, which had had good relations with Frelimo in exile, would be permitted to establish bases in southern Mozambique; and third, there was a fear that the Soviet Union, which had assisted Frelimo in the struggle for independence, would acquire significant influence in southern Africa. Pretoria's response was to put economic pressure on the Maputo government. After all, Mozambique was bound by geography, history and transport infrastructure to South Africa; in addition, its economy was dependent on services provided to South Africa and Rhodesia/Zimbabwe, and if these countries chose not to use Mozambique's ports, railways and labour, the Frelimo government would suffer.

At about the same time, some Portuguese businessmen who had relocated to South Africa, and some Rhodesian intelligence agencies, founded and nurtured the MNR to try to destabilise the government of then President Samora Machel. Although some South African intelligence agents were peripherally involved in the scheme, it was not supported by the Vorster régime. The hands-off policy by Pretoria changed after Zimbabwe attained independence in 1980, by which time Botha was the South African prime minister. By that time also, the international political climate had changed dramatically, especially following the Soviet intervention in Afghanistan.

During this period, Mozambique faced numerous natural and man-made disasters. Poor economic planning and management, compounded by a widespread and long-lasting drought, floods and cyclones had taken a heavy toll on the popularity of the Frelimo government. The country was also suffering a chronic shortage of skilled personnel and a drop in world prices for its agricultural exports. On the other hand, MNR forces, unorganised and devoid of any ideology, had been able to thwart relief efforts outside Maputo. The civil war, combined with South African economic pressure, severely damaged Mozambique's economy in the 1980s. In the light of these problems, Frelimo leaders realised that the costs of maintaining order in the face of economic misery, internal unrest and external threat were beyond their immediate means.

Mozambique approached various countries – including in the early 1980s Western European countries – for aid but with little success. Eventually the United States agreed to provide limited economic support on condition that it reduced ties with the Soviet bloc and mended fences with South Africa. For these reasons, the vulnerable Maputo government approached Pretoria at least three times before the final phase of negotiations leading to Nkomati. South Africa did not reduce its pressure until it was absolutely certain that Maputo was prepared to end ANC activities in its territory. Even after signing the Nkomati agreement, there was circumstantial evidence that Pretoria had not severed its aid to the MNR. According to the agreement, Mozambique was required to prevent the ANC from using its territory for attacks against South Africa, and likewise Pretoria agreed to withdraw its covert support for the MNR.

Although Mozambique publicly stated that it believed that the South African government was determined to make the accord successful, it was not satisfied with Nkomati's security benefits, and Pretoria's clandestine support for the MNR continued to be a source of friction between the two states. Economic activity was, however, vigorous, and Mozambique was interested in a range of benefits. These included the revival of trade, renewed use of Maputo's port, increased sales of hydro-electric power from the Cabora Bassa dam to South Africa and the revival of South African tourism. Mozambique also hoped for developmental and budgetary aid. Accordingly, a series of economic agreements were reached in late March 1984, in which South Africa consented to pay higher charges for electricity from Mozambique's Cabora Bassa dam and to pay Mozambique for access to the power. South Africa also took active measures to help

Mozambique with the faltering railways and harbours infrastructure, and to supply drought and, ironically, flood relief. Pretoria also launched programmes to relink South African private enterprise with opportunities in Mozambique. Talks were also opened between Botswana, Mozambique, South Africa and Zimbabwe about building a storage dam on the Limpopo river. Other economic and technical assistance flowed from South Africa to Mozambique. But the MNR would not go away.[28]

The civil war in Mozambique continued throughout the decade, but by the late 1980s, a delicate process of internal reconciliation was under way, backed by Kenya, South Africa, the UK, the USA, the USSR and Zimbabwe. Indeed, by early 1990, MNR activities had declined.

The picture which has emerged so far is that South Africa has used virtually all resources available to it – military, diplomatic and economic – to try to consolidate its hegemony over southern Africa. It has subverted some nearby states, dislocated their economies and engaged some of them militarily, but it has not defeated them. The restraints on Pretoria's regional policy have been internal, regional and global.

EXTERNAL CONSTRAINTS

External constraints on South Africa have often emanated from the moral outrage against apartheid, which has been condemned by the world community as a crime against humanity. For more than a generation, a large section of the international community has regarded South Africa as a pariah state and some international organisations have taken active measures to try to isolate it. It was forced out of the British Commonwealth in 1961, and has since then regularly been criticised by the Commonwealth heads of government meetings. The Commonwealth has taken more measures against South Africa than any other international organisation, apart from the United Nations.[29] This is perhaps because, as a former British dominion like Australia, Canada and New Zealand, South Africa has historically had close links with the Commonwealth. The Non-Aligned Movement has also persistently condemned apartheid since the 1960s.[30]

By far the most concerted international efforts against South Africa have been made at the United Nations, where most African and Third World states have tried to isolate Pretoria diplomatically. The United Nations General Assembly has passed numerous resolutions designed to punish South Africa until apartheid has been dismantled. The UN imposed an arms embargo in 1963 and made it mandatory in 1977; it also imposed economic sanctions in the 1980s. Most of these sanctions have not been effective, largely because of the willingness of some Western powers, together with Israel, Japan and Taiwan to circumvent them. Moreover, South Africa's destabilisation policies, especially its persistent attacks on Angola's and Mozambique's transport systems, have made it impossible for the independent African states in the southern African region to have alternative routes to the outside world. As a result, they have become so dependent on South Africa that for them to cut links with Pretoria would be committing economic suicide.

The sanctions and other international measures have had the effect of constraining South Africa's regional adventures, but they have also aided its great-power ambitions by compelling it to develop an advanced industrial infrastructure. South Africa virtually neutralised the effects of the arms embargo by buying arms on the black market and by developing its own arms industry through ARMSCOR. In these efforts, South Africa is said to have received crucial support from Israel – another country that has persistently ignored UN resolutions.

The establishment of an indigenous arms industry has had two unanticipated consequences. First, South Africa has been able to manufacture small arms well-suited to low-intensity conflict. These arms have found a ready market in Angola and Mozambique, and as far north as Somalia. Second, South Africa has surreptitiously acquired nuclear weapons technology and is said to have tested a nuclear device in 1977. It is believed official Israeli and private West Germany interests gave assistance to Pretoria in its search for a nuclear capability.[31] A nuclear weapons capability by South Africa would have repercussions far beyond its immediate region, and has also been of some concern to the superpowers.

The Great Powers

South Africa's relations with the great powers have been influenced by a range of factors, including apartheid, South Africa's regional policy and the international political climate. Western powers, including the United States, have occasionally protested against apartheid, but at the same time they have been quite willing to do business with the Pretoria régime. The South African régime has often tried to portray itself as a bulwark against Communism, and while it pursued regional goals which advanced the Western cause of anti-Communism, Western powers occasionally felt, especially in the 1980s, that close identification with Pretoria might hurt their wider ambitions. In its efforts to strengthen ties with the UK, the US and other Western powers, the South African régime until 1990 portrayed its opponents, especially the liberation movements, as Communist surrogates in an effort to exploit East-West relations to its advantage. South Africa's relations with the Soviet Union and other Communist powers have, in general terms, been cool. This is because the Communist powers endorsed the armed struggle against apartheid and provided arms to some of the victims of Pretoria's aggression.

US relations with South Africa have vacillated over the years, depending on a particular administration's preference. Under the Carter Administration between 1977 and 1981, US policy towards southern Africa and indeed, much of the Third World, was torn between, on the one hand, the 'regionalists' represented by the Secretary of State Cyrus Vance and the ambassador to the United Nations Andrew Young, and, on the other hand, the 'globalists', represented by the National Security Advisor Zbigniew Brzezinski. Regionalists, who occasionally prevailed on President Carter, argued that southern African problems should be seen in the regional context rather than in the East-West dimension. Brzezinski, on the other hand, felt that the US should 'not ignore the Soviet-Cuban military presence in Africa to the point that the conservative whites in South Africa would be fearful of accepting any compromise solution'.[32]

The debate between regionalists and globalists subsided, however, following the Soviet intervention in Afghanistan in 1979 and the emergence of the 'second Cold War' between the superpowers. But on southern Africa, regionalists prevailed during the entire Carter period. However, despite President Carter's rhetorical disapproval of apartheid, his administration maintained the economic links that were vital to the white minority régime's survival, doing virtually nothing to discourage investment in the country.[33] Moreover, in 1978, the Carter Administration used its veto power to defeat a UN Security Council resolution proposing mandatory economic sanctions against South Africa.

The Reagan Administration, on the other hand, was more inclined to see the situation in southern Africa in East-West terms. Alexander Haig, Reagan's first Secretary of State, indicated early in 1981 that there would be less pressure on South Africa, especially over Namibia. Reagan's Assistant Secretary of State for African Affairs, Chester Crocker, the architect of the policy of 'constructive engagement', argued that the US policy was to build a more constructive relationship with South Africa, one based on shared interests, persuasion and improved communication. It was, indeed, the Reagan Administration which initially proposed linkage between Namibian independence and the withdrawal of Cuban troops from Angola.

Instead of championing human rights, as the Carter Administration had done, the Reagan Administration stressed the need to meet the Soviet threat in southern Africa and the West's stake in the South African economy, because of its possession of strategic raw materials. Although the Reagan Administration did not completely abandon the demands for change in South Africa, its policies had the effect of easing pressure on Pretoria. But, the increasing strength of the anti-apartheid lobby in the US, coupled with the large outflow of capital from South Africa by corporations which felt it was no longer safe to do business in the country, persuaded Congress to pass various legislations imposing economic sanctions against Pretoria.

European powers, especially the UK, Germany and France, have also sought to change the South African system through dialogue. Although they did not approve of apartheid, they did not want to isolate South Africa, largely because of their huge financial investments in the country. Aware of Soviet interests in the region in the 1970s and 1980s, these countries sought to exert pressure on the South African government to reform through dialogue. They felt that as long as apartheid existed, Moscow would exploit it to its own advantage. The anti-apartheid movement in Europe eventually caused the European Community to impose economic sanctions on South Africa in the mid-1980s.

Western countries were also concerned with progress on Namibia's independence, and they formed the 'Contact Group' consisting of France, West Germany, the United Kingdom, Canada and the United States in 1977. The main objective of the Group was to negotiate the terms for Namibia's independence. The Contact Group's cohesion suffered in the early 1980s when, against opposition from other members, the US went ahead with linkage between Namibian independence and the withdrawal of Cuban troops from Angola. The accords that expedited progress towards Namibia's independence were concluded in New York in December 1988, capping 11 years of Western diplomatic pressure. However, the battle of Cuito Cuanavale and the disillusionment of the white electorate with the war were also important in determining South Africa's withdrawal from Namibia.

The Soviet Union and its allies, on the other hand, were more inclined to support the liberation fighters, who advocated the armed struggle internally and the isolation of South Africa externally. The Soviet Union did not have a strong interest in southern Africa until the Angolan civil war of 1975, when Moscow gave its support to the MPLA. The MPLA's challengers, UNITA and the FNLA were supported by South Africa and China, respectively. The USSR had provided modest assistance to the MPLA since the early 1960s, but that aid was insubstantial until 1975, when the Soviets airlifted and transported thousands of Cuban troops and tons of heavy weapons to Angola.[34]

To the extent that massive Soviet support for the MPLA was prompted by South Africa's involvement in the Angolan civil war, the Soviet military presence served as a constraint on South Africa's regional ambitions. Following several South African incursions into southern Angola in the early 1980s, Angolan, Cuban and Soviet representatives met in Moscow in January 1984, after which the Soviet Union announced a new military agreement with Angola. During the next eighteen months, Moscow supplied Angola with large quantities of arms, including T-62 tanks, Mi-24 assault helicopters and advanced surface-to-air missiles. The Soviet and Cuban presence in Angola lasted until the late 1980s.

Under Gorbachev, Soviet policy towards South Africa and its neighbours changed drastically. The Soviet Union, facing serious domestic political and economic problems, started to withdraw from Third World conflict areas, including southern Africa. The withdrawal of the Soviet presence had several implications. First, it removed the rationale for South Africa to claim that the enemies of apartheid were Communist surrogates; this meant that Pretoria had to look for a different rhetoric to uphold its policy of destabilisation. Second, it terminated support for liberation movements in South Africa, and more importantly, for the Angolan government, thereby exposing it to greater pressure from South Africa and the Western/South African-funded UNITA. Finally, the withdrawal of the Soviet presence left Western powers, especially the United States, as the main external determinant of developments in southern Africa.

Up to the late 1980s, the Soviet military presence in southern Africa served as an important constraint on South Africa's regional ambitions, especially by arming Angola and Mozambique and other forces in the region. Western powers also occasionally protested against South Africa's incursions into neighbouring territories, but they did not provide anti-apartheid forces with arms. Their constraint on South Africa's regional military adventures was much more subtle, and often came in the form of threats to reduce the level of mutual co-operation. The third group of states that served as a constraint on Pretoria were African, most of them being victims of South African aggression.

Pan-Africanist Pressure

Pan-Africanism, as a movement, was concerned with the dignity and freedom of the African. It also aimed at achieving continental unity for the independent African states. The Organisation of African Unity (OAU), formed in 1963, was designed to forge unity on the African continent and help liberate the remaining parts of Africa.[37] African leaders, especially the late President of Ghana, Kwame Nkrumah, and former Tanzanian leader Julius Nyerere, argued in the 1960s that the independence of individual African states was meaningless until the whole continent was liberated.[38] Through the OAU, African states have sought to put pressure on the South African régime to give the majority black population its full political rights. They have used two forms of pressure. First, they have excluded South Africa from the OAU and tried to isolate it diplomatically. Malawi was the only African state with full diplomatic relations with South Africa by early 1991. Second, the OAU Liberation Committee also organised various forms of assistance for the liberation movements and some member countries, especially the Frontline states, provided them with sanctuary. The Frontline states have consistently tried to put political pressure on Pretoria since the 1960s. Their support for the ANC and SWAPO was a constant worry to Pretoria, but they were too weak to threaten it either militarily or economically.

Some states have sought to check South Africa's economic might through the Southern African Development and Coordination Conference (SADCC) which includes Angola, Botswana, Lesotho, Malawi, Mozambique, Swaziland, Tanzania, Zambia and Zimbabwe. SADCC was formed in April 1980 primarily to coordinate the economic policies of the member countries with a view to reducing ties with South Africa. Besides that goal, SADCC also aims to achieve collective self-reliance and to create operational and equitable regional integration. To realise these objectives, it has sought to mobilise domestic and regional resources to carry out national, interstate, and regional policies to reduce dependence. It is a voluntary association of roughly equal entities. Botswana and Zimbabwe have much healthier economies than the other states; their economic potential is thus a key asset to the organisation.

Broadly shared political and economic goals are the basis of cooperation within SADCC. The organisation's annual consultative meetings in the first ten years have been occupied with debates on how, and to what extent, SADCC countries can move towards economic independence from South Africa. SADCC believes that even if South Africa were majority-ruled, its members would still need to diversify their trading and transport links to gain greater independence from the region's economic giant.[39]

Although SADCC has sponsored various transportation, communications, mining and agricultural projects, it faces major problems. Its member countries share broad political goals, but they also profess diverse economic philosophies and policies towards trade, the private sector and foreign investment. There has also been hesitation on the part of its members to facilitate intra-SADCC commerce and remove trade barriers. In the light of these difficulties, SADCC has not been a big hindrance to South Africa's regional economic ambitions. Extra constraints on Pretoria have come from the wider international system.

The International Political Climate

The general international political climate has also influenced South Africa's regional policy substantially. In periods of improved US-Soviet relations, South Africa has often pursued cautious policies within the region. In times of great hostilities between the superpowers, on the other hand, the South African government has had virtually a free hand to pursue its regional political and military agenda. It is, however, too simplistic to attribute vacillations in South Africa's regional policy to the international political climate alone. As mentioned above, other factors within South Africa, and the wider southern African region, have also played a role.

During the early 1970s, when the superpowers improved their mutual relations, Pretoria launched a diplomatic blitzkrieg aimed at establishing détente with African states, but it had very limited and short-lived success. Prime Minister Vorster held secret meetings with Presidents Leopold Senghor of Senegal and Felix Houphoet Boigny of Ivory Coast in September 1974; he also met President William Tubman of Liberia in February 1975. Later that year, Vorster had a highly-publicised meeting with President Kenneth Kaunda of Zambia, and the two discussed joint efforts to end the Rhodesian/Zimbabwean war. The independence of Angola and Mozambique in 1975, however, removed two important portions of a buffer between South Africa and independent African states, and signalled a change in South Africa's regional policy. Indeed, by the end of 1975, Pretoria had found itself once again isolated in the region, following its intervention in the Angolan civil war, but because of its anti-Communist stance it still remained close to American interests.

By the late 1970s, the international political climate had changed again. Washington had abandoned the policy of détente, blaming its demise on Soviet activism in Third World conflict areas, including Angola in 1975, the Horn of Africa in 1977–78, and Afghanistan in 1979. The two superpowers were once again moving towards a new Cold War. Meanwhile, P. W. Botha, who had become prime minister, was inclined to use military force to assert South Africa's regional role. Following the inauguration of the Reagan Administration in 1981, Washington exercised virtually no constraints on South Africa in its regional activities, especially when it invoked the Communist threat. During this period, South Africa took advantage of the new Cold War to advance its regional objectives.

South Africa also exploited the willingness of Western nations in the 1980s to engage in dialogue. After coercing neighbouring states in the early 1980s, South Africa went out to sell its 'reign of peace' abroad. In May and June 1984, shortly after the Nkomati Accord, Prime Minister Botha embarked on a much-publicised tour of Europe, visiting Portugal, the United Kingdom, West Germany, Italy, the Vatican, Belgium, Switzerland and France, the first official overseas tour taken by a South African prime minister in over two decades. He tried, though unsuccessfully, to deflect threatened sanctions and international isolation by portraying South Africa as a broker of regional peace and not an ostracised pariah. The tour, however, convinced Botha that he needed substantial progress in political reform if sanctions were to be avoided, and a year later in August 1985, he announced more reforms.

Botha and SADF were not, however, willing to give Namibia independence. They were obviously still searching for a way to circumvent the UN Security Council resolution 435, which was passed on 29 September 1978, the day after Botha became prime minister. His predecessor, Vorster, had agreed to the terms of the settlement proposals, but Botha, as defence minister, had vehemently opposed the whole scheme, because he felt UN-supervised elections were a prelude to a victory by SWAPO. But, as it was stated above, by the late 1980s, South Africa felt it needed a settlement. The war with SWAPO and Angolan forces was very expensive for Pretoria, economically and politically.

With the independence of Namibia and the release of Nelson Mandela in 1990, F. W. de Klerk felt he had done enough to signal his determination to change the political complexion of South Africa. He toured several European countries and the US in 1990, pleading for the lifting of economic sanctions. The international community has, however, been cautious, giving approbation where necessary, but persistently urging more reform.

The improvement in US-Soviet relations since the late 1980s, the momentous events that swept away Communist régimes in Central Europe in 1989, and the continuing doubts about the efficacy of Communism in the Soviet Union, have also indirectly affected the regional balance in southern Africa. The South African régime can no longer plausibly portray its opponents as Communists surrogates. Moreover, Western powers now urge rapid political reform in the Third World and want South Africa to liberalise its political system.

CONCLUSIONS

South Africa's performance as a regional great power has been characterised by its economic and military domination of southern Africa. It has dominated the economies of Botswana, Lesotho and Swaziland for several decades. It has also served as the main trading partner of Malawi, Zambia and Zimbabwe for many years. In addition, South Africa dominates the transport systems of virtually all countries in the region. Whenever these states have sought alternative routes, South Africa has used its military and other security agencies to sabotage them. These activities have been an integral part of South Africa's regional preponderance over a long period of time.

Central to South Africa's vigorous diplomatic activity in the late 1980s and early 1990s, both in the region and worldwide, has been a desire to project an image of a flexible government on the move. It has sought to portray the image of a reformist state determined to dismantle the archaic apartheid system on the one hand, and a state striving to live at peace with its neighbours on the other. The reality is, however, quite different.

The ruling Nationalist Party has since the late 1980s argued that it would like to implement a multi-racial system in South Africa gradually, but its view of multi-racialism involves the entrenchment of group rights, which most black leaders have rejected. After many years of oppression and exploitation, South Africa's non-white population appears impatient with the pace of reform, hence the continued violence. Moreover, the widespread boycott of the 'coloured' and Indian parliamentary elections since the mid-1980s has signalled dissatisfaction with the new constitutional arrangements, which President de Klerk planned to change by mid-1991. Since the early 1980s, nationwide unrest – transport and consumer boycotts, rent strikes, labour dissatisfaction, school strikes and boycotts, protests, and extensive violence – has posed a direct challenge to the reform process started by Botha and continued by de Klerk. One of the problems arising from the reform process has been the lack of a nationally acceptable leader in the country.

The tendency towards anarchy within South Africa has been a constraint on Pretoria's regional supremacy. A South Africa that is ungovernable cannot exert influence abroad for long. The unbanning of the ANC and other political groupings has also removed the pretext for South Africa to send forays into neighbouring states. But that has not heralded an end to Pax Pretoriana. The MNR, originally created by Rhodesian intelligence and later handed over to South Africa, has refused to abide by Pretoria's dictates. It continues to receive funding from Portuguese business interests in South

Africa and Portugal, and from some South African security agents without official approval. The UNITA factor has also prevented peace in Angola. Although South Africa might argue that UNITA receives assistance from some Western governments, it is generally believed that without South Africa's active support, UNITA would not have remained a potent force.

As the richest and militarily the strongest state in southern Africa, South Africa still dominates the region, and the political significance of its economic power has grown as Western countries have increasingly shifted their attention to Eastern Europe.

NOTES

The author acknowledges useful comments on earlier drafts of this chapter from Arne Tostensen of the Christian Michelsen Institute, Bergen, Norway; Rick DeAngelis of Flinders University, South Africa; and Pia Broderick, Hugh Collins and John de Reuk of Murdoch University, Perth, Australia. He alone is, however, responsible for the chapter's shortcomings.

1. J. P. Hayes, *Economic Effects of Sanctions on Southern Africa* (London: Gower, 1987).
2. Kenneth W. Grundy, *The Militarisation of South African Politics* (2nd edn; Oxford: Oxford University Press, 1988).
3. The apartheid system has been analysed in numerous studies. See, for instance, Robert W. Peterson (ed.) *South Africa and Apartheid* (New York, NY: Facts on File, 1971): T. D. Moody, *The Rise of Afrikanerdom* (Berkeley, CA: University of California Press, 1975).
4. E. N. Tjønneland, *Pax Pretoriana: The Fall of Apartheid and the Politics of Regional Destabilisation* (Uppsala: Scandinavian Institute of African Studies, 1989), p. 7.
5. For a summary discussion of reforms in South Africa in the late 1980s and 1990, see *Strategic Survey 1989–1990* (London: Brassey's International Institute for Strategic Studies, 1990), pp. 66–74.
6. For a good analysis of South Africa's relations with its neighbours, see Robert S. Jaster, *South Africa and its Neighbours: the Dynamics of Regional Conflict*, Adelphi Papers No. 209 (London: International Institute for Strategic Studies, 1986); Joseph Hanlon, *Beggar Your Neighbours: Apartheid Power in Southern Africa* (London: James Currey, 1986).
7. Namibia was colonised by Germany in the 1880s. Following the German defeat in the First World War, the territory was transfered to South Africa under a League of Nations mandate in 1920. After the Second World War, South Africa refused to turn over its defunct League mandate to the League's successor, the United Nations, and instead proposed

to incorporate Namibia. That was the beginning of the long struggle between South Africa and the UN over Namibia, which ended only in 1990. In 1966, the UN General Assembly declared Pretoria's mandate over Namibia ended and established the UN Council for Namibia as an alternative government to run the territory *in absentia*. The UN Security Council in 1970 declared South Africa's occupation of Namibia illegal, because its application of apartheid to the territory violated the terms of its mandate. In 1978, the UN Security Council passed the now famous resolution 435 setting forth procedures for Namibia's independence. See, for instance, David Soggot, *Namibia: The Violent Heritage* (New York, NY: St. Martin's Press, 1986).

8. A statement by a certain Giliomee, cited in Stanley Uys, 'Whither the White Oligargy?', in Jesmond Blumenfeld (ed.), *South Africa in Crisis* (London: Croom Helm, 1987), pp. 56–76.
9. See Tjønneland, *Pax Pretoriana*, p. 16.
10. For a concise analysis of P. W. Botha's legacy to South Africa, see Brian Pottinger, 'The Botha Era: An End or Beginning?', *CSIS Africa Notes*, No. 104. (Washington, DC: Center for Strategic International Studies, African Studies Program), 30 October 1989.
11. Tjønneland, *Pax Pretorians*, p. 7.
12. See Tjønneland, *Pax Pretoriana*, p. 6.
13. See Jaster, *South Africa and its Neighbours*, especially Chapter 1.
14. See Hanlon, *Beggar Your Neighbours*, p. 1.
15. See, for instance, Kenneth W. Grundy, 'Pax Pretoriana: South Africa's Regional Policy', *Current History* LXXXIV (1985): 150–4.
16. See Robert S. Jaster, *The 1988 Peace Accords and the Future of Souith-western Africa*, Adelphi Papers No. 253 (London: International Institute for Strategic Studies, 1990), pp. 17–23.
17. Tjønneland, *Pax Pretoriana*, p. 16.
18. For a concise discussion of this problem, see John de St. Jorre, 'Destabilization and Dialogue: South Africa's Emergence as a Regional Superpower', *CSIS Africa Notes*, No. 26, 17 April 1984.
19. There is a lot of literature on the Angolan civil war in 1975–76. See, for instance, John A. Marcum, *The Angolan Revolution, Vol. 2: Exile Politics and Guerrilla Warfare (1962–1976)* (Cambridge, MA: MIT Press, 1978). See also the informative account of the disillusioned head of the CIA Angola Task Force, John Stockwell, *In Search of Enemies: A CIA Story* (London: Andre Deutsch, 1978).
20. For a very good discussion of these issues, see Raymond L. Garthoff, *Detente and Confrontation: American-Soviet Relations From Nixon to Reagan* (Washington, DC: The Brookings Institution, 1985), Chapter 15.
21. For a useful analysis of the Reagan Administration's policy towards Angola, see Michael McFaul, 'Rethinking the "Reagan Doctrine" in Angola', *International Security*, XIV (1989–90): 135.
22. For a useful discussion of some of these issues, see Sam C. Nolutshungu,

'Namibian Independence and Soviet-US Cooperation' in Anatoly A. Gromyko and C. S. Whitaker (eds), *Agenda for Action: African-Soviet-US Cooperation* (London: Lynne Rienner Publishers, 1990), pp. 243–50.

23. See, for instance, the Appendix in Jaster, *The 1988 Peace Accords and the Future of South-western Africa*, p. 72

24. For a very good analysis of these issues, see Jaster, *The 1988 Peace Accords and the Future of South-western Africa*, especially Chapters 1 and 2.

25. See Chris Pycroft, 'Changes in White South Africa', in Ben Turok (ed.), *Witness From the Frontline: Aggression and Resistance in Southern Africa* (London: Institute for African Alternatives, 1990), pp. 95–8.

26. See, Hanlon, *Beggar Your Neighbours*, p. 2.

27. For an account of Zimbabwe's move to independence, see Henry Wiseman and Alastair M. Taylor, *From Rhodesia to Zimbabwe: The Politics of Transition* (New York, NY: Pergamon, 1981).

28. For a perceptive analysis of these problems, see Hanlon, *Beggar Your Neighbours*, pp. 185–218.

29. See, for instance, Gillian Gunn, 'Post-Nkomati Mozambique', *CSIS Africa Notes*, No. 38, 8 January 1985.

30. For an example of the Commonwealth's criticism of South Africa, see the findings of the Commonwealth Eminent Persons Group on Southern Africa, *Mission to South Africa: The Commonwealth Report* (Harmondsworth: Penguin, 1986).

31. As an example, the Non-Aligned Movement's sixth conference in Havana in 1979 condemned South Africa's aggression against neighbouring states and the actions of Western powers which buttressed apartheid through their economic involvement in the country. See Peter Willetts, *The Non-Aligned in Havana* (London: Frances Pinter, 1981), pp. 87–97.

32. See Robert S. Jasper, 'Pretoria's Nuclear Diplomacy', *CSIS Africa Notes*, No. 88, 22 January 1988.

33. Zbigniew Brzezinski, *Power and Principle: Memoirs of the National Security Adviser 1977–1981* (New York, NY: Farrar, Straus, Giroux, 1983), pp. 139–40. For Vance's views on the issue, see Cyrus Vance, *Hard Choices: Critical Years in America's Foreign Policy* (New York, NY: Simon and Schuster, 1983), pp. 256–313.

34. See Hedley Bull, 'The West and South Africa', *Daedalus*, CXI (1982): 255–70.

35. See Kurt Campbell, 'Soviet Policy in Southern Africa: Angola and Mozambique' in Kurt M. Campbell and S. Neil MacFarlane (eds), *Gorbachev's Third World Dilemmas* (London: Routledge, 1989) Chapter 8.

36. For some analysis of the politics of the OAU, see, for instance, Zdenek Cervenka, *The Unfinished Quest for Unity: Africa and the OAU* (London: Africa Books, 1977); and Olajide Aluko, 'The OAU and Human Rights', *Round Table*, No. 283 (July 1981), pp. 234–42

37. See O. Agyeman, 'The Osagyefo, the Mwalimu and Pan-Africanism: A study in the growth of a dynamic concept', *Journal of Modern African Studies* XIII (1975): 653–75.

38. For a useful analysis of some of the problems and aspirations of SADCC, see C. D. R. Halisi, 'Cooperation for Southern African Development and Regional Security', in Gromyko and Whitaker, *Agenda for Action*, pp. 225–36.

8 Vietnam as a Regional Great Power: a Study in Failure

Stein Tønnesson

In the twentieth century, two attempts were made to build an Indochinese bloc as a springboard for regional power. Neither of them succeeded. The French conquest of the Viet, Khmer and Lao kingdoms from the mid-nineteenth century led to the establishment, in 1887, of French Indochina, a federal state led by a Governor General. By adding Tonkin and Laos to their established possessions, the French hoped to open the road for their capital to the promising markets of southern China, and also to use the whole of Indochina as a basis for the French claim to be an Asian power. The history of French Indochina lasted less than seventy years: mortally wounded during the Second World War, it perished in 1954, at Dien Bien Phu.

A group of Viet communists around Ho Chi Minh, who in 1945 – and again in 1954 – took over the French government in Hanoi – Indochina's capital – saw the anti-colonialist struggles of the Viet, Lao and Khmer as steps on the way to the creation of a powerful socialist bloc. With the withdrawal of the Vietnamese troops from Cambodia in 1989 and the dismantling of socialist institutions, it became clear that the attempt to establish an Indochinese socialist bloc had also failed.

This chapter examines the regional power potential of Indochina and explores the reasons for the failure of the two attempts. The focus will be on the pre-1945 and post-1975 periods, whereas the intermediate years, when Vietnam was split in two régimes, shall be ignored. As a consequence, the American interlude in Indochinese history (1961–73) shall also be left aside.

INTRODUCTION

Before the Second World War, it was normal to speak of the Indochinese peninsula as an entity including not only Vietnam, Laos and Cambodia, but Burma, Thailand and Malaya as well. Here we shall reserve the term

'Indochina' for the political entity created by the French, consisting of Cochinchina, Annam, Tonkin, Laos and Cambodia. The Indochina Union, led by French Governors General, existed from 1887 to 1954. The creation of the Indochinese state – with a federal government, army and police – curtailed the authority of the monarchs in Hue, Phnom Penh and Luang Prabang, and contradicted the ambitions of the nationalist movement emerging among the Viet élite after the Chinese Revolution of 1911. With a firm basis among the Viet, the predominant ethnic group in Indochina, Vietnamese nationalism aimed at the creation of a unified and independent nation-state on the territory of Tonkin, Annam and Cochinchina.[1]

The only indigenous political group that accepted Indochina as their political frame of reference, was the Indochinese Communist Party (ICP), formed in 1930 under the leadership of Ho Chi Minh. Ironically, this party was to realise the nationalist ambition of creating a Vietnamese nation-state. During the Japanese occupation (1941–45), the communists adopted the ambitions and rhetoric of the nationalist movement. The party as such nearly disappeared from public view; instead its cadre worked through a national liberation front, the *Viet Minh*, which in turn became the framework for the Democratic Republic of Vietnam, proclaimed on 2 September 1945. However, until the very moment of the proclamation, it remained uncertain whether the aim of the communists was an Indochinese federal state on the model of the Soviet Union, a Vietnamese nation-state throughout Indochina, or a Vietnamese nation-state limited to the territory of today's Vietnam (Tonkin, Annam, Cochinchina). The latter solution materialised, but this was the result not of a deliberate choice by the communist leadership, but of the particular circumstances of August 1945: with the sudden Japanese surrender, a power vacuum opened up, and revolts broke out. They brought Viet Minh activists to power in Tonkin, Annam and Cochinchina, but not in Cambodia and Laos.[2] In November 1945, the ICP was officially dissolved. When it reemerged six years later, it decided to form three national parties: the Vietnam Workers' Party, and independent parties for Cambodia and Laos.[3] The communists ceased to pronounce themselves as Indochinese and instead assumed the leadership of three separate national liberation movements.[4]

In 1954–55, when France pulled out of Indochina after having recognised independent states in Vietnam, Laos and Cambodia, the Indochinese Federation disappeared from the French as well as from the communist agenda as an explicit political project. Instead there were four states: North Vietnam, South Vietnam, Laos, and Cambodia. However, with the end of the Vietnam War in 1975, the 1976 unification of North and South Vietnam, and the establishment of socialist régimes in Laos and Cambodia, the prospect of an Indochina bloc resurfaced, this time as a vehicle for Vietnamese regional power.

At the end of the Vietnam War, there were around 55 million people in the three Indochinese countries taken together. In 1990 there were approximately 77 million; 7 in Cambodia, 4 in Laos and 66 million in Vietnam. On the map, the Vietnamese state, as it emerged from the August Revolution of 1945 and the 'national unification' of 1975–76, forms an S-shaped coastal strip at the southeastern corner of continental Asia. The Red River Delta in the north has an exceptionally fertile soil; a sophisticated system of dikes has for more than two thousand years allowed an extreme concentration of rice-cultivating villages. During the two last centuries, the southern part of the Mekong Delta has also been densely populated. From 21 million in 1945, the Vietnamese population grew to about 66 million in 1990. Ethnic Viet were traditionally confined to the lowland deltas, leaving the higher hinterland to a variety of ethnic minorities, some of which maintained a hostile attitude to the Delta population. Although the Viet were more profoundly influenced by Chinese Confucian culture than any other people in Southeast Asia, they maintained a separate identity also in relation to China. Geographically, this can be ascribed to the highlands barring the densely populated Tonkin Delta from the heavily populated regions of China; historically, to a long dynastic and bureaucratic tradition in Hanoi and Hue with preserved records of revolts against bad Chinese rulers; and, anthropologically, to local customs such as the cult of the family and village ancestors. Ancestral worship contributed to make Viet hamlets and villages some of the tightest and most stable social organisations in the world.

The Vietnamese nationalist movement emerged in the second decade of this century, but was severely suppressed by the French Indochina régime. In the 1930s, organised communism gained hegemony among the young generation of the Viet élite. As a modern nation, Vietnam was born in 1945. First, a nationalist imperial government installed by the Japanese unified the country, adopted the name 'Viet Nam', a flag and an anthem. Then, at the Japanese capitulation, the 'August Revolution' brought to power a generation of communists born in the first decade of the twentieth century. Their leader, Ho Chi Minh (1890/94–1969), was a little older than his collaborators: the virtuous mandarin Pham Van Dong (1906–), the cynical strategist Vo Nguyen Giap (1910–), the doctrinary ideologue Truong Chinh (1907–88) and the party apparatchiks Le Duc Tho (1910–90) and Le Duan (1908–86). They were the most influential among the tiny group of leaders who spent much of the 1920s and 1930s in jail or exile, emerged as national leaders in 1945 and remained in power until the late

1980s. They demonstrated a remarkable cohesion, due to the magic aura of 'Uncle Ho', one of the twentieth century's most gifted national leaders.[5]

The Region

In 1935, Robert Burnett Hall prudently defined 'the geographic region' as 'what a regional geographer studies'. Since there were as many concepts of the region as there were regional geographers, whatever haziness of thought might appear in his contribution was 'backed by abundant precedent'.[6] Towards the end of the Second World War, Indochina started to be considered as part of a region called 'Southeast Asia'. The concept originated in the 1943 set-up of the British South-East Asia Command (SEAC). Only a few years earlier, when R. B. Hall discussed the regional concept, westerners still commonly referred to Southeast and East Asia as the 'Far East'. Traditionally, there were little else than trade relations between Indochina and the islands that constitute the states of Indonesia, the Philippines, Malaysia and Singapore. Nor did these states pose any military threat to Indochina. This accounts both for the colonial and the post-colonial period, although the formation of the South-East Asian Treaty Organisation (SEATO) in 1955 and its more economically oriented successor ASEAN (Association of Southeast Asian Nations) from 1967, somewhat augmented the regional role of these recently decolonised states. It may make sense, when dealing with the 1970s and 1980s, to see the Indochinese and the ASEAN member states (Indonesia, Malaysia, the Philippines, Singapore, Thailand, Brunei from 1984) as two rival groupings competing for regional power. However, when discussing the regional performance of French Indochina and Vietnam, it is more fruitful to consider Thailand apart, and to draw China into the picture. These two states have always figured most prominently in the foreign policies of the governments in Hue and Hanoi. The importance of ASEAN increased considerably after the Vietnamese invasion of Cambodia in 1978. The threat perceived by Thailand, Malaysia and Singapore from the Indochinese bloc served as a catalyst for cooperation in ASEAN.[7] Indonesia was the strongest power in the group, but in the post–1975 rivalry between Vietnam and Thailand, Indonesia served almost as much as a mediator as a Thai ally. Still, when analysing Indochina's relations with the surrounding powers, it does not make sense to limit one's interest to ASEAN. Rather than an Indochina-ASEAN rivalry, we should analyse the posture of Vietnam in terms of a triangular Sino-Thai-Viet relationship, with Laos and Cambodia as small buffer states.

Each time China was united under a new expansionist régime or dynasty, it constituted a threat both to Vietnam (variously called Dai Nam, Dai Viet,

An Nam, and Nam Viet) and to Thailand (Siam). China was then able to play on the rivalry between Vietnam and Siam. In this rivalry, the several Lao principalities, the Khmer kingdoms (and formerly the kingdom of Champa) were buffer states. The establishment of French Indochina was a result of successful French campaigns against China and Siam, and the French state was maintained during a period when Siam and China were both weak. Thailand was allowed to survive as a buffer between the French and British empires in Asia. After the period of decolonisation, Thailand was first an important US ally in Southeast Asia and later a key member in ASEAN.

Vietnamese Power Potential

Relative to China with its population of 1.1 billion (1990), Vietnam remains a dwarf; Indonesia also had two and a half times as many inhabitants in 1990 as Vietnam (175 million as opposed to 66 million). Militarily, however, Vietnam represented a formidable opponent to any power in the region. Since 1975, Vietnam may in fact be said, on a regional level, to have satisfied the classic requirement of a great power that it should be able to defend itself against any coalition of rival powers. In the late 1970s, Vietnam maintained and expanded its army of between 1 and 1.4 million troops, commanded by an officer corps with almost unequalled fighting experience. It was not till 1989 that Vietnam started to reduce the size of the army. In the late 1980s, Indonesia and Thailand's armed forces were only one fourth the size of the Vietnamese (between 250 and 300 000 men). Malaysia had only a little more than 100 000. In all of these countries, the army was not a purely military organisation, but was also heavily involved in activities generally considered to be civilian. Vietnam, however, distinguished itself by having an army under strict party control. Conflicts between the army and civilian politicians were not as visible as in other Southeast Asian countries.[8]

A major problem for Vietnam, as for so many other Asian and African countries, was overpopulation. Despite the many lives lost in war, the Vietnamese population grew tremendously in the latter half of the twentieth century – in the 1980s by more than 2 per cent per year. The density of the population was extremely high: 176 per square kilometre in 1984, as opposed to 108 in China, 98 in Thailand, 40 in Malaysia, 39 in Cambodia, and 15 in Laos. For a state, a dense population is a double-edged sword. If there is enough territory, and the labour force is mobile, population growth can be an economic growth factor. If people are locked up in underfed city suburbs or villages, unwilling or unable to migrate, the density is instead a constraint. The density and poverty of the population in the Red River

Delta already constituted a dilemma for the French Indochina régime: investments in agricultural improvement were most needed in the north, but more profitable in the south. Increased agricultural outputs in the north would be consumed by underfed peasants. After 1975, the communists faced the same dilemma: should Socialist Vietnam give priority to increasing the production of rice in the north even though it would be consumed locally? Could a socialist régime oblige unwilling peasants to move to new economic zones? Would it be better to rely on the productive potential of privately owned land in the south?

Economically, Indochina was in bad shape in 1975. In many regions, there was tremendous destruction. In North Vietnam, economic management had been dedicated to the needs of war, and Hanoi depended heavily on Chinese and Soviet aid. There was barely an export sector at all, and the population was expecting to be better off once the war was over. The South Vietnamese economy, which in the 1950s and 1960s had been blown up by the influx of US aid and the purchasing power of the US army, had been abandoned in a disrupted state. Herbicides, bombs and mines were formidable obstacles to agricultural development.

In 1975, optimistic assessments of Indochina's power potentials therefore had to be based on future economic possibilities: the Mekong Delta could again become a big rice exporter; there were prospects of finding oil in the South China Sea; a people having demonstrated remarkable abilities in war might also be mobilised for a production effort. Since most of the Mekong countries (Vietnam, Cambodia, Laos, Burma and China) were ruled by socialist régimes, they might also be able to cooperate in regulating the Mekong, a project US advisors had been obliged to give up.[9] Expectations can be important in assessing the power potential of a state or bloc of states, sometimes more important than actual economic strength. No GNP figures were available for the Indochinese countries after 1975, and it was not known to what extent US bombing had destroyed North Vietnamese industry. Neither was it known that agricultural productivity in North Vietnam had in fact seriously decreased during the final years of the war.[10]

Socialist Vietnam was to prove incapable of solving the country's growth problems. Attempts to achieve growth and an even distribution of rice through collectivisation was met with staunch resistance from the peasants. For more than ten years they fought against government policy, primarily in the Mekong Delta, by using the only means at their disposal: deliberate laziness. The 'production strike' succeeded. In the late 1980s, Hanoi gave up its experiments and permitted a return to family-based farming.[11] The unwillingness of the southern peasants to accept socialist agriculture must be considered a major internal constraint on Vietnam's development.

Attempts at industrialisation did not succeed either. During the French colonial period there was much discussion as to whether or not to industrialise Indochina. Little was done in this direction. After the crack and crisis of 1929–30, the colonial market served as a safety net for outmoded French industries; fears of competition and of creating a rebellious proletariat combined to forestall the realisation of ambitious modernisation programmes.[12] During the Indochina wars, what industry there was served the war, and after 1975, US and Chinese economic embargo policies deprived Vietnam of access to investments, markets and modern machinery. Soviet and East European aid was generally of low quality, the infrastructure was in shambles, and one major industrial project after the other turned out to be unprofitable.[13] During the reorientation starting in 1986, the Hanoi leaders abandoned a model of development based on heavy industry, and instead emphasised agriculture, handicraft, small scale industry and tourism. The industrial failure was another major constraint on Vietnam's development.

Through the 1980s, young educated Vietnamese grew more and more ashamed and frustrated with their country's bad performance in the economic field, blaming it partly on the US embargo, partly on the orthodoxy of their old uneducated leaders. The contrast between the worn-out and antiquated Gia Lam and Than Son Nhut airfields and the modern streamlined airport outside Bangkok became a symbol of injured national pride. Somehow the generational conflict was initially contained and controlled but it remains potentially explosive.

When assessing Vietnam's relative strength in the region, a good starting point is to compare it to Thailand, the closest and main rival. Thailand is centrally placed in Southeast Asia, and is less exposed to the Chinese threat than Vietnam, but Vietnam has a larger population than Thailand (66 as opposed to 56 million in 1990). The population growth of Thailand and Vietnam in the 1980s was roughly the same (2–2.1 per cent); Thailand had a somewhat lower birth rate than Vietnam while Vietnam had a higher death rate. Economically, however, the Thai were considerably better off than their neighbours. In the 1980s, Thailand had a GNP of between 800 and US\$ 900 *per capita*, while that of Vietnam was estimated at between 100 and US\$ 200 *per capita* (figures for Vietnam remained unreliable and were often not included in international statistical surveys).

In the regional rivalry between Vietnam and Thailand, Thailand's main strength after 1975 was its economic growth. The strength of Vietnam was its armed forces, as demonstrated by the rapid and well coordinated invasion of Cambodia in 1978, and the successful defence against the Chinese attempt of February 1979 to 'teach Vietnam a lesson' by invading its northern provinces. There was an extreme contradiction between Vietnam's formidable military and weak economic performance. In the late 1970s and early 1980s, Vietnam was one of the states in the world giving highest priority to its army. Vietnam 1975–89 therefore constitutes a unique case for studies of how military capabilities can underpin – or undermine – regional power.

REGIONAL PROFILE

The French perception of Indochina's status in Asian affairs was intertwined with the French self-perception as a world power. French Indochina was created as a compensation for the French loss in the 1870 war with Germany. Through the history of French Indochina the colony served, together with the colonies in North, West and Central Africa, as symbols of French status as a world power. The symbolic importance of the colonies became acute during the Second World War when two rival French régimes sought to save the great power status. More specifically, Indochina was the basis for the French claim to be a Far Eastern power, on a par with Great Britain, the United States, Japan and the Netherlands. These were the main Asian powers in the first three decades of the twentieth century. The system broke down with the Japanese advance into Indochina in 1940–41. After the Second World War, France tried to regain its lost position by rebuilding an Indochinese Federation under the umbrella of the French Union (the French Commonwealth organisation). France never quite adopted, however, to the limited perspective of the region created by the war experience: Southeast Asia. The new region was a result of the decolonisation process triggered by the Greater Asian War; within it there was no room for France.

The main heirs of the French outlook were the Indochinese communists. From September 1945 to April 1975, the independence and unification of Vietnam overshadowed their other goals, but 1975 was perceived as a new start. Since Socialist Vietnam maintained a closed political system, and since the ambitions of its ageing leaders were mostly shrouded in communist rhetoric, it is difficult to know what their exact foreign policy aims were. The safest is perhaps to take their professed ideology seriously. In 1975, the generation of communist leaders who had led the successful wars against France, the United States and the South-Vietnamese régime, had accomplished the impossible. They were bearers of an amalgam of nationalism and doctrinal communism which stood out as utterly successful and drew enormous sympathy from a radical generation of youth throughout the world. The cadres who had lived in the aura of Ho Chi Minh saw their people as a vanguard in a world-wide national liberation struggle. It is highly unlikely that Hanoi had the ambition to attack neighbouring states such as Thailand militarily and topple 'dominoes' with armed force, but Hanoi probably hoped to see successful communist-led rebellions in one country after the other. Alternatively, it may be true, as has been argued, that Vietnam (somewhat like Israel), was obsessed with its security, seeing itself surrounded by enemies.[14] In the years 1975–79, Hanoi's optimistic outlook quickly gave way to an inflexible and suspiciously defensive policy. World events did not fit with expectations, and old men do not easily revise long nurtured visions. They probably saw their new problems as a temporary retreat on the march towards a socialist international order.

The leaders of the victorious Vietnamese were extremely proud to have been the first to beat US imperialism in war. In Korea, the local communists and the Chinese had been obliged to accept the border line at the 38th parallel, but in Vietnam victory was militarily complete. This pride gave an enormous impetus to their self-esteem: 'The epoch-making victory of the Vietnamese people,' said a 21 May 1975 editorial in Hanoi daily *Nhan Dan*, 'has contributed to bringing about an important change in the world balance of forces'.[15] With the hindsight of the 1990s – when we know that Western liberalism was revived under Reagan and Thatcher, that Asian NIC countries were to succeed in their industrialisation programmes, and that the communist régimes in Central Europe were to fall – it may be difficult to recollect that in the mid-1970s, it still looked as if the world was moving in a socialist direction. For many years, the Hanoi leaders remained prisoners of their 1975 optimism.

There is little doubt that in 1975, Hanoi expected Indochina to form an influential bloc in international affairs. This expectation was not primarily based on estimates of concrete capabilities, but rather on a general assumption that a people which had managed to beat both France and the United States in war would also perform well in the country's reconstruction. Considerable aid was expected to flow from China and the Soviet Union, and good relations with neutral and non-aligned countries such as India, Sweden and Yugoslavia enhanced the potential for Vietnamese power and influence. The régimes of Laos and Cambodia were expected to tolerate a fair degree of Vietnamese influence.

Eventually, these prospects were insufficient. Instead of increasing its regional power, Vietnam's international posture relative to its regional challengers decreased dramatically from the late 1970s onwards. Only militarily did Vietnam remain a formidable power, and this seemed to be of little use in the early 1990s when a new generation of leaders gave priority to economic development. In 1986, after the ascendancy of Mikhail Gorbachev in Moscow, the Vietnamese Communist Party elected Nguyen Van Linh, a moderate reformer, as Secretary General. He embarked upon a process of careful reappraisal and renewal *(Doi Moi)*. Under his leadership, the Vietnamese Communist Party gradually abandoned what ambition it might have had to gain regional power through socialist ideals and military power. The main goals were reformulated as increasing the agricultural output through de-collectivisation of land, breaking the US economic blocade, and attracting foreign investment. Other ambitions were adjourned to a distant future.

Relations with Great Powers

The main great powers in Asia during the French colonial period were the United States, Great Britain and Japan. In French Indochina's immediate neighbourhood, the main rival powers were China and Siam (Thailand). French power in Asia was based on a close alliance with the other European powers, in particular the French depended on the presence of the British Navy: Singapore was a cornerstone in the Far Eastern power system. The French endeavoured to protect Indochina from US and Japanese economic penetration and to avoid it being influenced by the liberal colonial policies pursued by the United States in the Philippines.

French Indochina's relations with China and Siam (Thailand) were always difficult. Treaties had been signed, but the main mission of the French colonial army was always to establish a reliable defence system against possible Chinese or Thai incursions. The power balance broke down in 1940. Weakened by the defeat to the German army in Europe, and unable to achieve military assistance from Great Britain or the United States, the Governor General in Hanoi felt obliged to allow a Japanese military entry through China. In 1941, after a brief war, French Indochina also ceded sizeable Cambodian and Laotian territory to Thailand.

During the Cold War, the Viet Minh and, later, North Vietnam were supported by both China and the Soviet Union. North Vietnam had relations only with the socialist camp while South Vietnam had relations only with the pro-American camp in world affairs. This changed in 1969–72, when ping-pong diplomacy brought President Nixon to China. The visit led to a partial resurrection of the special Sino-American relationship which had existed before and during the Second World War. This in turn brought a deterioration of Sino-Vietnamese relations. China reduced its aid to Vietnam already in 1975. After the death of Mao Ze-dong and the demise of the 'Gang of Four' in 1976, China liberalised its economy and generally improved relations with capitalist countries. One effect of the new Chinese posture was to drive the Vietnamese Communist Party away from its traditional neutrality in the Sino-Soviet controversy and throw Hanoi completely into the arms of the Kremlin. This happened at a time when the Brezhnev régime was conducting an overambitious foreign policy out of proportion to Soviet economic and productive capabilities. Vietnam was a major benefactor – or victim – of this policy.

At one point there was a chance for Vietnam to change the pattern. This was in late 1976, when the 'Gang of Four' had just been arrested and a new Chinese leadership was susceptible to external initiatives. Hanoi made a modest attempt to test the attitude of the new leaders by dispatching a request for aid, but did not grasp the occasion for a more calculated initiative. A 'race' was going on between Beijing, Hanoi – and Phnom Penh – for improving relations with the governments of the ASEAN states. This race, which involved the cancellation of both Chinese and Vietnamese aid to communist insurgents in ASEAN, was won by China.[16]

The improvement of the Sino-US relationship and the hostile Chinese policy towards Vietnam must be seen as the prime movers behind Vietnam's diplomatic isolation. Hanoi felt insecure as a result of its loss of Chinese sympathy, and in this situation Pol Pot's Democratic Kampuchea launched provocations across the Vietnamese border. After some hesitation, Vietnam responded with the 1978 full scale invasion, and installed a pro-Vietnamese régime in Phnom Penh. After the Vietnamese invasion, China first made the mistake of invading northern Vietnam by armed force, leading to humiliating losses, and rapid withdrawal. Then China applied a more cynical and effective policy: an economic embargo in conjunction with the USA, and a flow of military assistance to Khmer Rouge guerrillas in the Thai-Cambodian border region, binding substantial Vietnamese forces in Cambodia for ten years (1979–89). By sustaining the Pol Pot régime in Cambodia, Beijing had first outmanoeuvered Hanoi diplomatically. When Hanoi responded militarily, China at first also reacted militarily, but then turned to a policy of fighting by proxy.

During the first years after 1975, USA and the Soviet Union did not enjoy much influence inside Indochina. After the Vietnam débâcle, Washington lost much of its interest in the region and gradually came to entrust China with the task of containing the 'local Soviet satellites'. Policy formulation was to a great extent left to the regional powers themselves. Even if the Soviets provided substantial amounts of aid to the Indochinese countries, the Soviets gained little influence. The Vietnamese were eager to achieve Soviet aid and keen to support the Soviets in international fora; they were also prepared to grant the Soviets military facilities, but they did not take advice on what they regarded as their own matters. Vietnam also took care to prevent the establishment of too close relations between the Soviets and the leaders of Laos, later also with the Heng Samrin régime in Cambodia.

Relations with Regional Challengers

After 1975, it was normal to see Vietnam and Indonesia as the two expansionist powers in Southeast Asia.[17] However true this may be, it did not make them serious rivals. Indonesian foreign policy was not as anti-Vietnamese as that of other ASEAN powers. As a maritime and insular state with a large population, Indonesia was more concerned with the possible Chinese threat than with the ambitions of an Indochinese bloc. In addition, Indonesian expansionism was principally directed eastwards, thus representing a potential menace to Australia. Malaysia, the Philippines and the South China Sea served as buffers between Indochina and Indonesia.

Rather than entering into rivalry with Indonesia, Socialist Vietnam inherited the two main regional challengers of French Indochina: China and Thailand. Yet there were important differences. On the one hand, the Vietnamese régime could count on active popular support and a formidable military force whereas the French colonial army had never been sufficiently strong and popular to defend Indochina if it were left without powerful allies. On the other hand, French Indochina had, until 1940, enjoyed a far better diplomatic position than did Socialist Vietnam in 1975. China was weak and ridden by internal strife during the whole history of French Indochina and, until Japan entered the picture, Thailand had no allies to rely upon. French Indochina had a powerful ally in Great Britain, and maintained a correct relationship with the United States. In contrast, during the formative years of socialist Indochina (1975–78), China was strong and unified, and Thailand was a member of ASEAN. Vietnam's only ally in the regional power game was the distant Soviet Union. In addition, whereas the French-led Hanoi régime had always been able to control Laos and Cambodia (partly by using Viet personnel), the socialist régime in Hanoi faced an extremely hostile régime in Cambodia. The small Cambodian state cannot of course be seen as a regional challenger to Vietnam, but since Cambodia became the main issue in Vietnam's relations with its regional challengers, the crisis leading to the 1978 Vietnamese occupation of Cambodia must be discussed here.

The emergence and development of the conflict between Vietnam and Cambodia cannot be separated from Hanoi and Phnom Penh's relations with China. It was basically a triangular affair at first, with lesser roles to play for the other powers in the region. The Khmer Rouge leaders in Phnom Penh had two main concerns: their hatred for the Vietnamese, and their need for Chinese support. Shortly after the establishment of their régime in 1975, they started to prepare for the unavoidable war against the 'hereditary enemy'. The border incidents of 1978 between Vietnam and Democratic Kampuchea need not be explained by anything Hanoi did. They were caused by the irrational chauvinism of the Pol Pot group, and made possible by China's support. What is open for discussion, is the way Hanoi reacted to the problem. If Vietnam had possessed powerful allies in the region and had tried to mount an international campaign against Pol Pot's genocidal policies, Hanoi might have achieved international under- standing for a temporary military intervention to protect the Cambodian people. Instead, Hanoi disregarded its own weak diplomatic standing and undertook the invasion of Cambodia in a way which led to massive international condemnation. By occupying the country, establishing a pro-Vietnamese régime, and failing to promise early withdrawal, Vietnam further alienated all its neighbours. Despite the fact that it had failed to gain the friendship of any of the ASEAN countries, Hanoi proclaimed China to be Vietnam's historic enemy. The result was a military alliance of the two major regional rivals, China and Thailand, sustained by all the surrounding powers except Burma and India, and also by the United States. It was as if Hanoi had forgotten Ho Chi Minh's dictum always to divide the enemies from each other. Vietnam's only remaining assets on entering the 1980s, were a powerful army and the Soviet alliance.

EXTERNAL CONSTRAINTS

Over the last hundred years, one particular factor has figured prominently in great power perceptions of Indochina: the natural deep sea harbour at Cam Ranh Bay, used successively by the French, US and Soviet navies. From the British perspective, naval access to Indochinese waters and cooperation with the French navy was an important factor in securing the searoute from India over Singapore to Hong Kong. In general, French Indochina was perceived of as a buffer against potential threats to the British possessions in Asia from China or Japan. The United States' view was more equivocal. On the one hand, French Indochina was part of a system guaranteeing stability. On the other hand, French colonial policies did not take sufficient account of the aspirations of the Asian peoples, and also hindered the creation of open Asian markets. In this respect, the two main rival powers in the Pacific, USA and Japan, had similar interests in a liberalisation of French policies. In the beginning of the century, and again from the early 1920s onwards, Tokyo hosted a pretender to the Vietnamese throne, Prince Cuong De, but French Indochina first gained real importance to Japan in the late 1930s. In 1939–40, it was imperative for the Japanese to close the flow of goods to Chiang Kai-shek's China through the port of Haiphong. At the next stage, in 1941, French Indochina became the stepping stone for the Japanese advance into Southeast Asia.

In 1975, Vietnam stood as proof of the correctness of Moscow's national liberation strategy, and Vietnam became the Soviet Union's main ally in Asia. The Brezhnev régime had won a victory over China in their rivalry for hegemony within the socialist camp and for influence in the third world. By obtaining Vietnamese membership in the Comecon and access for the Soviet navy to base facilities at Cam Ranh Bay, the Soviet Union incorporated Vietnam in its economic and military system. However, assistance to the Indochinese countries represented a severe drain on the Soviet budget, and the alliance with Vietnam hampered Moscow's relations with other Southeast Asian states. Under Gorbachev, the Soviet Union introduced the 'new thinking' which did away with the national liberation strategy, and generally started to conduct a pragmatic foreign policy based on the existing international system. The exclusive alliance with Vietnam became a liability.

US perceptions of Vietnam since 1975 seem to have been influenced by two main factors: vengefulness and the alliance with China. In 1975, North Vietnam broke the 1973 Paris agreement and took over all of South Vietnam. The dramatic evacuation of US personnel and their Vietnamese collaborators from Saigon in 1975 represented a humiliation of the United States. President Carter genuinely desired reconciliation, but Vietnamese insistence on reparations, in combination with the further rapprochement between Washington and Beijing prevented normalisation of US-Vietnamese relations. The Vietnamese invasion of Cambodia offered the CIA a golden opportunity to turn the means used against the United States during the Vietnam War against Vietnam itself: at low cost, the United States, Thailand and China were able to keep a drawn-out guerrilla struggle against the Vietnamese occupation forces in Cambodia going. The United States has also been able to enforce and maintain an international embargo, preventing any loans to Vietnam from the World Bank, the Asian Development Bank and the International Monetary Fund.[18]

Vietnam's two main regional challengers have been defined here as Thailand and China. In the first half of this century, Thailand (Siam) perceived French Indochina as an antagonistic power. In the nineteenth century, Laos and Cambodia had been under Siamese suzerainty; the western provinces of Laos and Cambodia were considered also by Thai nationalists as naturally belonging to Thailand; from 1941 these provinces were indeed Thai territory, but in 1946, they were forced to retrocede them to French Indochina, after US mediation. The border conflict induced Bangkok with considerable sympathy for the struggle of the Viet Minh against the French régime. Thai sympathy evaporated with the onset of the Cold War, when Bangkok had to face internal guerrilla forces sustained from China, which had contacts both to the Malayan insurgency and the Viet Minh. During the Vietnam War, Thailand served as a major US ally in the region. In 1975, the same threat perception which had existed during the French period, re-emerged with the unification of Vietnam and the establishment of socialist régimes in Laos and Cambodia. Before the French colonisation, the main issue in Thai-Vietnamese relations was their respective influence in the lesser states of Laos and Cambodia. A Vietnam-united Indochina bloc could not but be perceived as a deadly threat in Bangkok, not only because it brought the Vietnamese army nearer, but also because the bloc represented a formidable demographic and potentially productive power.

The two other states whose perceptions should be considered are Laos and Cambodia. During the colonial period, the Lao princes and population were more loyal to the French than were the Viet, and the Khmer also offered far less resistance to French policies than they did. Although the French régime used a great number of Viet personnel in the administration of Laos and Cambodia, the French presence also constituted a guarantee against ethnic Viet dominance. After the French withdrawal from Indochina, Laos was ridden by internal strife between princely factions allied either with Thailand and USA or Vietnam, while Cambodia adopted a neutralist foreign policy. The coup against King Norodom Sihanouk in 1970 led to the establishment of a right wing nationalist and extremely anti-Vietnamese régime. When it fell in 1975, it was substituted with an extreme left-wing régime with a similarly hostile attitude to the Vietnamese. The Lao élite chose a far more careful approach. Those unwilling to accept Vietnamese dominance fled the country. The remaining élite tried to do the best out of the situation and to preserve as much autonomy as possible while adjusting to Vietnamese desires. However, there is reason to believe that the so-called communists in Laos, and also the pro-Vietnamese Heng Samrin régime installed in Cambodia in 1979, always kept looking for ways to reduce the Vietnamese influence and assert their own independence.[19] If ever there was an opportunity to create a multi-ethnic Indochinese nation, it was lost in 1945. After this, the Cambodians, and even the leaders of the various Lao clans – communists, princes and conservatives alike – maintained not only local customs, but also independent national identities.

Conflicting Perceptions?

In the crucial 1975–78 period, Indochina was caught in a web of intense, conflicting threat perceptions: Vietnam felt threatened by Cambodia, by China and, to a lesser extent, by Thailand. The newly established communist régime in Cambodia feared absorbtion in a Hanoi-dominated Indochinese bloc, and decided to assert itself demonstrably against Vietnam. China resented the re-establishment of a powerful and unified state at its southern flank and saw the Cambodian animosity towards Vietnam as an opportunity to keep Indochina divided against itself. Thailand was wary of Vietnamese attempts to establish a military presence in Laos and Cambodia.

The conflicting perceptions came into play at a time when the United States had withdrawn from its paramount role in the region and when China was embroiled in the power struggle following the death of Mao Ze-dong. No patterns had been established for regional conflict resolution. Phnom Penh's policies had an explosive potential. When Pol Pot purged all pro-Vietnamese personalities from the ranks of the Khmer Rouge and launched military raids into Vietnamese territory, Hanoi responded with the full use of its military force. The result was more than ten years of warfare, and Indochina's diplomatic isolation. For more than a decade, while ASEAN grew into an important regional grouping, Vietnam was prevented from wielding influence in regional affairs.

The International System

Between the 1920s and 1990s, Indochina's place within the structure of the international system changed repeatedly. The instability of external influences within the region is indeed a major characteristic of modern Southeast Asian history. Between the two world wars, the Far Eastern regional system was multipolar, with Great Britain, the United States, France, Japan, and the Netherlands as major powers. In the 1930s, under the threat of the rising sun, a bipolar system emerged, forcing all decision-makers to choose between West and East. With the Japanese capitulation in 1945 came a temporary return to a multipolar regional system under which the Philippines, Burma and Indonesia won independence, while Great Britain and France were engaged in anti-insurgency wars in Malaya and Indochina. With the 1949 communist victory in China, Southeast Asia returned to a basically bipolar system, with the USA and its client states on one side; the Soviet Union, China and a range of national liberation movements on the other. A temporary moderation of the Sino-Soviet attitude following Stalin's death made it possible for the declining European powers to negotiate an Indochinese settlement in 1954, but the bipolarity of the system survived and provided the background for the US war in Vietnam.

The Sino-Soviet split, which became manifest in 1969, led to reappraisals of Western policies towards China. This eliminated the US strategic rationale for continuing the Vietnam war. With the transformation around 1969–72 from bipolarity to tripolarity in Washington's perception of Asia, the enormous US expenditures in Vietnam lost strategic relevance. In the détente period of the mid-1970s, Southeast Asia entered a new phase with a new multipolar regional system which gave the regional powers themselves greater leeway. The external influences which had dominated the region for more than a century were drastically reduced. The European presence was at a minimum. Japan, although once again a formidable economic power, had still no say in the region. In the open landscape of 1975, the Hanoi leaders had reason to feel confident that they could occupy a prominent place. Instead the changes of the international structure in the mid-1970s worked against Vietnam. Under President Jimmy Carter, Washington gave priority to cementing its re-established ties with Beijing. China sought to contain Vietnamese power by sustaining an anti-Vietnamese régime in Cambodia. Thailand was given Chinese military assistance, and since all the ASEAN member states were apprehensive of Vietnam's military capabilities, they moved closer together than before. In 1978, Hanoi's response to its diplomatic encirclement was to hinge its foreign policy completely on the alliance with the Soviet Union, and invade Cambodia to set up a friendly régime. The result was a complete loss of leverage in the international arena.

The Soviets also gained little from their aid to Indochina. Even the much talked about port facilities at the deep sea harbour of Cam Ranh Bay, which the Soviets had taken over from the retreating US Navy after 1975, were of limited value since they were far away from the nearest Soviet port. For the French, Cam Ranh Bay had been useful until 1940, because they could count on naval co-operation with the British. For the USA, Cam Ranh Bay was valuable because it was linked to a chain of bases in Asia and the Pacific. For the Soviets it was of significantly less value. It is not surprising that Gorbachev gave up the facilities at Cam Ranh Bay. For an external great power to gain influence in a region where there are several medium and small powers, it is not very useful to have just one client state, especially not if it is in conflict with everyone else. A stake (like base facilities) in one beleaguered state will only give that state the necessary leverage for exacting more and more aid. To gain regional power, the external power must preferably be influential in more than one of the local states so as to play them out against each other. It is also in the interest of internal powers to maintain relations with more than one great power. The mutual dependency between Vietnam and the Soviet Union was a liability for both. [20] It can be compared to the relationship between Israel and the USA. Washington has increased its leverage in the Middle East by criticising Israel and cultivating relations with Egypt, Saudi-Arabia – and during the 1990–91 Gulf war – even Syria. In the late 1980s, Moscow tried the same in Southeast Asia by depreciating ties with Vietnam and improving relations with Beijing, Bangkok, Djakarta and other regional capitals.

The modest role of the two former superpowers in Southeast Asia after 1975 was the effect of the tripolar power structure (USA-Soviet-China) that developed in the détente period of the 1970s. Since Beijing and Washington fell down on the same side in 1979, when the Cold War temporarily resumed between Washington and Moscow, there was no return to the old dichotomy in Southeast Asia. A new bipolar regional structure emerged, this time with an 'Indochina bloc' pitted against all the other states in the region.

From the late 1940s to the late 1960s, Washington was obsessed with the idea of 'falling dominoes'. After the 'fall' of the whole of Indochina, there was much talk of whether or not the Soviet Union would fill the vacuum left over by the United States. We may now conclude that it did not. The vacuum, if there was one, was filled by the regional states themselves: Vietnam within the borders of Indochina; China and ASEAN within the rest of the region. If new dominoes fall, they shall fall in the opposite direction. Any Cambodian leader (with a possible exception for the Khmer Rouge) will have to put emphasis on economic development, and therefore look west, and to Japan. Vietnam has little to offer, except help in the military protection of the régime. As late as in 1986, the Sixth Congress of the Vietnamese Communist Party defined the consolidation of the relationship between the three Indochinese countries as 'a law governing the survival and development of all three fraternal nations'.[21] In 1991, however, it seems improbable that Vietnam will intervene militarily in Cambodia once again, regardless of whom the country falls to.

The failure of Vietnam to gain regional influence should be explained on multiple levels: internal constraints; hostile perceptions held by neighbouring states; Hanoi's inflexible foreign policy; changing patterns in the tripolar relationship between USA, China and the Soviet Union.

CONCLUSIONS: VIETNAM – A FAILED ATTEMPT TO GAIN REGIONAL POWER

If we define a regional great power as a state which can defend itself militarily against any coalition of other regional powers, French Indochina certainly did not qualify, not even at the height of French power in Asia. The colonial state was established through successful military campaigns against China and Siam, but after the First World War, French Indochina depended on the strength of the British Navy as well as on a workable relationship with a weak China.

Vietnam after 1975 probably qualified as a regional great power. In 1978–79, by successfully intervening in Cambodia and subsequently inflicting heavy losses on a massive Chinese intervention force in Tonkin, the Vietnamese army demonstrated its formidable strength. However, when dealing with the contemporary world, a definition focussing exclusively on the military factor is unacceptable. Economic factors and diplomatic manoeuvering are instrumental in power relations between states. Once some degree of regional influence is incorporated into the definition, Vietnam cannot be considered anywhere near the status of a regional great power. Indeed the states in Southeast Asia that did increase their regional influence in the 1980s were Vietnam's rivals in ASEAN: Thailand, Malaysia and the mini-state Singapore. They stood to gain in every domain where Hanoi failed. Thailand experienced an impressive economic growth (around 7 per cent yearly), transformed its capital into a major international metropolis and centre of tourism, maintained close ties with two of the world's great powers (USA and China), sustained a low cost guerrilla struggle against the Vietnamese army in Cambodia and contributed to developing closer cooperation within ASEAN.

Geopolitically, Vietnam is squeezed between China and Thailand. Although both French Indochina and Socialist Vietnam tried to direct attention to the sea (fisheries, islands, oil, building of a merchant fleet), the basic ingredients in their security policy were the relationships with China and Thailand.[22] In both cases these relations were difficult, but France had the advantage of facing a weak China and an isolated Thailand. Neither the French colonialists nor the Indochinese communists were able to carry out a modernisation strategy leading to substantially increased living standards. Neither group was able to solve the overpopulation problem. While the French régime relied on a balance of power approach to foreign policy, Socialist Vietnam based its security on the maintenance of an enormous army, and an alliance with the Soviet Union. In either case, Indochina did not become what we may legitimately call a regional great power.

Why did it fail? In 1930, and again in 1940, the French Indochina régime had to confront major popular rebellions in all three Viet countries (Tonkin, Annam, Cochinchina). The French never managed to establish an educated pro-French middle class. This should not, however, be seen as the main reason for the French failure. The French régime had little difficulty in suppressing these rebellions. As long as the French were able to maintain their highly effective police system, internal revolts could be put down.[23] The French failure should first of all be explained by the Second World War. In 1940–41, changes in the balance of power forced France to accept Japanese occupation of Indochina. In 1945, the Japanese removed the French régime and, after Tokyo's surrender, witnessed the August Revolution without doing anything to stop it. The French returned temporarily, but in early 1950, when the Chinese provinces Yunnan and Guangxi were incorporated in the People's Republic of China, it was no longer possible to maintain a French Indochina, not even a decolonised version.

The failure of the Indochinese communists to build a strong and powerful Indochina is intriguing. How can it be that the victor of the First Indochina War of 1946–54 and the Second one of 1959–75, eventually felt obliged to withdraw from what is often called the Third Indochina War, and, moreover, were outdistanced in the competition for regional influence by less militarily strong rivals? This chapter has pointed at the many internal and external constraints on Vietnamese policy after 1975. They shall not be repeated here. Instead the focus shall be on three main characteristics of Hanoi's political line: emphasis on the Soviet alliance; maintenance of a huge army; dogmatic, inflexible leadership. The priority given to the Soviet alliance and to the army led Vietnam to diplomatic isolation and a continued state of economic backwardness.

Vietnam in the years from 1975 to 1989 provides a case of how risky it is to build one's foreign policy on a combination of military might and dependence on a distant power, however ideologically committed it may be. The influence of distant powers tends to be ephemeral, while neighbouring states remain present. The Vietnamese experience also shows how counterproductive it can be for a national leadership bent on gaining regional influence, to overemphasise its armed forces. Vietnam 1975–89 is a case of military over-stretch. The Vietnamese had already proven their military power before 1975 and did not need a powerful army to deter foreign interference. What was needed was consolidation internally and reassurance externally. The decision to maintain an army of well over one million men was a major mistake. With the exception of times of generalised warfare, regional influence cannot be achieved through military force alone. By keeping a huge army, and using it to occupy Cambodia, Vietnam attained the opposite of what its interests were. It made it more difficult to gain friendly relations with other states in the region; drove the ASEAN states and China together in a *cordon sanitaire*; and weakened Vietnam's economy by depriving the civilian sectors of talent and resources.[24]

For rational actors within the modern state system, the armed forces serve three main purposes: (1) their existence deters undesirable action by foreign powers; (2) they are kept as a last resort, to be used if the country comes under attack; (3) certain parts of the armed forces are used for active missions, under particularly favourable conditions; they should be such as to make it extremely likely that the use of armed force will yield the desired results rapidly, and without causing an unacceptable degree of hostility from other states. If success is not extremely likely, and it is still felt that armed force should be used, the rationally operating state will prefer to fight by proxy, that is, arming terrorist or guerilla groups within the territory of the state it wants to thwart (such as China, USA and Thailand did in Cambodia).

For the leaders of the Indochinese nations in 1975, the use of armed force had been a continuous ingredient of interstate relations since 1940–41. Before the Second World War, the same leaders had lived under suppression from an omnipresent French police. The use of violence thus appeared as an evident ingredient of politics. If we make an exception for North Vietnam and the NLF's propaganda effort during the Second Indochina War, which was largely carried out by non-communists, skill in practising non-violent means of diplomacy and propaganda was not developed to much sophistication by Hanoi. The best brains and the most experienced decision-makers were army officers or party apparatchiks.

The way the Khmer Rouge demonstrated *their* newly won power was simple and vile: violence in a multitude of forms, internally as well as externally. On the moral level, no comparison is possible between the racism, paranoia and terror of the Pol Pot régime and the well organised bureaucracy of Socialist Vietnam, but the Vietnamese leadership also had its main qualifications in the calculated use of violence. After 1975 it was no longer an advantage in their quest for regional influence.

The ascending powers in Southeast Asia after 1975 – Thailand, Malaysia and Singapore – emphasised economy and diplomacy, while avoiding violent internal conflicts.[25] The same applies for outside powers. At low cost, USA and China were able to isolate and bog down Vietnam in a drawn-out counter-insurgency. On the other hand, the inflexible policies of the USA and China allowed other powers to play a more active and constructive role in the region. In the latter half of the 1980s, powers such as Indonesia, Japan, Australia and France quietly increased their influence through economic investments and diplomatic initiatives. Their increased influence was visible in the negotiation process for the attempted Cambodian peace settlement in 1989–90.

As for the third characteristic of Hanoi's policy – caustic, inflexible leadership – it should be ascribed to the arrogance of recent success, doctrinal orthodoxy, and old age. From 1975 to 1986, and to some extent even later, Vietnam was directed by a generation of communists born in the first decade of the twentieth century, who had dedicated their lives to the struggles against French colonialism and US imperialism. For this generation, the August Revolution of 1945, the victory at Dien Bien Phu of 1954, and the conquest of Saigon in 1975, were the landmarks of their lifetime. They harboured a feeling that the Vietnamese nation was destined to fight evil and establish not only a unified nation, but also a bright shining socialist world. Two of Ho Chi Minh's greatest talents had been his persistence and his ability to adjust his policies to the needs of the situation. His successors shared the former, but not the latter. Marxist-leninist ideology does much to explain the deficiency. It is better suited for gaining power than for using it rationally once it has been conquered. Gorbachev's reform policies from 1985 and the events of 1989 in Beijing and Eastern Europe bewildered the Hanoi leaders. They had already lost touch with the young generations, who grew tired of ideology and instead looked west for pop music, commodities and opportunities. In 1989, Hanoi's vision of the world broke to pieces.

Did Hanoi adjust to the changed world? To some extent it did; both its foreign and domestic policies changed drastically between 1986 and 1991. The government aimed at getting out of the quagmire to take up competition with Thailand and other countries in the economic field. Prime Minister Chatichai Choonhavan (1988–91) and his vision of an Indochinese market-place were tremendously popular in Vietnam. In the cultural and political fields Hanoi hesitated to grant democratic liberties. This was no doubt resented by the young intellectual élite, but it contributed to hold the state together and prevent social and political disorders while the economy was being re-transformed from socialism to capitalism.

Dramatic cuts in Soviet and East European aid forced Hanoi to give up its reliance on its distant socialist alliance partners, and instead seek partners locally as well as among the leading capitalist countries. In Vietnam's regional policy, this reinvigorated the traditional dilemma of choosing between Thailand and China. On the one hand, Vietnam could seek a close partnership with Thailand, and join ASEAN, while placing less emphasis on its relations with China. This would provide the safest road to rapid economic development, but would also entail a security risk, as well as the evils of uncontrolled capitalism: dependence on foreign capital, social injustice, regional imbalances, unemployment, corruption, pollution, prostitution – strikes and demonstrations. On the other hand, Vietnam could give priority to improving relations with China. This seemed to be the option of the old generation in Hanoi. It would make it easier to maintain the Party monopoly – and hence national cohesion, but it would not be attractive to the educated youth, and it might lead to continued economic backwardness. If Vietnam did not stand out as more dynamic and democratic than China, foreign investors might prefer the enormous Chinese market to the smaller Vietnamese.[26]

The Vietnamese élite of the 1990s definitely favour the Thai model rather than the Chinese: they aspire to become part of a dynamic Indochinese marketplace, encompassing the whole peninsula. Vietnam is likely to remain a formidable military power, but the attitude of the country's new élite is opposed to military as well as ideological adventures. They are longing for prosperity.

NOTES

In addition to the editor and the other authors of this volume, I would like to thank Duong Quoc Thanh, Jon Lidén, Henning Simonsen and Arthur Westing for their comments to earlier drafts of this article.

1. In English the Viet used to be called 'Annamese' or 'Annamites'. They are called 'Viet' here, and not 'Vietnamese', in order to distinguish between Viet ethnicity and Vietnamese nationality. Vietnamese nationals can be ethnic Viet, Tay, Khmer, Cham, Nung, Tho, Man, etc.
2. S. Tønnesson, *The Vietnamese Revolution of 1945. Roosevelt, Ho Chi Minh and de Gaulle in a World at War* (London: SAGE, 1991).
3. B. Kiernan, *How Pol Pot Came to Power* (London: Verso, 1985), p. 79. M. Vickery, *Kampuchea. Politics, Economics and Society* (London: Pinter, 1986), p. 11. M. Stuart-Fox, *Laos. Politics, Economics and Society* (London: Pinter, 1986), pp. 19–20. *The Vietnam-Kampuchea Conflict (A Historical Record)* (Hanoi: Foreign Languages Publishing House, 1979), p. 6.
4. After the Vietnamese invasion of Cambodia in 1978, the Khmer Rouge accused Hanoi leaders of all along having preserved the federation as their secret goal. A useful survey of the discussion caused by this allegation can be found in MacAlister Brown, 'The Indochinese Federation Idea: Learning from History', in J. J. Zasloff (ed.), *Postwar Indochina.*

Old Enemies and New Allies (Washington, DC: US Department of State, 1988).

5. Among the many books and booklets published on the occasion of Ho Chi Minh's 100th anniversary, the one that really sheds new light on his career is D. Hémery, *Ho Chi Minh. De l'Indochine au Vietnam* (Paris: Gallimard, 1990).

6. P. B. Hall, 'The Geographic Region: A Résumé', *Annals of the Association of American Geographers*, XXV (1935): 122–30.

7. A. Jørgensen-Dahl, *Regional Organization and Order in South-East Asia* (London: Macmillan, 1982).

8. An interesting discussion of the relationship between the military and economic development can be found in J. Soedjati Djiwandono and Yong Mun Cheong (eds), *Soldiers and Stability in Southeast Asia* (Singapore: Institute of Southeast Asian Studies, 1988).

9. W. R. Sewell and G. F. White, 'The Lower Mekong. An Experiment in International River Development', *International Conciliation,* No. 558 (May 1966) 5–63. G. F. White, 'The Mekong River Plan', *Scientific American,* CCVIII, No. 4 (April 1963): 49–59.

10. M. Beresford, *Vietnam. Politics, Economics and Society* (London: Pinter, 1988), pp. 134–5.

11. D. Hémery and Nguyen Duc Nhuan, 'Crise du communisme et du développement. L'Indochine en état de fragile espérance', *Le Monde Diplomatique* (October 1989): 12–13.

12. A lucid analysis of French economic policy in the colonies can be found in J. Marseille, *Empire colonial et capitalisme français. Histoire d'un divorce* (Paris: Albin Michel, 1984).

13. S. de Vylder and A. Fforde, *Vietnam. An economy in transition* (Stockholm: SIDA, 1988).

14. J. J. Zasloff, 'Vietnam and Laos. Master and Apprentice', in J. J. Zasloff (ed.), *Postwar Indochina. Old Enemies and New Allies*, p. 38. In the early 1920s, Soviet foreign policy was marked by a similarly paranoid isolationism.

15. N. Chanda, *Brother Enemy. The War After the War. A History of Indochina since the Fall of Saigon* (San Diego, CA: Harcourt Brace Jovanovich, 1986), p. 24.

16. Ibid, pp. 74ff.

17. 'Deux expansionnismes régionaux : Vietnam et Indonésie', G. Chaliand and J. P. Rageau, *Atlas stratégique. Géopolitique des rapports de forces dans le monde,* (2nd edn; Paris: Fayard, 1983), p. 148 (an English translation of the 1st edn was published by Penguin).

18. N. Chanda, 'Indochina', in A. Lake (ed.), *After the Wars* (New Brunswick: Transaction, 1990), pp. 77–100.

19. J. J. Zasloff argues instead that the leading Lao communists, due to family ties and lifelong collaboration, were 'psychologically dependent' on the Vietnamese: 'Their links have been so strong that today they may not differentiate the Laotian interest from that of the Vietnamese';

'Vietnam and Laos. Master and Apprentice', in J. J. Zasloff (ed.), *Postwar Indochina. Old Enemies and New Allies*, pp. 41, 43–4.

20. While recognising the alliance with Vietnam as a Soviet asset, L. Buszynski also states that 'the alienation of ASEAN has been the major cost of the acquisition of Vietnam for the Soviet Union and insofar as it has been a feasible aim to develop political influence within the ASEAN states, the consistent inability to do so may be considered a failure for Soviet foreign policy.' *Soviet Foreign Policy and Southeast Asia* (London: Croom Helm, 1986), p. 248. There are, however, signs that this may change in the middle to long term.

21. S. T. Johnson, 'Vietnam's Politics and Economi in mid-1987', in J. J. Zasloff (ed.), *Postwar Indochina. Old Enemies and New Allies*, p. 5.

22. P. B. Lafont (ed.), *Les frontières du Vietnam. Histoire des frontières de la péninsule indochinouse* (Paris: l'Harmattan, 1989).

23. P. Morlat, *La répression coloniale au Vietnam (1908–1940)* (Paris: l'Harmattan, 1990).

24. Nayan Chanda has remarked that Vietnam could avoid 'a hard debate on guns and butter' because its immediate needs were filled by Soviet aid: N. Chanda, 'Defence and Development in Vietnam', J. Soedjati Djiwandono and Yong Mun Cheong (eds), *Soldiers and Stability in Southeast Asia* (Singapore: Institute of Southeast Asian Studies, 1988), p. 323.

25. C. Jeshurun and S. Paribatra have discussed the reasons why Thailand's military expenditures did not increase more dramatically after 1975 than they actually did. He concludes that Thai threat perceptions 'found expression through other means such as diplomacy and foreign policy rather than blatant and uncontrolled defence spending': C. Jeshurun, 'Threat Perception and Defence Spending in Southeast Asia. An Assessment', p. 17; S. Paribatra, 'Thailand: Defence Spending and Threat Perceptions', pp. 90–5; both in Chin Kin Wah (ed.), *Defence Spending in Southeast Asia* (Singapore: Institute of Southeast Asian Studies, 1987).

26. For a discussion of Vietnam's foreign policy dilemma by a Vietnamese expert on international relations, see Duong Quoc Thanh, 'Back to the world. Recent Changes in Vietnamese Domestic and Foreign Policy', *Bulletin of Peace Proposals*, XXII (1991): 25–9.

Conclusion

Iver B. Neumann and Øyvind Østerud

To what extent do the seven case studies presented above make up more than the sum of its parts? One may immediately make the generalisation that quantitative criteria in themselves are not enough to substantiate claims to regional great powerhood. The cases of inter-war Poland and Vietnam after 1975 are good reminders that a state without the necessary economic foundation for regional great powerhood will sooner or later be caught out, however strongly the claims to that status are made. Indeed, this is an interesting regional echo of the systems-level debate on the rise and fall of hegemons which took centre stage in the literature during much of the 1980s.[1] However, the cases of Israel and Brazil call attention to the fact that *any* designation of a set of sufficient quantitative factors will prove insufficient. Israel has, paradoxically, been able to turn small population, small area and regional hostility into an asset. Brazil, which has had a regional preponderance in almost any quantitative set of criteria imaginable, has still, due to a certain lack of interest in its region, nevertheless declined to play an active regional role. In order to assess regional great powerhood, then, a structural, geostrategic orientation is in itself simply not enough. The roles, ambitions and influence held by a given candidate *vis-à-vis* the other states which make up the region, what may perhaps be called the intersubjectivity of states, must also be taken into consideration.

Which are those other states? A number of the contributors make much of the academic problems involved in drawing up regions, and of the differences in perceptions among local powers themselves, between local powers and great powers, and among the great powers on this score. However, the *decision makers* in the states under special scrutiny seem to have few qualms about where that region is within which they want to play a role as regional great power. To them, perhaps, the region equals the sphere of influence striven for. If this is made into a criterion of regional great powerhood, of the cases examined here India, Israel and South Africa come nearest to fulfilling it, whereas Poland's is the greatest failure. However this may be, the dictum that regions are where politicians want them to be certainly finds substantiation here.[2] As with most if not all international relations concepts, the concept of region makes little sense when it is abstracted from policy ambitions and the calculus of power.

However, if the distribution of power on the system level cannot tell us much about the specifics of regional great powerhood, neither can the relative cultural homogeneity of the regions. Interestingly, the degree of cultural difference between the aspiring regional great power and the rest of the region *as seen from outside* the region and the cultures in question does not seem to be of much explanatory value, either. All the contributors stress the perceptions of cultural distance between states in a given region, be that between Poland and Czechoslovakia, or between Indonesia and Malaysia. This is a reminder that cultural differences *in themselves* are perhaps of little importance for the student of international relations, but that *their representations* in the form of perceptions of a relevant 'other' are crucial.[3] Such 'otherness' is given pride of place in Butenschøn's treatment of Israel, which, in his presentation, comes close to following the tribal pattern of, for instance, the Maasai, where Maasai land is defined as the land where the Maasai live at any given time. Indeed, all the contributors highlight the importance of state genealogy and the character of the nation building process to self-perception and regional relations. It is here, in the mythologies of nations and states, that 'otherness' has its roots, and not in any 'objective' cultural reality. It is, arguably, no coincidence that states which stress their embattled position in the world in their self perception (Israel, Poland, South Africa; Indonesia during the *konfrontasi*) are also the ones whose bids for regional great powerhood are the most tenacious. Moreover, the domestic relationship between dominant ethnic groups and minorities are often tumultuous in these states. Precarious relations between internal minorities and adjacent states have affected the state security perceptions and thereby fed into the regional policies of Israel, India and South Africa, as well as of North Vietnam and of Poland in the inter-war period. Weak internal cohesion and the existence of external and internal irredenta combine to weaken the state's effectiveness in foreign policy. Arnfinn Jørgensen-Dahl approaches the importance of internal cohesion from a different angle when he stresses the importance of continuity in foreign policy for any aspiring regional great power.

If one may speculate about the inner-driven roots of assertiveness, one may also speculate about similar mechanisms at the systemic level. What do the case studies reveal about responses to the anarchy between states generally, and assumptions about a perpetual quest for power specifically? Is there a sense in which small states aspire to regional great powerhood, while regional great powers aspire for the status of a fully fledged great power? Perhaps an attempt could be made to explain the unfolding of Indian foreign policy in this light. However, in the case of Vietnam it is stressed how reliance on military capabilities alone can be counterproductive. And then again, there is the counter-example of Brazil the abstainer. As Andrew Hurrell puts it in his chapter, whereas India from the 1960s on preached peace but built up a regionally overwhelming military force, Brazil preached conflict but chose to remain extremely weak militarily. India, certainly, had border area conflicts of a more precarious nature, while a stable *status quo* seemed acceptable to both Brazil and its neighbours.

In opposition to Realists, Rationalists predict that states will rise to the challenge of anarchy by maximising order among states. Where formal institution-building is concerned, its role is hardly central in the cases covered. Following the bid for improved regional standing by Vietnam in 1979, political cooperation within ASEAN was strengthened, with what might be argued to be positive effects on Indonesia's leverage as a regional great power in Southeast Asia. In the chapters on Brazil and India, their roles in regional organisations have hardly been mentioned. The existence of SADECC and the Arab League makes for a backhanded tribute to the importance of regional organisations by having been set up mainly to thwart the ambitions of a regional great power.

Moreover, India and Vietnam have unilaterally undertaken policing functions in their regions. Brazil has been known to carry out cross-border anti-subversive activities, as have, on a larger scale, Israel and South Africa. The latter have also funded armed insurgents within other regional states. In most of the cases treated here, moreover, there have been attempts at meddling in regular domestic politics elsewhere in the region. However, regional interaction has only to a very limited extent produced anything functionally similar to the 'international society' which Rationalists identify on the global level.

This point brings us to the general question of similarity between inter-state interaction on the regional and system-wide levels. Øyvind Østerud in his theoretical opening chapter stresses heavily that the very existence of great powers, which by definition have interests spanning more than one region, is an all-important constraint on regional interaction, and in and of itself warrants a negative answer to the question of structural similarity. When the international posture of Vietnam decreased rapidly during the late 1970s, this was not only due to internal constraints and counter-pruductive military policies, but also to the change of Chinese policy, which drove Hanoi more firmly into the arms of the Kremlin. Similar instances have been identified by most of the other countributors.

Which conclusions can be drawn about the relations of regional great powers to great powers proper? As witnessed by the negative example of

Poland, where differing regional perceptions of the designs of the different great powers made up a serious impediment to the success of Polish regional policy, similar perceptions of great powers by the states of a region may make it easier for an aspiring regional great power to be recognised and to act as such. In his chapter, Stein Tønnesson emphasises how Vietnam in the years from 1975 to 1989 can be seen as a case of how risky it is to build one's foreign policy on a combination of military might and dependence on a distant power, however ideologically committed it may be. The influence of distant powers tends to be ephemeral, while neighbouring states remain present, he reminds us. The contrary viewpoint, that the prudent policy for small powers and indeed for all regional powers is to ally with a distant great power, could also be argued for Vietnam (and Tønnesson does so where economic aid is concerned), and indeed for Israel. Brazil briefly dabbled with the strategy of attaching itself to the closest superpower, a strategy which was labelled 'sub-imperialism' by its *ad hoc* detractors. Indonesia, Poland and, arguably, India tried, with varying degrees of sincerity and success, to distance themselves from great-power rivalry. In the case of Poland, the result was a collusion against it by the two great powers in the immediate proximity, whereas in the case of India, the relations between its main regional challenger Pakistan and the United States have been close. Still, India has based its power projections on a close relationship with the USSR, although without the sort of guarantees that Israel has enjoyed from the USA.

In the late 1960s, the Nixon administration formulated a new strategy of containment where strong regional allies were given a crucial role.[4] This strategy collapsed not only with the fall of Saigon in 1975, but equally dramatically with the fall of the Shah in Iran four years later. Regional powers that also played a role in the Soviet-American contest lost a valuable card, a situation which was further intensified with the waning of the contest. On the other hand, some states have tried to exploit the leeway made available to aspiring regional great powers by the end of the Cold War. Baathist Iraq is certainly a case in point. The changing intersections of regional and global balances of power stimulated the abortive Iraqi projection towards Kuwait in the early 1970s, towards Iran during the 1980s and again towards Kuwait in 1990. Evidence of lingering debates about the relative importance of the regional versus the global setting in Washington is given by Samuel Makinda in his contribution on South Africa.

The concept of regional great power seems useful inasmuch as it brings out the inequality of states in their immediate political setting. However, no clearcut case of a regional great power has been identified above, although Israel and India come close. Interestingly, Israel is a deviant case in a number of respects, whereas India seems to aspire for full great powerhood. If these are the predicaments of the two best candidates, it further undermines the existence of such a thing as a stable category called regional great powers. 'Regional great powers' are clearly not replicas of great powers proper at the regional level. What is substantiated in this book is, above all, the importance of the complex interplay between local configurations and the wider international context for the understanding of the regional hierarchy of states.

NOTES

1. Robert Gilpin, *War and Change in World Politics* (New York, NY: Cambridge University Press, 1981); Robert O. Keohane, *After Hegemony. Cooperation and Discord in the World Political Economy* (Princeton, NJ: Princeton University Press, 1984); Paul Kennedy, *The Rise and Fall of Great Powers. Economic Change and Military Conflict from 1500 to 2000* (London: Fontana, 1989).
2. Joseph S. Nye (ed.), *International Regionalism* (Boston, MA: Little, Brown, 1968), pp. vi–vii.
3. Iver B. Neumann and Jennifer M. Welsh, 'The Other in European Self-Definition: An Addendum to the Literature on International Society', *Review of International Studies*, XVII (1991): 327–48.
4. Øyvind Østerud, 'Decay and Revival of *Détente*. Dynamics of Center and Periphery in Superpower Rivalry', *Cooperation and Conflict*, XXIII (1988): 15–28.

Index